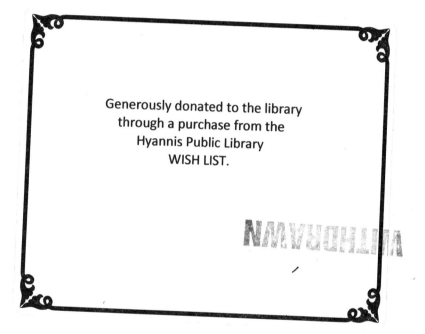

My Berlin Kitchen

My Berlin Kitchen

A Love Story, with Recipes

Luisa Weiss

VIKING

VIKING
Published by the Penguin Group
Penguin Group (USA) Inc., 375 Hudson Street, New York, New York 10014, U.S.A. • Penguin Group
(Canada), 90 Eglinton Avenue East, Suite 700, Toronto, Ontario, Canada M4P 2Y3 (a division of
Pearson Penguin Canada Inc.) • Penguin Books Ltd, 80 Strand, London WC2R 0RL, Eng-
land • Penguin Ireland, 25 St. Stephen's Green, Dublin 2, Ireland (a division of Penguin Books
Ltd) • Penguin Books Australia Ltd, 250 Camberwell Road, Camberwell, Victoria 3124, Australia
(a division of Pearson Australia Group Pty Ltd) • Penguin Books India Pvt Ltd, 11 Community
Centre, Panchsheel Park, New Delhi – 110 017, India • Penguin Group (NZ), 67 Apollo Drive,
Rosedale, Auckland 0632, New Zealand (a division of Pearson New Zealand Ltd) • Penguin Books
(South Africa) (Pty) Ltd, 24 Sturdee Avenue, Rosebank, Johannesburg 2196, South Africa

Penguin Books Ltd, Registered Offices: 80 Strand, London WC2R 0RL, England

First published in 2012 by Viking Penguin, a member of Penguin Group (USA) Inc.

10 9 8 7 6 5 4 3 2 1

LIBRARY OF CONGRESS CATALOGING–IN–PUBLICATION DATA
Weiss, Luisa.
  My Berlin kitchen : a love story, with recipes / Luisa Weiss.
  p. cm.
  ISBN 978-0-670-02538-1
  1. Weiss, Luisa.   2. Weiss, Luisa—Homes and haunts—Germany—Berlin.   3. Weiss,
Luisa—Marriage.   4. Berlin (Germany)—Biography.   5. Cooking—Psychological aspects.
6. Cooking, German.   7. Cooking, Italian.   8. Cooking, French.   I. Title.
  DD857.W34A3 2012
  943'.155—dc23   2012015042

Printed in the United States of America

For Max

The greatest thing you'll ever learn is just to
love and be loved in return.

—Eden Ahbez

Contents

Part 3

Part 4

Part 5

My Berlin Kitchen

Introduction:
A Strange Little Island

I LEARNED TO COOK AS A TEENAGER, EARLIER THAN MANY PEOPLE BUT not as early as an Italian farmer I know named Maria, who was sent to work for a rich family as a child and had to stand on a chair when she rolled out the family's daily pasta dough because, at seven years old, she was still too short to reach the table. I found my way to the kitchen along a much gentler path.

Before I learned to cook, I baked. My mother, who would rather have had a weekly appointment with a dental hygienist than be in charge of dinner, had in her possession an old unjacketed cookbook with a heart embossed on the spine. On the title page, the heart was bookended by the words: "The Way to a Man's Heart." Now I didn't know much about *that*, but what I did know was that *The Settlement Cook Book*, with its sensible title and pioneer spirit, reminded me of my idol, Laura Ingalls Wilder, whose books had been my constant companions in childhood.

I read it at bedtime and leafed through it industriously by day. I daydreamed about the birthday cakes I'd whip up for every single one of my friends. And then, eager to see results, I busied myself in the kitchen, making Applesauce Cake and Quick One-Bowl Cocoa Cake, learning how to melt chocolate and butter together in the double

1

boiler my mother always used to heat up her morning milk for her coffee, and how to cream butter and sugar until it looked like snow. I cooked chocolate fudge and patted out shortbread and even pulled saltwater taffy until my mother cornered me in the kitchen one afternoon and told me, in no uncertain terms, to *quit it.*

But as any mother knows, it's hard to get between one's child and her passion. And for me, cooking and baking were swiftly becoming the only things I really loved to do. Besides reading books, that is. There was little that gave me as much pleasure as spending time in the kitchen, watching butter, waxy and cold, turn into a creamy, yellow foam under the beaters of my electric mixer, seeing a sticky cake batter transform into an airy confection, or observing a puffy dome of risen bread dough, smooth and ever so slightly dry, like the underside of my grandmother's arm.

When I turned sixteen, my father gave me a paperback copy of Paula Peck's *The Art of Fine Baking*, which, besides leaving my mother in despair, taught me how to make génoise and pink fondant—glazed petits fours, flaky tart pastry, and Swiss meringue. And best of all, perhaps, it gave me the radical idea that the disdain with which my mother regarded my kitchen exploits was not universally shared.

Along the way to adulthood, I acquired one six-inch chef's knife, a dark green—glazed cast-iron pot, and the growing realization that baking and cooking were not just a sure way to end up with a pan of warm brownies or a kitchen full of the fragrance of beef stew. Busying myself in the kitchen was how I conjured the people and places I loved the most in the steam rising off the pots on the stove. And when I came down with a rare and chronic illness known as perpetual homesickness, I knew the kitchen would be my remedy.

I was born in Berlin in 1977, back when it was still known as West Berlin. In those days, you could still see the pockmarks from mortar fire in the façades of many buildings and the air smelled of coal smoke. West German schoolchildren sent to West Berlin on mandatory school trips rolled their eyes at the prospect of visiting the city. To them it was rather unlovely and so far away, requiring a long bus ride through the flat fields of East Germany, past checkpoints staffed by stern-faced guards with funny accents.

My father, a mathematician from Philadelphia, and my mother, an interpreter from Rome, fell in love and moved to Berlin together in the early 1970s, when Nixon was in his first term as president and the Baader-Meinhof gang was still a household term. My father wanted to escape from graduate school in Boston when he found a temporary teaching job in Berlin, and my mother, whom he'd met a year earlier at a German language course in Austria, came along for the ride. They were in their early twenties and ready for an adventure. West Berlin was a strange little island back then, its neighborhoods dotted with American, French. and British soldiers, its subways filled with spiky-haired punks. The city was kept alive by the occupying forces and by the West German government, which pumped money into West Berlin to keep it a vibrant bulwark against what loomed on the other side.

At first my parents lived in rented rooms in the quiet bourgeois neighborhoods of Neu-Westend and Schmargendorf, with grumpy landladies and thin walls. But the one year they thought they'd live in Berlin soon turned into two, and before long they decided to stay. My father got a job in the math department of the Free University and my mother took a translating position at a Berlin office of the European Commission, as it was then known, and they found an apartment on Bamberger Strasse in the quiet neighborhood of Wilmersdorf, in the heart of West Berlin. On one end of the street was a small weeping willow and a row of squat apartments built after the war and on the other was their pea green turn-of-the-century building with a marbled foyer, a gleaming wooden banister, and a defunct elevator shaft. Three floors up was their apartment. It had high ceilings, a windowless bedroom nook, and a kitchen that looked out over the trees below. All the streets in that corner of Wilmersdorf, known as the Bayerisches Viertel, were named after cities in Bavaria. Before the war, the Bayerisches Viertel had been home to a large number of Jewish Berliners, but now they were almost entirely gone.

My parents met many of their friends, mostly American expatriates married to Germans, through softball games and regular gatherings to discuss the 1972 presidential campaign of George McGovern. But as time passed and friendships developed, those once-earnest political meetings turned into gossipy afternoon chats fueled by gallons of tea and homemade cookies, much to the disappointment of the U.S. military surreptitiously wiretapping their telephones.

"Can you imagine how *bored* those guys must have been, listening to us?" my mother would say with a laugh. "Hearing me ask Nonna Adele for her eggplant Parmigiana recipe or making dates with Ann to go to the movies?" But there was nothing boring about the stories my parents would tell about their life together in Berlin. It was a glimpse into a world I didn't know, one in which they were still together. Because the truth is, I couldn't remember them not being apart.

My mother's first pregnancy was complicated and ended badly. As I was born two weeks early (with eyes wide open and a full cap of hair), my mother's doctor, Dr. Erich Saling, the head of obstetrics and a neonatal specialist at the birthing hospital in Neukölln, sent me straight to the incubator along with all the other babies born that day. The story of my birth was always inextricably tied up with his name, spoken reverently by my mother, as if he had been my gatekeeper into the world of the living. My father, on the other hand, liked to tell me about the first time he saw me gazing up at him from the incubator, alert and dark-haired as a monkey among all the plump, pale, bald German babies sleeping next to me. He's never told me much else about that day, just holds tight to the memory of his squirmy daughter, so alive, so eager to get out into the world. My parents named me Luisa, like my mother's great-aunt, but also because the name was identical in the three languages we would share: German, Italian, and English.

By all accounts, I was an easy baby who slept through the night at six weeks. After my parents went back to work a few months after my birth, their close friend Joan Klakow, an American expat with three children, became my de facto nanny. Joanie, as I called her, and her husband, Dietrich, easily incorporated me into their lives, bathing me in the bathroom sink, their children rocking me in eager arms while sitting in a beanbag chair, taking me with them to Puerto Rico to see

Joanie's mother. I loved the way their apartment smelled, like cinnamon and warmth. I loved feeling like I was their fourth child.

But even when you have everything you could want—in my parents' case, a longed-for child, easy childcare, a warm and loving community that was like family, in many respects a good life—it may not be enough. Soon after my birth, their marriage started to unravel. By the time I was three, it was all over. I don't remember much during the time my parents' marriage was falling apart. After all, life at Joanie and Dietrich's was safe and full of life. And I was so little.

When my mother made it clear that there was no marriage left to salvage, my father, sporting a mustache and a broken heart, decided to move back to the United States and took me with him. We went to Brookline, a suburb of Boston with leafy parks and rows of brick houses, while my mother stayed behind where we'd been, briefly, a family. Though I would continue to spend my summer and winter school holidays with her, flying diligently back and forth over the ocean, and, years later, would return to spend my high school years in Berlin, I never got over that early loss. Missing her, and Berlin, became a permanent state of mind. Growing up in Brookline, I never stopped thinking of Berlin's old apartment buildings with their faded façades, its overgrown parks with sun-bleached grass, the smell of onions browning in butter wafting out of a neighbor's window at lunchtime, the cobblestone streets that made the car rumble when we drove down them. I loved feeling that we were on our own little private island, that living within the Wall made us something apart, something special. And I missed the way my mother smelled, her smooth hands, her brisk steps along the hallway in front of my room.

My parents, who had promised to put me first and make the divorce as easy as possible, saw the easiest solution as turning me into an international commuter, flying back and forth between school years in Boston and vacations in Berlin. I traveled to and fro, learning to steel myself for so many goodbyes that it sometimes felt like my chest would explode. When I turned ten and couldn't bear the separation anymore, I moved back to Berlin to live with my mother. But after high school ended, I headed back to Boston for college. And each time I got on an airplane, my heart constricting, I wondered if this was how my life would always be.

As I grew up, moving around from Berlin to Boston to Paris to New York, I discovered that cooking was the most reliable way to feel less alone. My pots and pans became my constant companions, worn wooden spoons and a dull sheen at the bottom of my cast-iron pots a testament to how much I'd turned to them to find the tastes of home in my roving kitchens. Cooking was crucial: It couldn't shrink the Atlantic Ocean or lessen the six-hour time difference. But it made my world feel a little bit smaller.

It was in the kitchen that I could make the same tomato sauce with carrots and onions that my father always had in our sprawling Brookline apartment with the cluttered screened-in balcony and empty rooms, that I could grate bitter chocolate into a bowl of thin sour yogurt as my mother always had in Berlin when I still sat in a high chair, listening to the church bells peal on a Sunday morning as sun streamed through her kitchen window. When I stewed red peppers and onions with a cut-up chicken, the vapors brought my beloved Italian grandmother back to life. And I learned to knead Joanie's bread dough until I felt as strong and capable as she was. I couldn't will my beloved Berlin streets across the world or make the people I loved appear when I needed them, but by summoning the flavors of Berlin and the foods of my loved ones, my kitchen became my sanctuary, the stove my anchor.

Distance means nothing when your kitchen smells like home.

Part 1

1

I Never Want to Leave

I AM THREE YEARS OLD, SITTING ON A LITTLE WOODEN STOOL WORN BY years of use, right by the door to the kitchen. In front of me, on a small table that fits only three people, are a stack of newspapers, cookie tins, a woven basket full of cloth napkins, and a little ceramic dish, no more than an inch in diameter, filled with salt. My legs dangle from the stool and I face the stove.

Joanie, my *Tagesmutter*, as nannies are called in Germany, stands at the stove, melting butter in a pan. Joanie's long curly hair is gathered up in a bun at the top of her head. Wispy curls frame her face and the heat from the stove gives her ruddy cheeks. Her kitchen smells, as it always does, of lemon peel and damp wood, of warmed cinnamon and aniseed and something crisping nuttily at the edges. Blue and white crockery lines the kitchen walls, while jugs and bowls and teapots are clustered on top of cabinets and ledges.

On the bulletin board above my head are photographs of Joanie's three children, Nina, Nikolas, and Kim, and of me. In one picture, I am sitting under a tent made of bedsheets in Kim and Nikolas's bedroom wearing pointed fur-lined slippers that are a hand-me-down from the older kids. Kim, just outside the frame of the camera, has me laughing so hard I can hardly breathe. He is six years my senior and the closest I'll ever come to having a big brother.

Technically, I'm old enough to feed myself, but Kim still indulges me at lunchtime when he comes back from school, making elaborate takeoff, flight, and landing noises with each forkful he puts into my mouth. After lunch, we construct landscapes in his bedroom out of bedsheets and pillows and I submit happily to extended tickle sessions that always leave me gasping for air.

Joanie grew up in Washington, D.C., and in a sprawling apartment on Riverside Drive before moving to Berlin to study art as a young woman, which is where she fell in love with and eventually married a bearded young sculptor named Dietrich. She loves children and knows just how to talk to them, how to get them to fall in love with her, hook, line, and sinker. And in my eyes, Joanie is a goddess. She can do *any-thing.*

She sculpts busts of the maid she grew up with, her head thrown back in laughter, of her East German mother–in–law, of me, solemn-faced with a part down the middle of my head, and casts the busts in bronze that glows softly in candlelight. She makes dolls with long braids, soft limbs, and embroidered features. She sews tiny doll skirts and shirts and dresses out of fabric scraps and ribbon. She can bake bread and make flaky apple strudel. She knows all the words to beautiful folk and protest songs and when she sings, her high, clear voice always thrills me to the core. Joanie is pure love. She is love, safety, and comfort; sometimes it feels like my whole world revolves around her.

As the butter melts in Joanie's little pan, I knock my feet together expectantly. A frothy swirl of beaten egg goes into the pan and as the sides begin to set, Joanie chatters away to me. "Om–lett–uh con–fee-tuuu–ruh!" she trills and I repeat after her, "con–fee-TUUU–ruh!" The beaten egg, palest yellow and airy, puffs up like a small cloud. Joanie flips it deftly and when it's cooked through and light as air, she slides it onto a plate, dabs a stripe of raspberry jam down the middle, rolls it up, and dusts the top with a little powdered sugar. I love the way the cool, tart jam feels in my mouth as I eat the hot omelette.

After lunch it's time for a nap in Joanie and Dietrich's bedroom at the back of the apartment, down a long, book–lined hallway lit by a lamp in the shape of an enormous light bulb. The sounds of traffic on Hindenburgdamm mingle with birdsong and the voices of neighbors in the courtyard below. The alarm clocks on each side of the bed tick so loudly that I fall asleep with my heart beating like a metronome.

At the end of the workday, my mother, pixie-haired and smelling of lemony Eau Sauvage, will show up at the front door of Joanie's apartment. She'll come in, maybe stay for a cup of tea, but then she'll tell me in Italian to put my shoes on and Joanie will laugh every time, sounding out my mother's command. My mother and I speak Italian together, but Joanie and I speak English. These are the two languages of home for me: my mother and my father tongue. And in the world outside, there's German.

I am old enough to know that I'm not supposed to show disappointment when my mother tells me it's time to go home, but I never want to leave Joanie's apartment, where it always smells of something good and there are promises of tickle sessions and pillow forts, where we listen to *The Jungle Book* on the record player and Joanie reads us Rudyard Kipling stories and when I do something to make her laugh, her laughter peals through the apartment. At home, life is quieter and more solitary. There's a sadness in the air that I can't yet understand.

But my mother says it's time to go and I am nothing if not an obedient child. So I put on my shoes, say goodbye to Joanie, and walk down the two flights of stairs where a sign always affixed to one of the steps warns "*Vorsicht! Frisch gebohnert*," though I've never seen anyone ever wax the floors, and my mother and I drive home.

It is the beginning of the 1980s. Reagan is president of the United States, the Red Brigades are terrorizing Italy, and a Wall encircles the former capital of Germany, built under the guise of keeping East Germans safe from the insidious force of capitalism, though it's really meant to keep its people from hemorrhaging out into the world. And in West Berlin, in a third-floor apartment of an old building in a quiet leafy neighborhood rebuilt after large-scale destruction by Allied bombings in the waning months of World War II, I lie awake in my too-big bedroom, missing Joanie's cozy, fragrant kitchen.

Omelette Confiture

SERVES 1

It may seem odd to pair eggs with jam, but the combination of sweet-tart fruit with the moussey fluff of the omelette is delicious. It makes for a comforting snack for a small child or a light breakfast for a sweet-toothed adult. The best jams to use are ones with a tart bite: I'm partial to black or red currant. And don't skip the powdered sugar on top. The little explosions of sugar on the tongue are what make this omelette special.

   1 large egg
   1 tablespoon milk
   Small pinch of salt
   1 tablespoon unsalted butter
   1 to 2 tablespoons black or red currant jam
   ½ tablespoon powdered sugar, for garnish

1. Separate the egg white from the egg yolk. Beat the egg yolk with the milk in a small bowl until well combined. Beat the egg white with a pinch of salt in a spotlessly clean bowl until it just holds soft peaks. Fold the beaten egg white into the egg yolk mixture.

2. Melt the butter in a small nonstick skillet over medium heat. Pour the egg mixture into the pan and let cook for 3 minutes, until the edges have set, making sure the heat of the stove is not so high that the omelette browns or burns. Shaking the pan gently, flip the omelette and cook the other side for an additional 3 minutes. This takes some practice, but there's no shame in using a plate over the pan to invert the omelette instead of flipping it.

3. When the omelette is set and cooked through, slide it onto a plate. Dab the jam along the center of the omelette and then roll up the omelette—using a plastic spatula should help. Shake the powdered sugar through a sifter over the omelette and serve immediately.

2

The Apple of His Eye

MEMORIES ARE A FUNNY THING. SOME PEOPLE SAY THEY CAN'T remember anything before the age of ten and others have only hazy impressions of their childhood. I have laser–sharp memories of a lot of my childhood, like the smocking of a pink dress my Grandma Ann gave me when I was three or four years old. I can still see every single tiny satin rose sewed onto the bodice of the dress and remember how, when I tried it on for the first time while standing on a shag carpet in my American grandparents' impeccable midcentury house, it itched unpleasantly against my skin. Or how I used to lie on the changing table by the window of my bedroom in Berlin at dusk as my mother changed my diapers, singing off-key and tapping me gently on the belly as a cool breeze rustled through the printed curtains.

I can remember the color of the carpet in the first apartment my father rented for us when we got to Boston, how the toaster used to set off the fire alarm in the kitchen, and the kind face of Mrs. McCurdy, the elderly woman my father hired to look after me some days. Even what it felt like that one evening when I slipped and fell in the pink bathtub before bedtime, hitting my chin against the edge of the tub, and how those first terrible seconds of pain rendered me mute. But I have no memories of that flight I took with my father when we left Berlin for good.

A year after we arrived in Boston, my father found us an apartment

13

in Brookline, on the third floor of a pretty brick row house on Claflin Road. It was a big apartment, far too big for two people, one of whom was entering kindergarten. I think my father must have hoped that it wouldn't be just the two of us for the rest of my childhood. One room held nothing but my father's desk and a wooden chair and another had only a piano and a simple bench. My father liked to practice Mozart's "Rondo alla Turca" on the piano and later, during a short-lived phase of piano lessons, I banged out "Heart and Soul" on it regularly, the little white keys clicking satisfyingly under my fingers. Otherwise, it lay dormant.

I had a cozy little bedroom that was just the right size, a relief after the huge bedroom in Berlin that had always left me feeling adrift. In one corner was a pretty painted dresser my father had purchased at an antique store and in the other was the perfect spot for neatly lining up my dolls, teddy bears, and a grinning, bearded nutcracker doll on a little rug. We picked out the heavy fabric curtains, printed with Peter Rabbit and bundles of carrots, together.

But despite all this, I missed the apartment on Bamberger Strasse and the sound of the one loose floorboard in the hallway that always creaked when someone walked in the front door. I missed my mother and her lemony scent, her gentle voice, and the way she smiled at me. I missed Joanie, my guardian angel, and the way it felt when she gathered me up in her strong arms.

I knew even then that I shouldn't talk too much about what I missed. I knew my father was trying his best in a situation he must have hated. I had to help him, I figured. It couldn't have been easy to be a man in his early thirties, alone in a world he'd thought he'd left behind, raising his daughter largely by himself. I don't think he could help sometimes treating me like I was older or more capable than I was, and he didn't always do the best job of keeping his emotional turmoil hidden from me. So I had to be brave.

Soon we developed a little routine. My father, dressed in a tweed sport coat and tie, went to work every morning at Tufts, where he was chairman of the math department, dropping me off at the university's day-care center, where I took my afternoon naps under an itchy blanket he'd saved from his Boy Scout days, "Weiss" still visible in white chalk on the blue wool. I liked to imagine my father as a little boy camping in a tent somewhere as I drifted off to sleep under the dimmed rec room lights, though it was hard to imagine what he must have looked like without his mustache and his sport coat.

In the early evening, when work was done, he'd pick me up and we'd go home, where he'd make dinner and read me a few chapters from a book, the two of us sitting snug in the corner of the nubby cream-colored sofa in the living room, a beloved little brown bear that the Tooth Fairy once left for me tucked under my left arm. Then he'd sing me a song and put me to bed. This was our life together, day in, day out.

When I learned to read and started to skip ahead of him as he read to me, he grew irritable. And as much as I couldn't wait to read faster and faster still—I had so many books ahead of me to devour—I didn't want to stop our evenings together on the couch. So I let him keep reading aloud to me long after I learned to read, silently mouthing along in my head. I knew he didn't want to be left behind.

When you're an only child being raised by a mathematician who is easily distracted by all the empty notepads of the world waiting to be filled with formulas and musings on hypothetical buildings, finite algebraic equations, and other ungraspable thoughts, books are a natural escape. To my mind, there was nothing better. The only television set we had was a tiny black-and-white one stashed in the broom closet for the rare occasion when my father hired a babysitter. So I had nothing to distract me from my books and their other worlds that swallowed me whole, from Narnia to the Wisconsin woods, from a small town in Sweden to the red earth of Prince Edward Island. Nothing and no one interested me as much as my books. As a shy child who was dressed a little funny (short hair, gray flannel dresses, checked button-down shirts, blue suede shoes—painfully adorable to grown-up eyes, perhaps, but in early 1980s Massachusetts, just *strange*), I didn't have a lot of playmates to hold up against my books. Anyway, in their eyes I was always gone, always traveling back and forth between Berlin and Boston.

Instead of feeling out of place in my own world, I dove into the craggy hills of England, the enchanted boughs of a magic tree, and the gray-green banks of the great Limpopo River and left behind my preoccupied father, my loneliness, and my longing for my mother and for Berlin. I devoured every book I could get my hands on. I wanted that feeling of being slowly sucked out of my room and catapulted into a whole new existence that built itself up around me, again and again.

My father encouraged my literary obsession. We went to the library every week, where he would solemnly bid me farewell as I raced to the children's section, hands jittery because I didn't know where to start, and we bought stacks of books at the local children's bookshop, where I would spend hours walking up and down the gray-carpeted aisles, fingers running along the spines. He always gave me permission, once I'd finished my dinner, to read under the table of the dinner parties he took me to, where there were no other kids to play with.

Later, when I got older, he took me on literary pilgrimages. We drove to the Midwest to see Laura Ingalls Wilder's little log cabin, though I hadn't expected it to be quite so small and empty: in my mind it was still a cozy, vibrant home filled with animal pelts and oil lamps, a sleeping loft, and a happy family. We drove to Prince Edward Island to visit the Green Gables House and to walk in the red dirt that Anne Shirley loved so much. We went to Fruitlands, to see where Louisa May Alcott lived, and out to Plimoth Plantation, staffed with actors in period clothing, after I read a book about a little Pilgrim girl. I wondered feverishly if they hired children. My world was a strange mixture of literary escape and only child isolation.

When it came to dinner, my father and I had a little ritual for each day of the week. Mondays were Chinese takeout days. We'd call down to the Golden Temple restaurant on Beacon Street and order a white takeout box of moo goo gai pan and some steamed white rice. A little while later, we'd go pick it up, walking past the ice cream store on the corner that I always gazed at longingly but that we rarely went into. Tuesdays were my favorite, baked beans and broccoli days. My father would open a can of baked beans and boil some broccoli, dressing it with olive oil and lemon juice, and we'd eat the two together. I loved the way the sweet, vinegary beans stuck to my teeth. And each week we'd have one night at a local pizzeria with a jukebox. I was allowed to play one song while we waited for dinner. Once I figured out that I could get my usually solemn father to sing along to Michael Jackson's "Beat It" (and later, "Weird Al" Yankovic's "Eat It"), that was the only song I'd choose. We'd eat slices of a plain cheese pie, sitting by the window and talking.

Once a week, he'd defrost a package of frozen Brussels sprouts, steam them into pale green submission, and coat them with a little pat of butter. With the Brussels sprouts, we had to hash out a deal: he'd serve himself and then he'd put four on my plate, two little ones and two big ones. I had to eat them even though I didn't like them. They were bitter and squishy and looked like tiny little cabbages, which didn't endear them to me at all. Still, we'd negotiated that deal fair and square and I felt I had a bargain to uphold. So I choked down those Brussels sprouts week after week. And wouldn't you know, one day, as an adult, I found I actually liked them.

But best of all, my father gave me a family tomato sauce. He says he got the recipe from my mother's mother, Ninì, whom he adored, but my mother says that couldn't possibly be true, because Ninì hated to cook. They always liked to argue about who was right on this count. "Ree–chard, don't you think I'd *know* if my mother ever made that tomato sauce?" "Oh, get out of town. Are you telling me I don't remember who taught me how to make it?" I didn't mind the arguing; it was nice hearing their voices together in the same room. And besides, I didn't really care where the sauce came from—to me, it was his sauce.

It may seem a little funny to talk about tomato sauce. Chances are you scarcely need a recipe for one. The thing is, this is where it all starts for me. This sauce was one of the first things I ever made. It's the only thing I tend to cook when there's nothing in the kitchen and I need a quick dinner. It's what I cook when there's nothing I'd rather be doing less than cooking. It's what I make when I need steadying and reassurance. Its smell reminds me of my father and my Italian grandmother and I like to think that, one day, it'll be the first recipe my children inherit from me. If it's not a family heirloom, then I don't know what is.

To make it, he would dice up an onion and throw it along with a clove of garlic into a pot of olive oil warming on the stove. The smell of cooking onions would drift past the pantry into the living room, where I'd be sitting in anticipation. When the onions were soft and fragrant, he'd add chopped carrots and canned tomatoes into the pot and the whole thing would simmer together until it got sweet and saucy and I could hear my stomach growl. He'd boil a pot of water for spaghetti and break the long strands in half to cook them. Then he'd dress the spaghetti with the sauce and grate Parmesan cheese over the whole thing. We'd sit down at the drop–leaf table in the kitchen and we'd eat together and talk about the day.

Sometimes before bedtime, after he'd finished singing to me and he'd said goodnight, he'd turn at the doorway, ready to switch off the light, and tell me I was the apple of his eye, the love of his life. But I'm not sure he ever really needed to. I knew it all along.

Tomato Sauce with Carrots and Onions

SERVES 2 (CAN EASILY BE DOUBLED)

The only thing to keep in mind when making this very simple sauce is to make sure to let the onion cook thoroughly in the olive oil before adding the rest of the ingredients. This mellows the sometimes metallic bite of the onion and adds sweetness to the sauce.

    2 tablespoons olive oil
    1 clove garlic
    1 small yellow onion, finely diced
    1 medium carrot, diced
    1 14-ounce can good-quality peeled plum tomatoes in juice
    Salt
    Hot red pepper flakes, to taste (optional)
    5½ to 7 ounces dried spaghetti
    Grated Parmesan cheese, to taste

1. Pour the olive oil into a small saucepan set over medium heat. Add the garlic clove and diced onion and cook, stirring, for about 8 minutes. Don't let the onion brown. Add the diced carrot and cook for a few more minutes.

2. Add the canned plum tomatoes with their juice, shredding the tomatoes gently with your fingers before putting them in the pan. Season with a healthy pinch of salt and bring to a simmer. If you'd like your sauce to have a little heat, add the hot red pepper flakes. Turn the heat to low, put the lid on the pan, and simmer for 25 to 30 minutes, stirring now and then. Taste for seasoning. Discard the garlic clove.

3. In the meantime, put a pot of well-salted water on to boil for the spaghetti.

4. Cook the spaghetti until al dente and then drain in a colander, reserving some of the starchy pasta water. Toss the spaghetti with the tomato sauce, adding a little of the reserved pasta water if needed to loosen the sauce. Serve immediately, topped with grated Parmesan cheese.

3

A Distant Memory

I'M SITTING QUIETLY, AS INSTRUCTED, IN THE BACK OF JOANIE'S STATION wagon. Joanie's at the wheel and the rest of the car is crammed full of the usual stuff: old plastic bags, wooden toys picked up at the flea market, muddy boots that belong to the boys. It's late July, I am eight or maybe nine, and I'm in Berlin for the summer.

Every week, Joanie drives to Brieselang, a little village in the countryside just north of Berlin that has a small lake and one long main street to its name, to see her father-in-law, Hans. She brings him a few treats from the West and a little bit of company since his wife, Lottchen, died a few years earlier. Hans is a sculptor and lives in a small, cozy house that smells musty and faintly damp. Years later, I would realize that this was the smell of the East, not just of Hans's house; this and the stench of burning coal.

We're entering East Germany at the border crossing in Staaken, in the northwest of Berlin, one of the crossings that West Berliners can use to go into the East. The line of cars at the border is so long that people have switched off their engines in order to save gasoline. Whenever the line seems about to move, drivers get out and push their cars forward in neutral, legs straining against the asphalt, the midsummer sun warm on the roofs of the cars. The border looks like a traffic-jammed toll plaza, except instead of laconic toll officers taking change, somber East German *Grenzpolizei* check our papers. When the police get to our car, the air is thick with tension. Joanie has hidden some magazines in the stuffing of the front seat, illicit material in a country hell-bent on keeping West German progress, even something as banal as knitting patterns, far from its citizens.

Joanie and Dietrich were on vacation in Paris when the Wall went up overnight in August 1961. No one saw it coming and it was built in a matter of days. From one day to the next, the border between the Soviet sector—the eastern half of Berlin—and the French, American and English sectors—the western half of Berlin—was impassable. And Dietrich's parents were stuck on the wrong side. It would be seven years before Dietrich could see them again, even though they lived just sixteen miles away. Joanie, as an American citizen, could go to East Berlin for day trips, and later, after Joanie and Dietrich's first two children were born, the three of them could visit Hans and Lottchen in Brieselang. But Dietrich had to wait until 1968, when an agreement was hammered out between East Germany and West Germany that allowed former East German citizens back into East Germany for one day at a time. The West German government extracted a promise from the East Germans not to arrest returning former citizens for treason. People who had, by chance, found themselves in the West on or before August 13, 1961, like Dietrich, were no longer to be criminalized by the German Democratic Republic. But there was no way to protect those who had found a way to escape after the Wall went up.

In the trunk, we have a big bunch of bananas and several Swiss chocolate bars. Bananas are not for sale in East Germany and the chocolate bars available in the state-run grocery stores taste awful, like blocks of congealed fat mixed with cocoa powder. It's not illegal to bring bananas or chocolate over as presents. Things that *are* illegal: household appliances made in the West, teen magazines, too much currency.

In Brieselang, in Hans's cozy house, a pea green tiled oven heats the living room, and we lean against it to warm our backs. Hans's backyard is filled with plump snails, a few of his cast-iron sculptures, and a lush carpet of grass. Sometimes to my delight I even find a slug covered in sparkling dots of moisture. Hans's atelier is at the very back of the garden and just before it are great big tangles of berry bushes. The sweet–sour red currants are my favorite.

Joanie and I will spend the day there, keeping Hans company and visiting the neighbors on one side, who raise nutria and have rhubarb plants growing wild behind their house. They have a son my age named Martin and when we watch television together Martin proudly shows off the channels from the West that their television has only recently started to receive. The neighbors on the other side of Hans's house have a sour cherry tree that I'm invited to clamber up into. The cherries are bright red, almost orange, and when I pop a few in my mouth, they make the inside of my mouth pull together.

At lunchtime, Joanie will bake a *Quarkauflauf*, a rustic, lemon-scented soufflé made with sour cherries and Quark, a sour fresh cheese that tastes a little like a cross between cottage cheese and yogurt. Joanie, Hans, and I each have two helpings, spoons scraping congenially against our emptying bowls. Afterward, in the tranquil hours after lunch, I'll nap in the guest bedroom under a blanket that itches at my chin. It will be so quiet.

On the way into East Germany, the border police looked over everything in our car rather quickly, avoiding eye contact. It's on the way back into West Berlin, late at night, when I'm asleep in the backseat and the roads are bumpy and black, hardly lit at all, that the police will make us get out of the car as they take their flashlights and peer into the darkest recesses of the trunk, looking under the seats and behind the cushions while we stand under the klieg lights of the checkpoint, the countryside pitch black beyond the pool of light burning down on our heads.

I know what they're looking for and yet I don't really know. I see how thorough they're being, but I don't yet understand what it would be like to be a person hidden in someone's car, trying desperately to escape by cover of night from one Germany to another, in search of a better life.

Joanie's arm is around me as we wait, bleary–eyed, alone at the border, the line of cars from earlier that day a distant memory. Not many people leave East Germany at this time of night, but staying overnight would require a whole additional set of permits and stamps, not to mention advance warning of at least a week. In the next lane, a large truck carrying livestock idles. I see a white sheep's face poke through the slats in the side of the truck, and then another and another.

The *Grenzpolizei* finish their search and brusquely nod at us to leave, so we get back in the car and start driving, their uniformed figures receding quickly in the rearview mirror. I curl up in the backseat and close my eyes as we drive back home, back to the well–lit streets of West Berlin, where grocery stores are filled with bananas and dozens of different kinds of chocolate bars. Where Allied soldiers and their families live quietly among us, where the Wall is not an oppressive barrier to a different world, but a strangely invisible and seemingly inevitable part of daily life.

Parking in front of my mother's apartment, Joanie will try to rouse me. "Wake up, monkey," she'll say, as she gently shakes my leg. I feign sleep, eager to be held as she carries me up the stairs. And so, straining slightly, Joanie will gather up my floppy limbs and climb the three flights of stairs to my mother's apartment, the ornate, wrought–iron elevator shaft dormant since World War II.

Sour Cherry *Quarkauflauf*

SERVES 6

Quark is a staple in German kitchens. Flavored or plain, it is used as a breakfast spread or served alongside boiled potatoes. But it can also be used in sweet and savory cooked recipes, such as this rustic cherry soufflé of sorts. You can find Quark at well-stocked supermarkets and some green-markets. Local dairies such as New York's Hawthorne Valley Farm, Washington State's Appel Farms, Nebraska's Branched Oak Farm, Ohio's Blue Jacket Dairy, and California's Spring Hill Cheese Company produce their own Quark. (Some of these farms also do mail order.) The Vermont Butter & Cheese Creamery makes Quark that is distributed in specialty stores nationwide.

Butter for the baking dish

3 large eggs, separated

½ cup sugar

1 pound Quark

Grated zest of 1 organic lemon

½ teaspoon baking powder

½ teaspoon ground cinnamon

¼ cup farina (regular Cream of Wheat, for example, not the quick-cooking version)

2 cups pitted sour cherries, fresh or preserved (if preserved, drain and discard the juice)

Pinch of salt

1. Heat the oven to 375 degrees. Butter a baking dish that is at least 2½ inches deep and approximately 8 x 11 inches wide. Set aside.

2. In a large bowl, beat the egg yolks and the sugar together for a minute or two, until pale yellow and frothy. Then beat in the Quark, grated lemon zest, baking powder, cinnamon, and farina until smooth and creamy. Fold in the sour cherries.

3. Beat the egg whites with the pinch of salt in a spotlessly clean bowl until they have medium peaks. With a spatula, carefully fold half of the beaten egg whites into the Quark mixture to lighten it. Then fold in the remaining egg whites until no white streaks remain.

4. Pour the Quark mixture into the prepared baking dish and bake in the oven for 30 minutes, until the *Auflauf* has set and is starting to brown. There might be a crack or two in the top of the *Auflauf*. Remove from the oven and serve hot or warm.

4

An Unfair Advantage

THERE ARE SOME PEOPLE OUT THERE WHO ARE PRETTY SURE THAT having an Italian mother is an unfair advantage if you want to grow up to be a home cook. It's like having an ace in the hole or a secret weapon. But although my mother can knit socks, get stains out of anything—and speak *five* languages, for Pete's sake—she does not love to cook. In fact, I'd say she just barely tolerates it.

Over the years, my mother has taken a lot of ribbing for this from her older sister, who married into a Sicilian clan whose cooking is the stuff of legends. (More on them in a bit, I promise.) But most of the time my mother doesn't mind the ribbing; in fact, she thinks she deserves it. My Sicilian uncle can spend many happy hours in the kitchen preparing dinner, but in that same amount of time, my mother reasons, she could plant an entire bed of roses or read one of the three newspapers she consumes daily, and have more fun to boot. And in any case, she asks, why would she bake cookies when the Krumiri company makes better ones than any that have ever come out of her oven?

Now it's true that my mother will never be one to encase a duck in a pastry mantle and stuff it with a complicated French farce. She'd much rather order a roasted side of beef from the butcher than attempt to cook the meat herself. And forget about her ever baking a cake. Still, I think she's selling herself short. She may not have had the unbridled enthusiasm at the stove to light the fire of cooking under me, but my mother taught me quite a bit about cooking over the years.

She was the one who showed me how to sear thin-cut pork chops in a steel skillet with thin slices of lemon that sizzled in the pan, adding a clear, bitter note to the juicy chops. I watched her roast peppers slowly in a hot oven until they blistered and collapsed into silky-sweet heaps that she pulled apart with her fingers and dressed with minced olives, chopped parsley, breadcrumbs, and anchovies. She knew how to cobble together a delicious winter salad with a few Belgian endives, slices of blood oranges, and toasted walnuts. And in 1988, when I was in the sixth grade, she even taught me that stuffing a chicken with a lemon and sprinkling it with big flakes of salt before roasting it rendered the meat juicy and fragrant and the skin impossibly thin and crispy.

I got to spend that entire sixth grade year in Berlin with her. It happened to be the last year that Berlin was still a divided city, though, of course, we had no idea what was coming. After seven years in Brookline, I'd had enough of missing my mother and asked my father if I could go back to Berlin. When my father extracted a promise from me that I would only stay for a year, he let me go. But a ten-year-old is hardly a reliable bargain maker. Six months into my stay with my mother, I already knew that I wanted nothing more than to keep living in Berlin. I loved my school, fit in so much better with my classmates there than I did in Brookline. I felt like I was home again, even if staying with my mother also meant abandoning my father. But a promise was a promise, my father argued angrily with me on the night I asked him midway through the year if I could change my mind and stay. His answer was no. I'd given my word.

So I dutifully returned to Brookline six months later, roiling with resentment, and glumly endured the first semester of seventh grade at my old school. Then, just a few months after I left Berlin, an East German bureaucrat misread a directive at a press conference on a cold November evening in East Berlin and told the gathered reporters that the borders to the West were opening immediately to East German citizens that day, inadvertently causing thousands of East Germans to flock to the border crossings to the West in disbelief and glee, cajoling, chanting, and pleading with the increasingly overwhelmed *Grenzpolizei* to let them through the barriers. Miraculously, there was no violence. There were simply men in gray–green uniforms trying to do their jobs until they had the wisdom to step aside and let history take over, watching helplessly as the trickle of people passing by with tears and happy shouts quickly grew to a stream and then a great, pulsating river.

My mother was at a dinner party that evening with her boyfriend, Florian, and other friends, and though they'd heard the bureaucrat's announcement on the television by chance, it hadn't made any sense to them at the time. Much like it didn't make sense to anyone, really. They turned off the television and went back to their dinner. But on their way home later that evening, Florian and my mother saw steady streams of police cars racing in the direction of the Wall. Feeling adventurous, they turned the car around and followed them, recalling the cryptic announcement on the news earlier. Their curiosity paid off: that night, my mother danced on the Wall along with thousands of other Berliners who had emerged to see for themselves if what they had heard on the television and radio could be true. And at Christmas, just a few short weeks later, my father, my benevolent Gorbachev, let me return to Berlin for good.

I loved my mother's impulsiveness and sense of adventure. She could never stand sentimentality or traditional roles, much preferring to live life on her own terms with an intensity that belied her small frame. Lest you get the wrong impression, let me assure you that my mother also had her soft, maternal side, knitting me a dress of soft pink wool for my fifth birthday, sending me clandestine chocolate Santa Clauses in early December every year for Nikolaus when I lived with my father, and always knowing just how to soothe my fevered brow with one touch of her cool, dry palms. But cooking had always been more of a duty than a pleasure for her, much as it had been for her mother, Ninì.

Ninì, as my grandmother was called, came from Puglia, the home of such delicious things as *burrata*, focaccia made with a boiled potato mashed into the dough for claggy moisture, and homemade orecchiette pasta served with garlic–stewed bitter broccoli rabe. But she grew up in a poor family—her mother had been widowed at thirty–five, with five children, when her husband was mowed down in the first battle after Italy entered World War I—where food was fuel and not much else.

Ninì left her small village, Bisceglie, as soon as she was old enough and moved north to Ancona to teach high school philosophy. It was there that she met my grandfather and had three children, my mother and her brother and sister, before my grandparents decided to move the family to Rome when the children were very small. Somewhere along the way, Ninì picked up a few dishes that she cooked over and over for the rest of her life. You already know about the tomato sauce that is still a matter of dispute between my mother and father. There was also a very nice stew of braised chicken pieces with red and yellow peppers that my mother cooked faithfully until no one could bear to look at it again and she phased it out for good. But a humble pot of braised artichokes and potatoes, a dish that goes absolutely nowhere in the looks department, was my very favorite.

It's one of those homely Italian peasant dishes, the kind that looks pretty awful really, all sludgy and soft. A study in different shades of brown, if you will. No self-respecting French housewife would be caught dead serving it. But Italians have a different take on vegetables. They understand that low and slow is the way to transcendent vegetables. They figure that sacrificing looks is well worth it if you end up with a stewy pot of vegetables leached of color but packed with sweetness and flavor.

My mother wasn't quite sure what to think when I started taking over the dinner duties in high school. I didn't do much at first. I made a lot of tomato salads sprinkled with dried oregano, many pots of spaghetti, and I drove her to distraction with my cake baking and candy making. ("Who's supposed to eat all of this?" she'd wail, gesturing at the counters filled with chocolate-dipped shortbread.) But one day I roasted a chicken the way she'd showed me to, big flakes of salt going every which way. A few weeks later I tried my hand at roasting red and yellow peppers and dressed them the way she liked, with chopped olives and anchovies and plenty of parsley. Soon I was more than making up for all my sugary messes over the years and I had graduated from *The Settlement Cook Book* to Ada Boni's *Il Talismano della Felicità*, the only cookbook my mother ever consulted. It was as heavy as a doorstop and coming apart at the spine, with more than a thousand papery–thin pages covering everything from rustic vegetable *torte* to elegant *timballi*.

My mother had inherited the book from her aunt, whom she'd lived with as a child. My grandparents couldn't afford three children in the difficult postwar years, so the story goes, and my mother's aunt and uncle were relatively well off, living in a big, cavernous apartment in a nearby district of Rome. My mother's siblings stayed with my grandparents and sometimes even went hungry, while my mother, at her aunt and uncle's house, never wanted for anything. Except, of course, that while she may not have wanted for food or shelter or affection even, that feeling of belonging, of being wanted by her parents, was always missing, despite their best intentions.

Ninì died when I was little, of a fast–moving brain tumor that felled her in less than a year. Her death was a shock to the family, especially to my mother, who was still desperately making up for lost time. My mother never got over her death. I know she still misses Ninì more than anything in the world. So I think that she liked to cook chicken with peppers and those braised artichokes and potatoes as much for the memory of her mother as for anything else.

That was her way of conjuring up Ninì, of feeling close to her again. After all, she had never been one for wallowing in self–pity, always preferring to clench her firsts and barrel forward in life, clad in a thick coat of armor. And along the way, in addition to her braised artichokes and *peperoni al forno*, my mother taught me what it means to be strong.

Braised Artichokes and Potatoes

SERVES 4 TO 6 AS A SIDE DISH

Make sure to use baby artichokes for this dish, not the larger globe artichokes that are better steamed whole and eaten leaf by leaf. To clean baby artichokes, fill a large bowl with cold water and the juice of a lemon and set it next to your cutting board. Take a baby artichoke in one hand and start by breaking off most of the outer petals. The petals grow increasingly soft as you near the heart of the artichoke. When you've exposed most of the tender yellow flesh, take a sharp paring knife and peel the stem until all the dark green is gone and the stem is a clean, pale green. The stems are delicious, so don't discard them. Make sure, as you clean the stem, that you also pare away any dark green flesh at the base of the artichoke heart. Err on the side of cutting away too much—a mouthful of the artichoke's otherwise hard, fibrous texture will spoil your dinner. As you get more experienced cleaning artichokes, this will get easier. Finally, cut off the top of the baby artichoke's remaining petals, about half an inch. Cut the cleaned artichoke into quarters and drop the quarters into the acidulated water. Continue with the remaining artichokes until they are all cleaned and quartered and ready to cook. Remove the artichoke quarters from the water just before you put them in the pot to cook. Discard the trimmings and the lemon water.

½ cup olive oil

2 cloves garlic

1 pound Yukon Gold potatoes, peeled and cut into 1-inch chunks

6 baby artichokes, cleaned and quartered

1 teaspoon salt

½ cup white wine

Juice of ¼ lemon

4 big stalks flat-leaf parsley, minced

1. Pour the olive oil into a 3-quart heavy-bottomed pot set over medium heat. Add the garlic cloves and let cook for a few minutes, until faintly golden. Then add the potato chunks, lower the heat, and let them cook for 10 minutes, stirring vigorously every so often because the potatoes will stick to the pot (unless you're using nonstick). Add the quartered artichokes and the salt and stir well. Raise the heat to medium again. Cook for 5 minutes, stirring occasionally.

2. Add the wine to the pot, stir well, and bring to a simmer. Add the lemon juice, turn the heat down to low, put the lid on the pot, and let

braise for 20 minutes, stirring once or twice. If the vegetables start to look dry while they're cooking, add a few spoonfuls of water and stir well.

3. Just before serving, stir the minced parsley into the pot. Check for seasoning and serve. The dish keeps well for a day or two.

Peperoni al Forno Conditi

SERVES 4 AS A SALAD

This roasted pepper salad is a staple in my house and never fails to impress people. These days, many cookbooks and food personalities will tell you to roast bell peppers on a long-handled fork over an open flame, charring the skin (and often the flesh) of the pepper in order to peel it. But in Italy, peppers are roasted in the oven for close to an hour, guaranteeing silky-soft peppers and a transcendently scented home. I urge you to take the slow route: the results are sweeter and more delicious.

2 to 3 slices stale white peasant bread
3 red bell peppers
3 yellow bell peppers
¼ cup oil-cured black olives, pitted and chopped
3 anchovy fillets (optional), finely chopped
¼ cup salt-cured capers, soaked and drained
1 cup loosely packed flat-leaf parsley, minced
4 tablespoons best-quality olive oil, or more to taste
Flaky salt, such as Maldon

1. Cut the stale bread into rough chunks and blitz in a food processor until they turn to coarse crumbs. Spread the crumbs on a plate and set aside to crisp up and dry out.

2. Heat the oven to 375 degrees. Line a baking sheet with aluminum foil. Wash and dry the peppers and arrange them on the baking sheet. Put the sheet in the oven and bake for 45 minutes, turning the peppers every 10 to 15 minutes to make sure they cook evenly (I use my fingers, but you

could also use cooking tongs). By the end of the cooking time, they should be blistered all over, and their juices bubbling.

3. Remove the baking sheet from the oven and let cool on a wire rack until you are able to handle the peppers. Set out a clean plate or bowl next to the baking sheet and pull the skin off the peppers, working over the aluminum foil. Take care when you "unplug" the stem of the pepper: hot steam or liquid usually comes gushing out. Your hands will become quite wet as you work; periodically dry them to facilitate cleaning the peppers. Transfer the peeled peppers, devoid of any seeds, to the plate or bowl. As you transfer the pieces of pepper, use your fingers to tear the flesh into thin strips. Discard the aluminum foil and the pepper trimmings.

4. Sprinkle the plate of peppers with the breadcrumbs, olives, anchovies if using, capers, and parsley, and drizzle the olive oil over the peppers. Mix gently, and then add a few pinches of flaky salt to taste. Serve right away or let sit at room temperature, covered, for up to 4 hours before serving. If you're not going to serve the peppers right away, don't sprinkle on the breadcrumbs until the last minute. That way they retain their crunch.

5

My Sicilian Uncle

I AM OF THE BELIEF THAT EVERYONE NEEDS A SICILIAN UNCLE. NOT TO intimidate your first boyfriend or to shake down that weirdo in a three-piece suit who always leers at you on the subway, but to impart unto you everything he knows about cooking. Sicilian uncles know a lot, you see, about cleaning baby artichokes and grilling fish and de-salinating preserved anchovies to pack in olive oil and frying eggplant in such a way that it ends up practically greaseless. They have opinions about which pasta brands to buy; they put escarole on deep–dish pizza, and left alone with a pot of salted water and a pile of broccoli, they can make magic happen. A Sicilian uncle might just be your gateway to a life at the stove.

Without my Sicilian uncle Pietro, I would never have known the pleasure of prying tiny sea snails stewed in tomato sauce out of their black shells with a toothpick on New Year's Eve. He's the one who taught me how to stuff zucchini flowers with a baton of drained moz-zarella and an anchovy fillet before twisting up their tops, dipping them in a thin batter, and frying them to a greaseless crisp. I ate my first raw oyster at his behest (it stuck gelatinously in my throat as he watched from the other end of the table) and my first sea urchin too, spread on buttered bread, outside at a café in Nice at night. My best spaghetti dinners are the ones I learned by watching him, and I still know absolutely no one who can clean artichokes as well as he can and perform the kind of culinary magic with them that he's capable of (fried, braised, or stewed, they are *incredible*). Secretly, I call him the Artichoke Whisperer.

When I was a child, I was a little scared of Pietro. He was very tall and solemn, even stern, some would say. He commanded a lot of respect. Pietro had left Sicily as a teenager and moved to Brussels to work for the European Commission, where he met my aunt Laura, who'd also left Rome as a teenager to head north. In the 1960s, my mother tells me, Italy was a very provincial place. Anyone who could get out and see a bit of the world jumped at the chance. In a kind of Italian brain drain, these young people headed to Germany and Belgium and the United States in search of work. And that's how Pietro and my aunt ended up in Brussels.

Laura and Pietro returned to Italy each summer with their childern, just as my mother and I did. We'd all gather in the small village in the Marche where Laura and Pietro had a house, an old rectory complete with a chapel and an apricot tree in the garden, and where my grand-parents lived in a farmhouse that my grandfather bought and rebuilt after they retired and left Rome. My cousins and I spent our summers running back and forth between the two houses, which were con-nected by one of Torre San Tommaso's two intersecting streets, stop-ping only to buy popsicles at the lone general store to quench our thirst. Torre didn't have much else besides a scattering of farmhouses separated by wheat fields and spectacular views of the hills that Re-naissance painters had immortalized in paintings hung in nearby Ur-bino's Ducal Palace. It was perfect for us. Some days we'd head down to the beach in Pesaro, half an hour away, or go for a hike in the small hills around the village. But we always came home for lunch.

With rare exceptions, lunch and dinner were eaten at Laura and Pi-etro's house. They had a big dining table, big enough to seat two dozen people, and a kitchen large enough to accommodate us all. The fire-place alone could have fit a table of four. Plus, they were the cooks in the family. Just before lunchtime, my grandfather and my mother and I would get in his old Renault R4 and chug along the country road to the old rectory, just a few minutes away, the engine straining slightly at the incline. None of us ever wanted to miss an opportunity to eat what Pietro had prepared. It was always delicious.

Some days there were fat slices of Sicilian pizza for lunch. Pietro would make pizza dough, fitting the chubby dough into a cake tin and letting it rise a little. But instead of topping the crust with tomato sauce and mozzarella, he'd pile shreds of curly escarole onto the crust along with anchovy fillets, finely diced tomatoes, and cubes of scamorza cheese. It was an adult meal, slightly bitter and fishy, not the kind of pizza a half-American child who grew up eating cheese pies at Pizzeria Regina could always appreciate. But as the years passed, I came to love the stuff: bitter, salty, chewy, and puffy.

Another beloved lunch from Pietro's kitchen was a big bowl of penne slicked with a simple tomato sauce (bottled by our neighbors in Torre in a yearly end-of-summer group preserving initiative) stewed with basil and garlic and mixed with a generous dollop of sheep's milk ricotta from the dairy down the road, which left a rich, creamy film on the pasta. Pietro would cook while we kids were commanded to set the table and then, as we sat quietly, stomachs growling, Laura would dole out the steaming pasta into deep plates for all of us.

And on special occasions, Maria, who lived across the street, would butcher one of her rabbits or chickens for us and Pietro would roast the meat with big sprigs of rosemary from the garden. There were always roast potatoes too, cubed and studded with coarse salt, and plates of bitter boiled greens served with grassy-green olive oil and plenty of lemon juice.

Laura and Pietro prepared meal after meal for us, every day, all summer long. All we had to do in return was set the table and clear it afterward, filling the dishwasher and cleaning the tablecloth of any stray crumbs. (We also had to finish our plates, though that was never, ever a problem.)

For a few weeks each summer, Pietro's mother, Antonietta, would take the train up from Messina to Torre. Antonietta was as small and bird-like as Pietro was tall and imposing. She wore her silver hair in a graceful bun at the nape of her neck and antique earrings dangled from her ears. Antonietta wasn't my grandmother, but I called her Nonna Antonietta just as everyone else did—everyone except Pietro, who called her Mamma, and Laura, who always called her Signora. My grandmother Ninì's absence was huge and sometimes I think that having Antonietta around was a comfort even to my mother, though Antonietta was quieter and far more formal than Ninì had ever been despite her sly sense of humor. Best of all, she was an incredible cook. In fact, when Antonietta wasn't silently ironing everything from the bedsheets to my cousins' underwear, she was usually in the kitchen, bent over the counter, doing Very Important Things with vegetables and muttering gently to herself in Sicilian dialect, which none of us, except for Pietro, could understand.

I loved watching Antonietta work, her slim, elegant fingers rubbing seasoned breadcrumbs into tiny shreds of thinly sliced beef that she would then roll up and skewer. She'd make mountains of these skewered, breadcrumbed *bracioline* and just before dinner Pietro would take the platter of skewers and head out to the small grill propped up in the driveway. He'd stand there, patiently and expertly grilling the skewers, the breadcrumbs crisping and the meat softening over the smoldering coals, while we ran around in the kitchen, setting the table and sneaking pieces of the local unsalted bread, ravenous. When the *bracioline* were done, we'd plow through the skewers in minutes, letting the little rolls of meat, so tender and sweetly delicate, melt in our mouths, leaving behind only a whiff of smoke and herbs.

Antonietta also made the world's very best *bandiera*, which is sort of like an Italian version of ratatouille but about four thousand times more delicious. Despite my best efforts, I have never quite been able to replicate it. Instead of cooking all the vegetables separately, as the French would have you do, Antonietta methodically layered everything into one pot. Potatoes went at the bottom, because they took the longest to cook. Then came a layer of small carrot chunks, pieces of sliced peppers, red and yellow, a layer of cubed eggplant, a layer of zucchini, and on top and all around went shreds of plum tomatoes. She would pour in more olive oil than one would think necessary and sprinkle the vegetables with plenty of salt and basil. The pot would then stew for hour, the vegetables slowly braising, softening, slumping together in a rich, fragrant stew. There was never any resistance to the vegetables when the *bandiera* was done. It was slick and velvety and entirely impossible to stop eating.

Sometimes, as my cousins and I horsed around in the yard outside, I'd find myself drawn to the kitchen window. I'd peer inside and see Antonietta and Pietro working quietly side by side at the kitchen counter, peeling vegetables or cutting meat. Watching them made me curious about how the groceries Pietro bought each morning at the market in Urbino were transformed into fragrant, delicious lunches and dinners. I loved watching how Nonna Antonietta always salted a breadcrumb stuffing with just the right amount or how methodically Pietro cleaned an enormous pile of wild chicory, slowly, carefully, never rushing. It would be a while yet before I started to cook myself, but Pietro and his mother taught me that spending hours cleaning vegetables in a fugue state or preparing lunch for ten was a perfectly fine way to spend the day.

And years later, whenever I'd find myself in the kitchen for long stretches of time with a pile of greens to clean in front of me, say, I'd settle in and get comfortable, leaning my hips against the counter, just like Antonietta used to, and bending my neck quietly in concentration, just like Pietro does. Not only did my Sicilian uncle teach me how to cook, he taught me how to feed people too.

Pizza Siciliana

MAKES ONE 10-INCH ROUND PIZZA

This deep-dish pizza with its topping of anchovies and escarole is definitely for grown-up palates, but I'll think you'll be happy not to have to share it. It may seem strange to put a form of lettuce on pizza, but escarole is delicious when cooked and its bitterness mellows slightly in the oven. Don't be tempted to substitute mozzarella for the scamorza; it is too wet a cheese and will make the pizza soggy.

2⅓ cups Italian "00" or all-purpose flour, plus more, if needed
½ ounce fresh yeast
1 cup lukewarm water
Pinch of sugar
Salt
3 tablespoons olive oil
1 small head escarole (about 7 ounces), washed and dried
Freshly ground black pepper
6 to 8 anchovy fillets, chopped
10 ounces scamorza or provolone, cut into small cubes
2 plum tomatoes or 10 grape tomatoes, cut into small cubes

1. Put the flour in a mixing bowl and make a well in the middle. Crumble the yeast into the well and add half of the lukewarm water and the sugar. Using a fork, mix the yeast, sugar, and water together, drawing in just a little bit of flour from the sides of the well, until the yeast has dissolved. Cover with a dishtowel and let rest for 15 minutes, until frothy.

2. Add the remaining water slowly as you mix the frothy yeast and remaining flour together. Then add 1 teaspoon salt and 2 tablespoons of the olive oil and mix until you have a shaggy dough. Dump the dough out onto a floured surface and knead it gently with floured hands for several minutes, adding flour as needed, until the dough starts to come together. Try not to add too much flour—you want a very soft, floppy dough (a bench scraper will help keep the dough from sticking to the counter). When the dough is no longer sticky, form it into a soft ball.

3. Oil the bottom and sides of a 10-inch round metal cake pan with a drip of olive oil and put the ball of dough in the pan to rest. Cover with a clean dishtowel and let sit in a warm, draft-free place (a turned-off oven is a good choice) for about 1 hour, or until it has doubled in volume. While the dough rises, tear the escarole into small pieces and dress with the remaining olive oil, salt, and pepper to taste. Set aside.

4. When the dough has doubled in size, gently pat it out with your fingertips until it reaches the sides of the pan and is uniformly ½-inch thick.

5. Distribute the chopped anchovies over the pizza dough and top with two-thirds of the cubed scamorza. Then pile the dressed escarole on top of the cheese, and top with the cubed tomatoes. Let the pizza sit at room temperature, covered with a linen towel, for 20 minutes. In the meantime, heat the oven to 375 degrees.

6. Bake the pizza for 30 minutes. Then remove the pan from the oven and sprinkle the remaining cubes of cheese over the top of the pizza. Return it to the oven and bake for another 15 minutes. The top layer of cheese and the escarole should be golden brown (some edges of the escarole might even be a little singed). Take the pan out of the oven and, using an offset spatula and some elbow grease, check to see how the bottom of the pizza crust is browning. If it looks a little pale, put the pan back in the lower third of the oven and bake for an additional 15 minutes (you can tent some aluminum foil over the top if you'd like to keep the escarole from getting any darker).

7. Remove the pan from the oven, let it cool for a few minutes, and then carefully pull the pizza out of the pan. Slice and serve immediately.

Le Bracioline di Antonietta (Grilled Beef Skewers)

SERVES 4

Seasoned breadcrumbs are an Italian cook's secret weapon, gilding everything from vegetables to pasta to grilled meat. These *bracioline* are a little fussy to make, what with all the cutting and dipping and rolling and skewering required, but they are absolutely worth the trouble. The meat, quickly cooked over a charcoal grill or in the oven, is melt-in-your-mouth tender.

Approximately ¾ cup extra-virgin olive oil
Salt
1 pound thinly sliced beef carpaccio, cut into 2 x 3-inch pieces
1¾ cups plain breadcrumbs

½ cup finely chopped flat-leaf parsley
½ cup grated Parmesan cheese
Freshly ground black pepper

1. Pour ½ cup of the olive oil onto a large platter and season with a few pinches of salt. Slip the thin pieces of meat into the olive oil. Set aside at room temperature for at least 1 hour and up to 3 hours.

2. In the meantime, in a medium bowl or deep soup plate, mix the breadcrumbs with the chopped parsley, the grated cheese, and the remaining olive oil. Season with salt and pepper to taste. The breadcrumbs should be well seasoned and moist, but not greasy.

3. Heat the oven to 350 degrees. Take each piece of meat, shaking off the olive oil, and dunk it in the seasoned breadcrumbs so that the meat is well coated with crumbs. Roll up each breadcrumbed piece tightly and thread it onto a thin metal skewer. Repeat with the remaining pieces of meat, putting about 7 *bracioline* on each skewer. Set the skewers on a parchment-lined baking sheet.

4. Put the skewers on the sheet into the oven and bake for about 15 minutes, flipping the skewers over after about 8 minutes. If you have a grill, by all means use it: the flavor of the *bracioline* will be even more delicious. The *bracioline* are ready when they are browning and bubbling and the breadcrumbs have crisped. Remove from the heat and serve immediately.

6

The Matter of Breakfast

WHEN YOU GROW UP ALL MISHMASHED LIKE I DID, WITH AN American passport and Italian citizenship and a birth certificate issued in West Berlin, it might take you a little longer than usual to figure out your place in the world. You're this strange little hybrid of a person, easily adaptable, fluent in many languages, an outsider everywhere. It's the perfect background for becoming a spy, really. Though much to my chagrin the CIA has never approached me. Eavesdropping on tourists becomes a favorite pastime, as does identifying pedestrians on the sidewalk based on their footwear. But you have to come up with a straightforward answer when people ask you where you're from. You find yourself taking a deep breath and sizing up your questioner. How much do they need to know? How much time do they have? Are they going to be bored by the length of your story or lean in for more? Because there is never one straightforward answer.

Then you have to figure out where home is exactly. (Not, as you might imagine, an easy task either.) Since you're not exactly sure, you struggle with alienation, with commitment issues, and with a constant sense of isolation. We mishmashy folk can't pinpoint exactly where home is or even what it is, yet we're constantly longing for it. It's quite a pickle, to say the least.

And then there's the matter of breakfast.

Italians eat dry little cookies for breakfast, dipped into hot coffee and slurped up before the moisture–logged cookie can break off and drown in the murky depths of the coffee cup. My mother's favorite breakfast cookies when I was a child were *krumiri*, cornmeal cookies piped out into three-inch zigzag shapes and baked until toasty brown and crumbly. She stored her *krumiri* in a vintage tin that had an official-looking seal and a stern-faced man on the lid (Signor Krumiri himself, perhaps). Every time she went to Italy to visit her parents she came back with a few boxes of *krumiri* stashed in her suitcase. Aside from the extra crumbs at the bottom of the bag, the cookies were none the worse for the wear. I loved watching her transfer the cookies from the paper boxes into their rightful tin. Sometimes I even got to eat a few of the broken ones.

My father would not have approved. In Brookline he alternated between feeding me bowls of Raisin Bran (these were the days before high-fructose corn syrup came along, when the raisins in Raisin Bran sparkled in their coating of regular sugar, not the kind that is to blame for street riots, Attention Deficit Disorder, and the plunging stock market) and taking me to a little hole-in-the-wall deli down on Beacon Street. On those days, we'd sit at the counter and eat hot cream of wheat for breakfast, while an African American cook with a jaunty paper hat flipped eggs at a dizzying pace at the sizzling-hot griddle. I loved the creamy mouthfeel and wholesome taste of the hot cereal and always thrilled to find a little lump at the bottom of the bowl to chew. It would be years before I found out that lumpy cereal was something to be avoided. Even at my grandparents' house outside of Philadelphia there was hot oatmeal piled into a bowl and topped with a pat of butter at breakfast time. My grandmother had to coax me into eating it, but she didn't have to try very hard; I would have done most anything she asked.

As for the Germans, well, their breakfasts are legendary. Groaning boards piled high with thin slices of cheese, hams—boiled, smoked, and cured, sliced cucumber, boiled eggs, tomato wedges, coarse and smooth liverwursts, butter and Quark, plum butter and red currant jelly, all meant to adorn slices of dark, grainy *Vollkornbrot* or freshly baked crusty rolls split in half. In fact, German breakfasts are so good that at dinnertime people just turn back to that fabulous spread and keep going. *Abendbrot*, or evening bread, is what dinner is called in Germany. And though open-faced sandwiches for breakfast and dinner aren't everyone's cup of tea, the tradition definitely grows on you.

You see the conundrum. Crumbly cornmeal cookies dipped in coffee, wholesome grain cereal bathed in cold milk, or a slice of rye sourdough bread so fresh it's almost sticky, topped with a smear of cool butter and a paper-thin slice of ham—how's a girl supposed to know which breakfast is her birthright? It's enough to keep you up at night.

Just when I thought things couldn't get more complicated, along came the answer to my conundrum: poppy seed whirligig buns. These burnished, glossy orbs look like a dozen Princess Leia buns fused together in a pan. They're a little psychedelic and very beautiful, shiny and nut-brown. The buns are sort of like a classic American cinnamon bun, but the poppy seed filling, made almost pudding-like with milky semolina, is definitely German. And, just how the italians would want it, they are on the sweet side of breakfast, a little indulgent for more ascetic tastes.

So how's a girl supposed to choose? Turns out she doesn't really have to, not when there are poppy seed whirligig buns in the world.

Poppy Seed Whirligig Buns

MAKES ABOUT 15 BUNS

These buns seem complicated to prepare—yeast dough, cooked filling— but they're actually quite simple to make. What's important is that you buy poppy seeds at a store with a lot of turnover—you don't want rancid poppy seeds. Then all you have to do is make a quick, silky yeast dough, cook semolina, milk, and poppy seeds together into a filling that's good enough to spoon from the pot, and roll the two together. The buns bake up beautifully: big and fluffy with crisp edges and a pillowy-soft interior, the crunch of the poppy seeds contrasting nicely with the tender crumb of the bread.

They don't keep well, so make sure to eat them warm the morning they're made, with a big cup of steaming milk and coffee for dunking. The recipe is adapted from *Lust auf Genuss* magazine.

Yeast dough

¾ cup 2% or whole milk
¼ ounce fresh yeast
¼ cup sugar
4 cups all-purpose flour, plus more, if needed
2 large eggs, room temperature
4 tablespoons (2 ounces) softened butter
½ teaspoon salt
Neutral-tasting vegetable oil

Filling

2 cups 2% or whole milk
Grated peel of ½ large lemon
1 teaspoon ground cinnamon
1 teaspoon vanilla extract
⅓ cup plus 1 scant tablespoon sugar
Pinch of salt
⅓ cup plus 2 tablespoons semolina
1 cup poppy seeds

Butter for the pan(s)
1 egg yolk
2 tablespoons 2% or whole milk

1. First, make the dough: Heat the milk until lukewarm. Crumble the yeast into the milk and stir with a wooden spoon to dissolve. Add a pinch of the sugar. Let stand for a few minutes, until the mixture starts to foam slightly.

2. Pour the flour into a large bowl and make a well in the middle. Sprinkle the remaining sugar around the edges of the flour well. Pour the yeast mixture into the well and begin to stir with a wooden spoon, incorporating a little flour from the sides with each stir. Add the eggs, butter, and salt,

and begin to knead with your hands within the bowl. When the dough starts to come together, dump it on a lightly floured counter and knead until smooth and supple, about 3 to 5 minutes. You might need a little more flour or a little less, depending on the climate where you live.

3. Wash out the bowl and coat it with a small drip of vegetable oil. Place the ball of dough in the bowl and cover with a cloth. Put the cloth-wrapped bowl inside your oven (turned off!) or somewhere in your home that is warm and not drafty. Let rise for 1 hour, until doubled.

4. While the dough rises, make the filling: Put the milk in a 2-quart saucepan set over medium heat and add the lemon peel, cinnamon, vanilla, sugar, and salt. Bring to a boil; then slowly pour in the semolina, whisking continuously. Let the semolina cook for about 1 minute, stirring all the time. Then pour in the poppy seeds. Mix well to combine, and remove the pot from the heat. Let the mixture swell and cool somewhat, about 10 minutes.

5. Punch down the yeast dough and knead it on a floured surface for a minute or two. Let it rest for another minute or two. Then roll out the dough into a large rectangle, ½-inch thick. If you find the dough too elastic to roll, simply let it rest for a few minutes, then proceed. Spread the cooled poppy seed mixture evenly over the dough, almost to the edges. Roll up the dough lengthwise (I use a bench scraper here to help things along gently) and then wrap it tightly in aluminum foil. Place the foil-wrapped log in the freezer for 1 hour.

6. Butter two 10-inch round cake pans or one sheet pan. Remove the dough log from the freezer and discard the aluminum foil. Cut the roll into 1½-inch-thick slices. Place the slices in the buttered cake pans or the sheet pan. Cover with a cloth and let rise for 45 minutes. In the meantime, heat the oven to 375 degrees.

7. Mix the egg yolk with the milk and brush the buns with the mixture. Bake in the preheated oven for 30 minutes, until the buns are golden brown.

8. The buns are best eaten the day they are made. If you want to keep them, wrap the baked, cooled buns tightly in aluminum foil, put them in a freezer bag, and freeze them. Defrost, unwrapped, in a 300-degree oven for about 15 minutes.

7

Depression Stew

I DECIDED TO MOVE TO PARIS WHEN I WAS TWENTY–ONE YEARS OLD. I HAD just finished college in Boston, where I'd spent four years studying literature and catching up on all the American pop culture I'd missed during my high school years in Berlin. I'd long left behind *The Settlement Cook Book*'s cakes and candies and had taught myself to braise lamb shanks in the green cast–iron pot my father gave me for my nineteenth birthday and to cook polenta from scratch, stirring cornmeal and water together on the stove for nigh on an hour.

As college drew to a close, I had the vague idea that I wanted to work in book publishing. My childhood love of books had never diminished and I figured working with books made as much sense as anything else. I also liked the idea of staying in school. I was an English major but after a writing professor told me that going to an MFA program would be a cruel exercise in time wastage, I turned my eyes to my other major, French. My chic French adviser Carole, who sported a sexy mop of messy blond hair and artfully draped clothing, told me about a couple of one–year graduate programs in Paris I could apply to.

Paris, well now, *that* could be neat, I thought. I'd been to Paris on a few class trips in high school, but I'd really been charmed during college when I'd flown there during spring break to visit my father. He had an important colleague in Paris and spent a lot of time working there, subletting little apartments around the Bastille and in the Marais.

Every few days, he would call me in my dorm room in Boston with a phone card and tell me about the wonderful little streets he was discovering, the delicious bean stews he was making himself for dinner, the sharp little paring knives he bought at the outdoor market on boulevard Richard Lenoir, and how the accordion players in the Métro stations made him cry. My father *loved* Paris.

And when his wife, Susan, and I went to visit him one spring, the beautiful buildings, the crisp baguettes, the well-dressed children, and the elegant ladies charmed me too. I have a black-and-white photo from that trip, taken by Susan with an old film camera I used to use. My father and I are standing on a bridge near the Ile Saint-Louis and his arm is draped around my shoulders. We've just finished ice cream cones (I still remember how the boozy flavors of my scoop of prune ice cream spiked with Armagnac caught in my throat), and my father looks so proud, like it's *his* city glimmering behind us.

By the second half of senior year, it was decided. I was going to Paris to get my master's degree in French cultural studies. While my college roommates prepared to move to New York City for jobs in finance and advertising and publishing, I reread Jean-Jacques Rousseau and dug for discarded francs in my desk drawers.

I arrived in Paris during the first week of September. The master's program I had enrolled in matched each graduate student with studio apartment rentals scattered throughout the city and when I arrived at the address I'd been sent I was sure I'd hit the housing jackpot. My sixth-floor flat was in the courtyard building of a grand apartment on rue Bonaparte, in the legendary neighborhood of Saint-Germain-des-Prés, just steps away from Les Deux Magots, where Jean-Paul Sartre and Simone de Beauvoir used to sit and drink countless cups of café crème. There was a tiny kitchen and two pretty garret windows looking over the rooftops and there was even an elevator. My landlady, an imposing woman named Madame LaCarrière, lived with her family in the front building. She towered over me with a carefully coiffed helmet of blond hair and had a different rich, dark wallpaper in every room of her sprawling apartment. I was pretty sure her nearly grown children still addressed her and Monsieur LaCarrière with the formal *vous*.

That first day in Paris, groggy with jet lag, I unpacked my things, stashing them in the wooden wardrobe, and went on a long, meandering walk through the neighborhood, past the place Saint-Sulpice, where my mother told me to keep an eye out for Catherine Deneuve's rooftop apartment, past the tiny rue de Fleurus, where Gertrude Stein and Alice B. Toklas once lived, and through the nearby Jardin du Luxembourg, my shoes crunching in the gravel as young men in black socks and running shorts jogged past me. I watched little children float wooden boats in the fountain as their parents and nannies sat in metal lawn chairs arranged in a large circle around it. The sun threw its long rays across the neat lines of trees and everything looked just so, like in a painting. As I left the park at dusk to head back home, I bought a scoop of cassis sorbet from an ice cream vendor manning an old-fashioned stand by the park entrance. It was cold and winey in my mouth and it stained my lips a deep red.

During the first few weeks in Paris, I was just as awed by the beauty of the city as I'd expected to be. I spent days walking around, surprised to find the city smaller than I'd imagined. I could cross it in a few hours. As I traversed the city, I never tired of looking at the grand Haussmannian buildings and avenues, untouched by the war that had so ruined Berlin. I bought a fresh baguette every morning (and sometimes in the evening too), breaking off the crisp end, with a shower of crumbs, to chew as I walked. I spent hours at outdoor markets, ogling mounds of craggy oysters and bright pink langoustines piled on juicy-looking seaweed, deep, glowing heads of green lettuce stacked high, and the staggering circumference of a true Brie de Meaux, pockmarked and fragrant.

But there was another side to the city that I hadn't seen when I'd been just a tourist. First of all, I couldn't figure out how to meet people, beyond the handful of other students in my graduate program. So I spent an awful lot of time by myself. And there were only so many long exploratory walks I could take through Paris before I started to wish I had someone, anyone, there to share those strolls with me. The convoluted bureaucracy that governed everything from opening a bank account to paying an electric bill was frustrating in the extreme; it

sometimes seemed like public servants gloried in their role of stymie-
ing your every move. Most dispiriting, it was becoming increasingly
clear that the graduate program I'd enrolled in was not what I'd hoped
it would be. Finally there was all that rain. In the autumn of 1999, as
the Eiffel Tower glittered with thousands of lights counting down the
remaining days of the century, it must have rained 70 percent of the
time. I felt oppressed: by the wet, heavy skies, by my uninspired professors, and by my own inability to find my footing.

The few girlfriends I'd made in my graduate program were far
bolder than I was. They went out at night, to smoky bars and dimly lit
nightclubs, and found themselves the people they wanted to get to
know. They weren't shy about meeting men, about having love affairs
with mysterious strangers. And their stories were entertaining, for sure.
But I wasn't really interested in meeting men. I wanted girlfriends to
meet in cafés or for impromptu dinner parties in my tiny studio apartment, eating at the rickety little table that was my desk, my dining table, and my nightstand all at once. I wanted to see their Paris, to feel
like I was actually a part of the city instead of a silent, mostly invisible
observer. But I was shy and slightly terrified by how brave you had to
be to get anyone to notice you in Paris, especially women.

I went to classes by day and walked the streets alone in the evening, sometimes ducking into one of the city's myriad one-room movie
theaters tucked away in small side streets to escape the increasing se-
clusion I felt. I watched old French movies and black-and-white screw-
ball comedies and depressing contemporary Danish films and had to
fight for a seat at each Woody Allen retrospective I attended. When I
watched Annie Hall and Alvy Singer tussling with lobsters, I found
myself breathless with laughter and longing for that kind of easy companionship, for the friendliness of Americans, for lobsters.

My most frequent companion in those days was an eight-month-
old baby named Cassandra, for whom I nannied every week. Cassandra obligingly let me take her on long walks down the ever-inspiring
rue Mouffetard, where vendors hawked cheese and roast chicken,
piles of strawberries and loamy mushrooms, or down the boulevard
Montparnasse to the avenue des Gobelins. Each time I pushed the

stroller past the Closerie des Lilas I thought of Ernest Hemingway scribbling away in his notebook, so inspired by his surroundings. And I began to wonder just what it was about Paris that had bewitched so many people over the years. Had the beauty of the city really been enough for them? Had they not been as lonely as I was? How did they manage to find their way in a society that felt so impenetrable to me? At lunchtime, Cassandra and I would share a quiche that Cassandra's mother bought at a fancy pâtisserie in the neighborhood, chewing together in companiable silence.

My grad school friends filled me in on their romantic escapades as we sat in class in the mornings, and I would listen distractedly as my mind wandered to that other life I was supposed to be having, surrounded by French friends who had been easily won. This isn't to say that I didn't appreciate the company of the American girls who became my friends that year: Melissa, who introduced me to *Sex and the City* and would faithfully meet me for Sunday brunch every weekend, or Amy, who went with me to see Ariane Mnouchkine's Cartoucherie in the Bois de Vincennes, did her best to taste every lemon tart for sale in Paris, once cooked us a Taiwanese dinner in her tiny kitchen, where the shower stall stood across from the stove, hands flying as she made a stir-fry fragrant with soy and sesame, and introduced me to Pineau des Charentes, a sweet, pinkish wine served nicely chilled.

But I thought assimilating was part of the goal of the year. I had naïvely expected it would come naturally, which is why making American friends felt like cheating. It took me a while to understand that there was no shame in realizing that living in Paris was far less magical than visiting it.

The tiny sliver of a kitchen in my *chambre de bonne* at 47, rue Bonaparte was about as wide as my wingspan and only a little longer than I was tall. It was half the size of the bathroom, which felt like a spa with its huge tub, bidet, and washing machine set across from the sink. The kitchen had a small window with a dusty, guano-spangled grate in front of it, which gave the room the faintest impression of a penitentiary. Built into the narrow end of the kitchen were two burners, a sink, and no counters, which meant that if I wanted to cook myself something, I had to balance the cutting board over the sink when the burners were in use, and after I washed the dishes I had to wait for the burners to cool off before I could put them down to dry. I didn't really mind the setup, though. It just meant I couldn't make more than simple one- or two-pot meals, which was mostly how I liked to cook anyway.

At the market, I bought thin, pale green peppers that I fried and ate over rice—one turned out to be so hot that my lips swelled up like Jessica Rabbit's as I chewed—and enormous boiled beets, vendors piercing them with a long-handled fork and slipping them into paper bags that got stained and ripped on the way home. Back in the kitchen, I sliced the beets into silky rounds and dressed them with a pungent vinaigrette before eating the salad with pieces of baguette that crackled like a fresh fire when I bit into them. I made murky pots of sliced zucchini and tomatoes and onions, stewy and sweet, but hardly presentable. I kept a household rich in French honey and sharp little paring knives, chocolate-studded breakfast cereal, and cans of tiny sea foam—colored flageolet beans, just like my father had told me to.

I was still in college when my father taught me about Depression Stew. That's what he called the simple one-pot meal he made for himself when he was staying in Paris. He'd make the base of a tomato sauce, starting out with onion and garlic browning lightly in olive oil. Then he'd add some vegetables, perhaps a carrot or whatever was lying around the kitchen, really. It could be a stick of celery or a potato. After that, he'd throw in a can of tomatoes and then a can of drained flageolet beans. They were more delicate and delicious than regular cannellini or kidney beans. He'd season this mixture with salt and hot red pepper flakes, then he'd put the lid on and go do some math, the stew bubbling away quietly on the stove. You could tell when it was done, he said, when the vegetables were tender and the juices had reduced and the whole thing had come together in a slightly soupy, slightly stewy, but eminently spoonable way. The best way to eat Depression

of a deep soup plate with a heel of crusty baguette to
dregs. It was after that that he'd usually call to tell me how
nner had been.

her liked to think Depression Stew was the kind of food
you'd eat during a financial depression, cheap and filling and healthy.
But the way I saw it, you could also see it as a remedy for more personal lows. Cooking Depression Stew in my little Parisian kitchen reminded me of my father and the way he found things to love in every
city he went to, especially Paris. So whenever I was feeling blue, I'd
make Depression Stew, and just the act of it, peeling the carrot, sim-
mering the tomatoes, watching the tiny flageolet beans swim like a
school of pale green fish in the pot, made me feel a little less alone.

Depression Stew

SERVES 2

You can make this stew as rich in vegetables as you like, depending on
what's in your refrigerator. But it's just as good made with simply the basic
structure of tomatoes, onions, and canned beans. What's crucial is that it
be eaten with good bread. I recommend the heel of a crusty baguette or a
thick slice of fresh peasant bread that you've toasted, rubbed with garlic,
and drizzled with olive oil.

3 tablespoons olive oil
1 clove garlic
1 medium yellow onion, diced
1 carrot, diced
1 potato (optional)
1 small, firm zucchini (optional)
1 14-ounce can peeled plum tomatoes
Salt
Hot red pepper flakes (optional)

1 14-ounce can flageolets, drained (you may substitute cranberry
beans, also known as borlotti beans), or 1 box frozen baby
lima beans
Baguette or toasted peasant bread rubbed with garlic and olive oil, for
serving

1. Heat the olive oil in a small saucepan over medium heat. Add the garlic clove and the diced onion and cook, stirring, until the onion is translucent, about 5 minutes. Don't let it color. Add the diced carrot and cook for another few minutes. If you've got a potato or a small zucchini lying around, cut them into bite-sized pieces and add them to the pan. Stir well and let cook for another few minutes.

2. Add the peeled plum tomatoes and their juice, breaking down the tomatoes with your hands or a wooden spoon. Season with salt to taste, and hot red pepper flakes if you want a little heat. Stir well and let cook for 5 to 7 minutes.

3. Add the drained beans or frozen lima beans to the pot, stir well, and bring to a simmer. Turn the heat down to low and let the stew simmer, covered, for 30 minutes.

4. Serve hot with the heel of a crusty baguette, or place the garlic-rubbed, olive oil–moistened bread in a deep plate and ladle the Depression Stew over it. Eat with a knife, fork, and spoon.

8

At First Sight

PARIS DID HOLD A FEW SURPRISES UP ITS SLEEVE, THOUGH. A FEW months after arriving, I called an old friend from Berlin who had moved to Paris after high school, figuring that if I couldn't meet any French girls to be friends with, I'd at least get to see a friendly, familiar face from home. Malte told me through a crackling phone line that he was on an architectural assignment on an island in the Indian Ocean for a few months.

"But do you remember Max, from Berlin?" I did, vaguely. I'd met him once or twice in high school, but his face had blurred in my memory. All I could summon up were angular cheekbones, a strange haircut that consisted of buzzed-off sides and a long, drawn-back ponytail on top, and the fact that a few girlfriends of mine had had crushes on him, with his sharp features, tender mouth, and clear blue eyes.

"He's staying at my place for a few months," I heard Malte say with a slight delay. "He's doing some internship in Paris. You should call him! I'll give him your number too. You can have a drink together. I think he's lonely."

Okay, I thought. *I can take this guy out for a beer and we can commiserate about how hard it is to meet girls (for very different purposes, admittedly) in this weird, beautiful city. It will be nice to see an old face and it will be nice to be out of the house with another human being for a few hours one evening.* I had no idea that we were being set up. That Malte called Max after talking to me and told him the very same thing.

Max and I played phone tag for a few days, leaving messages on each other's answering machines, the slightly awkward, hyperpolite ones that people leave when they don't really know who's listening on the other end. Finally, we made plans to go to a gritty bar called Le Breguet in the 15th arrondissement. We agreed to meet on the platform of the Métro Pasteur and walk to the bar together, the way we'd both been accustomed to meeting friends in Berlin, before the Age of Cell Phones.

And so it came that on October 12, 1999, I got out of a subway car, turned around to wait for the train to pull away, and saw Max standing on the other side of the tracks. He was wearing baggy blue pants and a thin black jacket lined with red plaid fabric and his gold-rimmed glasses winked in the harsh underground light as we smiled at each other. I had wondered if I would recognize him; the last time I'd seen him had been six years earlier, in eleventh grade. But the blurred features in my head swam into focus as I saw him on the other platform. His funky haircut was gone, replaced by a full head of sandy blond hair and a neat side part. *Aha*, I thought. I *had* remembered the angular cheekbones correctly. But it turned out I hadn't remembered quite how nice his smile was.

Up at Le Breguet, which was smoky and graffitied and yet improbably cozy, we made our way through a pitcher of beer apiece over the course of the evening, though I hardly noticed the alcohol. While I had come to Paris for my graduate program, Max was completing an internship at Siemens in the north of the city. Like most other Germans, he'd only started university in his early twenties, a year earlier. His years after high school had been filled with military service and a multiple-year apprenticeship. While I had attended the German-American school in Berlin, founded in the 1960s and administered by the state of Berlin and the U.S. State Department, Max had gone to the Lycée Français, which had roots in Berlin going all the way back to the seventeenth century, when the Huguenots fled to Germany after being driven out of France.

So it turned out that Paris was an entirely different beast for Max than it was for me. He had friends galore, from high school and work. He didn't struggle with the language, nor did he spend much time wondering why Parisian girls were so hard to get to know. Besides, he wasn't anywhere near as shy as I was. It started to dawn on me that Malte hadn't been exactly truthful when he'd told me that Max was lonely.

We spent four hours talking and missed the last subway home that night. Out on the dark street, when we said goodbye, planting the easy double kiss on one another's cheeks, I was surprised by how happy and clearheaded I felt after the fog of the past few months in Paris. It had been so nice talking to Max. After all those weeks of mostly silent, solitary evenings, this one had been fun. Max was familiar, a reminder of my happy Berlin years. And there was something else too, a little spark of excitement that zinged through me that evening at our little table by the window. When we leaned in to say goodbye, I realized that I was thrilling at the thought of him getting close to me. This was so unlike me, ever cautious, ever shy. I chalked it up to the beer and the pleasure of seeing a familiar face, then turned up the collar of my raincoat and walked home through the dark streets. But I couldn't stop thinking of Max's crooked smile and the way his lips moved when he spoke.

In the days that followed, Max and I took the RER train out to Versailles and walked along a long canal behind the palace under steely skies. He made dinner for me at Malte's apartment, letting me watch as he spooned peanut butter and crème fraîche into a big pan full of sautéed chicken chunks, red peppers, and corn. The concoction was surprisingly good. No guy had ever cooked for me before, so I suspect that was half the charm. We went to the movies to see *Buena Vista Social Club* but instead of focusing on the Cuban singers on-screen, I could only think about the fact that I could feel the warmth from Max's arm, just a few inches away, that I could smell him, clean and fresh.

One night we bought a bottle of hard cider from an Arab grocer near boulevard Saint-Michel and then sat down on the promontory of the Ile de la Cité, legs swinging over the embankment as the city glowed around us, the Eiffel Tower glittering steadily in the distance. We took turns swigging at the bottle, the dry bubbles tugging at my throat. My palms were clammy and my heart raced.

It had only been a week, but it felt like a whole lifetime had gone by since we'd first met up on the Pasteur platform. My mind ran over each day that we'd spent together. Seven days wasn't much, but I had a funny feeling, deep in my belly, that something monumental was happening. Now, it was all I could do to keep from staring at Max whenever I was in his company. And the feeling seemed to be mutual: I'd never been looked at so intensely by anyone. I had the most pleasurable sensation of being swallowed up whole.

We finished the *cidre* at midnight and slowly stood up, shaking out the cramps in our legs chilled by the autumn evening air. Max walked me home, past the black river and bustling boule Miche. As I fumbled at punching in the security code at my front door, he stood next to me in slightly awkward silence. We walked through the courtyard, my shoes clicking against the old cobblestones, and then squeezed into the tiny elevator, our coat sleeves touching. Then he followed me through the front door to my little room. I left the lights off as we took off our coats and sat down on the narrow bed (where else was there to sit?) next to each other.

We stayed like that for some time, looking out at my neighbors' dark windows across the courtyard while the clock in the kitchen ticked far louder than I'd never noticed before. Then Max leaned in and kissed me and everything around us gently fell away, the room, the clock ticking, the velvet night sky. I thought I might even have heard the gears of the earth coming slowly to a full stop. I heard him whisper, "I'm falling in love with you."

When I walked to class the next morning, groggy but zinging with a terrifying and wonderful kind of nervous energy, it was like the world had been scrubbed clean overnight. Everything sparkled and the edges of the buildings were thrown into sharp relief. I could have walked into a lamppost I was so tired, but I'd also never felt so awake, so alive. The crazy thing was, I hadn't even known that part of me had needed waking.

Max and I set out to discover Paris together, which was, I decided, how it was supposed to be discovered, *à deux*. We climbed up Ménilmontant and slurped Chinese noodle soups in a tiny hole-in-the-wall that displayed stewed chicken feet in the front window. We spent late nights at Le Breguet and sat on the steps of the Sacré-Coeur for hours, watching the sky over the city change from gray to periwinkle to the palest, palest pink. Max came with me to the little movie theaters I'd discovered on my solitary walks and took me to the grittier north of the city, where he worked. We went dancing on a boat anchored in the Seine and Max introduced me to *grec frites*, a warmed pita wrapped around shredded pork and French fries and eaten out of hand, best long after midnight. And sometimes we'd just sit in silence and look at each other. I wanted to memorize every inch of him. It was the strangest thing: he fit like a puzzle piece into a part of me I had never before realized was still empty.

Soon I had Max sitting at the little round table that moonlighted as my desk, my nightstand, and my dining table. He'd open a cold bottle of *cidre* and I'd make simple things like saffron-tinged risotto or spaghetti for dinner. Sometimes I put together a salad with mâche, the soft, dark green leaves as tender as new grass, and wedges of sour blood oranges, their juice staining the dressing red. Best of all were the indoor picnics. We'd get a good baguette at the bakery down the street and then head to the Monoprix supermarket for little rounds of chalky goat cheese, slices of *rosette de Lyon* salami, a bit of pâté that reminded us of liverwurst from back home, olives, and cherry tomatoes. We would pile everything onto the table and then eat dinner with our hands. But the braised endives might have sealed the deal. Those really made his eyes grow wide.

I'd first eaten braised endives with my father earlier in the year at a simple lunch spot in Paris where a three-course meal cost the equivalent of nine dollars and the kitchen specialized in classic French bistro dishes like *hachis Parmentier*, leeks vinaigrette, and *blanquette de veau*. The braised endives appeared on our plates looking entirely unspectacular. They were limp and a little wan-looking, really. But a fork sank into them like a knife through butter and what they didn't have in color they made up for in taste: bitter and creamy at once, faintly caramelized and zinging with citrus flavor. They tasted so interesting, so unlike most other vegetables I liked to eat. They were a little strange, but I couldn't stop eating them. I liked that about them.

A few months later, my father found a recipe for braised endives in a rather generic–looking French cookbook he'd come across in a bargain pile at his favorite bookstore in Boston, the New England Mobile Book Fair. He called me excitedly to give me the recipe over the phone. There wasn't much to the dish, really. All you had to do was halve the endives and fry them in olive oil until the cut sides were a feathery golden–brown. Then you turned the endives, sprinkled them with a little bit of salt and sugar, which you quickly caramelizd and added the juice of a lemon. With the heat turned almost all the way down and a tight lid on top, the endives braised in the sweet–sour juice, mellowing and softening, in just about half an hour.

The world wants you to believe that the way to a man's heart is with a big steak, maybe, or a stack of pancakes and bacon the morning after a long night in bed. But I'm here to tell you that it might just be a slightly bitter braised vegetable that does the trick. After all, braised endives were what made the man I was starting to adore turn to me after dinner, sighing contentedly, and say, "I *love* that you love to cook."

Braised Endives

SERVES 2 AS A SIDE DISH

In this simple side dish, lemon juice adds a sour note to balance the endives' bitterness. To amplify the lemon, you can zest some of the lemon peel to add at the very end of cooking. Or, if you like the combination of oranges and endives, substitute the juice of half an orange for the lemon juice. Serve alongside roast chicken or a piece of pan-fried fish for an easy weeknight dinner.

 3 or 4 Belgian endives
 3 tablespoons olive oil

Pinch of sugar
Salt and freshly ground black pepper to taste
Juice of 1 lemon
1 tablespoon butter (optional)

1. Wash and dry the endives and pull off any discolored outer leaves. Cut them in half lengthwise and trim off the root end but leave the endive halves intact. Cut out the inner core.

2. Heat the olive oil in a heavy, lidded 3-quart sauté pan over medium heat. Put the endives, cut side down, in the pan. (If your endives are huge or if you double the recipe, you may have to do this step in batches.) Let the endives cook for 3 to 5 minutes on each side, letting them brown but not burn.

3. When all the endive halves have been browned on both sides, squeeze them into the pan and sprinkle them with the sugar, salt, and pepper. Let the sugar melt for a few seconds. Then add the lemon juice, immediately turn the heat to low, and cover the pan.

4. Let the endives cook for 15 minutes. They should be fork-tender and caramelized. Remove the endives from the pan and put them on a serving plate. Raise the heat to medium and reduce the cooking juices in the pan to a thin syrup, stirring for 2 to 3 minutes. If you want a richer sauce, add the tablespoon of butter to the pan and stir it in until it has melted and emulsified, creating a silky sauce, an additional 3 to 5 minutes. Butter or no butter, pour the sauce over the endives and serve immediately.

9

Not At All Ready

I DON'T KNOW HOW YOU WERE AT TWENTY-ONE, DEAR READER, BUT IN hindsight I guess you could say I was a little set in my ways. I'd long gotten over my childhood aversion to different foods touching on my plate, it's true, but I still avoided things like mayonnaise and mustard and pickles like the plague (a difficult feat in Paris, as you might imagine). I spooned the cilantro delicately off my Vietnamese soups, avoided perfectly lovely gravlax edged with hideous, feathery dill (ooh, how I loathed it), and was very, very nervous about love at first sight.

Love at first sight is pretty much the biggest cliché in the world. And it is an even bigger cliché if it happens to you in Paris. Now if you are a person with any normal kind of heart, you can't scowl at the circumstances or feel embarrassed by the fact that you have managed to become a walking cliché. You just have to open yourself up and let it all in. Which is just what Max did. He wrote me adoring letters and exulted in his good fortune. He kissed me with alacrity on every street corner, told me how lovely I looked, even when I wasn't at my best, and if he could have shouted his love from a rooftop, I do believe he would have. He gave himself up to love with relish.

But I teetered on the edge for quite some time. I was terrified by the depth of my feelings and by the depth of his. I'd never experienced anything like it before in my life, and, if I'm honest, I was a little suspicious of the whole thing. It couldn't possibly be real, this all-consuming love we felt for each other. There had to be a catch somewhere. There just had to be. You know, it was sort of like loathing pickles your whole life (those slithery, sweetish things) and then eating a cornichon for the first time, crisp and sour and perfect, and not wanting to accept that this wondrous thing that you'd like to spend the rest of your life popping into your mouth like candy is the very same thing you spent your whole life mistrusting. (Are you still with me?)

There were moments when I felt I needed absolutely nothing more from the world than Max's arms around me. That sense of the world falling away, of there being only the two of us, was nothing short of life changing. I felt complete, whole, when he was with me. But I was nervous too. I spent too much time worrying that it was all too intense, too quick, that we were being too passionate for our own good. I alternated between moments of ecstasy, the kind of natural high I'd never before experienced, and extreme suspicion. What was going to come of all this? Wasn't true love at first sight just a load of baloney? It couldn't possibly be like this in real life. I was on my guard.

I could die, I'm so happy, I thought one day. And the next, *I need to be careful. This is crazy. I'm only twenty-one and I hardly* know him.

And then there was the matter of geography. By the end of the year, Max's internship was over and he returned to the small Bavarian town where he was enrolled in university while I stayed in Paris. With my father's approval, I found the nerve to quit my graduate program and, with the help of Madame LaCarrière, who undoubtedly did not want to lose a paying tenant so quickly, got a job at a publishing house around the corner from my apartment. Max and I wrote hundreds of e-mails and mailed dozens of postcards and letters to each other over the months that followed. Occasionally, he'd come to Paris to see me and I'd fly to Passau to visit him, but our daily romance was conducted by the pen and the computer. There was a lot of room for misunderstanding. We were in love, desperately, head over heels, but the reality of our lives wasn't quite matching up.

I loved the job I'd found, working in the English-language

department of a French publishing house, proofreading translated cookbook manuscripts and art books. Some days I was even tasked with alphabetizing the department's massive library of cookbooks. I would sit cross-legged in front of the bookshelves and, when I had a quiet moment, I'd transcribe irresistible recipes for tricolor omelettes, French chocolate cake, or *Riz Impératrice* onto pages of loose-leaf paper that I folded and stashed in my pockets. At lunchtime I would walk home and warm up leftover Depression Stew or I'd head to my favorite bakery and buy a baguette sandwich lined with salami and sliced cornichons, since they'd become my new obsession, and eat the sandwich perched by the fountain on place Saint-Sulpice. Max loved cornichons and ate them by the jarload when he came to visit. He was the one who got me to fall in love with them too, with their nubby skin and their intensely puckery flavor.

But once Max left, living in Paris didn't get any easier. Despite the very nice colleagues I had at the publishing house, their friendliness never extended past the threshold of the company door at 5:00 P.M. And Amy and Melissa had long since found boyfriends with whom they spent most of their time. Max was far away and the e-mails, postcards, and letters he faithfully sent didn't make up for his absence. Evening after evening alone in my apartment, eating cornichons from the jar and cooking single-girl dinners of spaghetti topped with breadcrumbs and capers, I felt like was I shriveling up inside.

At the end of my year in Paris, when the summer was drawing to a close, I decided to leave. I'd made it an entire year, which had seemed nigh on impossible all those months ago when I was mired in grad school classes with professors droning on about the imperative case. I gave myself permission to see it as enough. The next time Max came to visit, we packed up my paring knives, my recipe clippings, and the rollerblades we'd bought to zip around the city with together, and rented a car, which we drove from Paris to Berlin over the course of two days, stopping to sleep at a bleak highway motel near Düsseldorf, where the hum of cars passing in the night and the distinct sense that a chapter of my life was ending kept me awake all night. We barely spoke.

My plan was to find a job in Berlin. Once I got there, installed in my mother's guest bedroom, I spent weeks job hunting, mailing my short little resumé to the few publishing houses left in Berlin after the end of the World War II, when most businesses and industries high-tailed it to prosperous West German cities and stayed there. But I got no responses in return. It soon became abundantly clear that with my American high school diploma (I had opted out of the German diploma track in high school) and my American college degree, I wasn't going to get very far. The academic reforms that would change the way Germany recognized foreign degrees, especially American ones, were still years away.

The limits of my existence in Berlin soon became uncomfortably clear. I may have been born there, claiming the cobblestoned sidewalks as my own, but when it came down to brass tacks, I was an outsider, a foreign national with an education that didn't account for much in the eyes of the establishment, despite my near-perfect German and the fact that I didn't know where else to call home. It was deeply upsetting to realize that I didn't have much of a practical future in the city I'd always figured I'd grow old in. And I realized why my father had, in part, been compelled to leave Berlin after his marriage fell apart. As a foreigner, even an assimilated one who wanted nothing more than to be a contributing, responsible member of German society, there was still a glass ceiling, a polite but firm barrier.

Once I realized that there wasn't much available to me in Berlin, I felt stifled. I was at the beginning of my working life. Finding myself empty-handed in Berlin, while in New York jobs were opening up left and right, made me want to leave right away. Max, on the other hand, wouldn't be done with university for years. If I stayed in Berlin for him, without any job prospects, wouldn't I start to resent him sooner or later?

Beyond the work situation, I was scared of the commitment Max wanted. I hid my fear of commitment behind my professional concerns, but Max wasn't fooled. He told me in desperation that this kind of love—all-consuming, life-completing—wouldn't come around again. It was a once–in–a–lifetime thing. Didn't I *get* that? The thing was, I didn't believe him. When I was ready for it, when I was old enough, I was sure it would. It was wiser to leave.

And soon it was decided: I would make my way to New York, stopping at my father's in Boston while I lined up a job in the big city. Some girlfriends on the Upper West Side had a room opening up just at the right time. My path was clear and the future suddenly seemed very safe. I gave up on Berlin and, in that instant, it felt like a relief.

Max couldn't believe the speed with which I made my decision. And I wondered, late at night in those days before I left, if I wasn't making a terrible mistake. But I left anyway. I didn't know what else to do. And that, sometimes, is all you can say.

Spaghetti with Breadcrumbs, Capers, and Parsley

SERVES 1 (CAN EASILY BE DOUBLED)

2 tablespoons olive oil

1 clove garlic, smashed

1 dried chile, crumbled

1 anchovy fillet (optional)

Salt, if needed

3 tablespoons plain breadcrumbs

2 tablespoons minced flat-leaf parsley

2¾ to 3¾ ounces dried spaghetti

1. Bring a pot of salted water to a boil.

2. While the water is heating up, put 1 tablespoon of the olive oil and the smashed garlic, crumbled chile, and anchovy (if using) in a small pan set over medium heat. Break up the anchovy with a wooden spoon as the oil heats, letting it dissolve into the oil. (If you're not using the anchovy, add a pinch of salt to the pan.)

3. Add the breadcrumbs and cook, stirring constantly, until the bread-crumbs are golden brown and crunchy (do not let them burn). Discard the garlic clove, add the minced parsley, and taste for salt. Set aside.

4. Cook the spaghetti in the boiling water until al dente. Reserve a few spoonfuls of the starchy cooking water before draining the spaghetti.

5. Toss the spaghetti in the pan with the breadcrumbs and the second tablespoon of olive oil. If the spaghetti seems a little dry, add a bit of the starchy water to loosen the sauce. Serve immediately.

Part 2

10

I Fell Hard and Fast

MY GRANDPARENTS TOOK ME TO THE RAINBOW ROOM AT THE TOP of the GE Building in Rockefeller Center when I was four years old. The dance floor was polished and gleaming, there were waiters in white dinner jackets and black tuxedo pants, and we ate duck for dinner, its tender flesh and deep, gamy flavor a revelation. For dessert, a kindly waiter brought me a black-and-white cookie on a little china plate. Lest you think something as special as an evening at the Rainbow Room would be lost on a four-year-old, don't worry: I'll never forget it. Though it may be hard to believe, however, that wasn't actually when I fell in love with New York, even if I was awfully charmed.

The weekend I fell in love came along several years later. I was nine, and my father and I were visiting the city with my grandparents again. My Grandma Ann had grown up in Brooklyn, and my Grandpa Dave, one of eight children, had grown up in the Bronx. They'd moved away from the city as a young married couple when my grandfather got a job at the Philadelphia Navy Yard and had settled in a quiet suburb of Philadelphia, where they would go on to raise their sons and spend the rest of their lives. But they left their hearts in New York. The Philly suburbs were a pallid substitute for the big vibrant city they'd grown up in, and even after fifty years in Philadelphia, when asked where they were from, my grandparents always said "New York!"

Grandma and Grandpa surrounded themselves with other New

Yorkers and often returned to Manhattan on day trips, taking a bus into town, where they'd catch an afternoon performance at the opera or go to a matinee at the theater. Afterward they'd have an early-bird dinner with their friends at an Italian restaurant in Queens with thick white tablecloths, Neapolitan waiters, and red-sauced pasta before heading back home again.

One weekend in 1986, my father and I met them in Manhattan. We went to see *Madame Butterfly* at Lincoln Center, where I sat on my grandmother's lap as the long-haired, doomed lady in a kimono sang, and we rode across town in a yellow cab driven by a man with an old-time Brooklyn accent. We met old friends of theirs for lunch and walked up Fifth Avenue, the city pulsating, alive, around us.

I gaped at everything: the masses of cabs, the looming buildings, the people, as colorful and wild as anything I'd ever seen. I loved the narrow streets of the East Twenties and the glitter of the Plaza Hotel. We walked past vegetarian kosher Indian restaurants and power-suited, big-shouldered businesswomen on Fifth Avenue. And I fell hard and fast. I bought a canvas "I ♥ New York" tote bag from a street vendor and came home bubbling, proclaiming it, and knowing it in my bones: *One day, I'm going to move to New York.*

And so, fifteen years later, I did.

I left Paris and Berlin behind, along with all the confusion and sadness that lurked there, and I found myself a job at a publishing company in Rockefeller Center. I had a little desk outside the publisher's office and I answered his phone, fending off agents and authors, took notes in meetings, went out to book parties with other assistants, and reveled in bagfuls of free galleys. I walked over the Brooklyn Bridge at sunset, skin tingling, with a still glorious Lower Manhattan in plain sight, and felt a smug pride when I learned to navigate the West Village without a map.

I had a small room in an apartment with two girlfriends on the Upper West Side, just across from Zabar's and a few blocks from Central Park. My roommates worked in publishing too, and after work we'd watch old Meg Ryan movies set in the streets around our apartment. On weekends we stayed out late or threw dinner parties with borrowed chairs and Christmas lights strung up over the windows, and in winter we fought with our landlady about the heat.

That first year in New York, I spent every day in a febrile state of joy: discovering the thrill of black-and-white movies on Sunday afternoons at Film Forum, having Bloody Marys in pint glasses for dinner at the Tile Bar in the East Village, shaking Bill Clinton's hand at a book party in Tribeca, taking buses all around town just so I could see each neighborhood all the way through, hearing the laconic subway conductor announce Times Square as the "crawss-roads of the world" every morning on the way to work, and seeing all my fellow passengers break out in a smile.

I never felt alone in New York. None of the solitude that had so dogged me in Paris was anywhere to be found. Even on long solitary walks in Central Park and on early morning cab rides home after a long night out with friends, I felt like I was surrounded by people, in the best possible way. I never minded the crowds. After the heartbreak of leaving Max behind, it felt like New York was healing me.

But there were many moments when I felt guilty too. I'd saved myself at his expense. It wasn't meant to be, I'd try to console myself, even though the words rang hollow in my own ears. The timing wasn't right. And, I'm sure he's moved on by now. Which only tied me up in more knots. So I put my head down and tried to forget about Max.

Being in New York made me feel like I'd won the lottery. I had moved to the center of the universe and it was even better than I had ever imagined. Many evenings during my first years there I'd come home and change, make something quick for dinner, and then head out again, crisscrossing the Upper West Side from the Seventy-ninth Street Boat Basin to Central Park, from the grand Apthorp apartment building to the shuttered Metro Theater on Ninety-sixth and Broadway. Sometimes I walked all the way up to Columbia at 116th Street, passing the wrought-iron gates on Riverside Drive, wondering which apartment building Joanie had grown up in; then I would head over to Amsterdam Avenue, which at that height was still a little dicey, and back down to the hubbub of the mid–Eighties, where restaurants and bars were crammed full of young people carousing and spilling out onto the sidewalk.

Our street—hidden among the beautiful brownstone–lined blocks around us—was a little gritty. There was a famous vintage clothing shop at the end of our block, a gentlemen's bookstore a few doors down, where dodgy-looking characters would head in with their eyes averted, and sometimes, on the way to work in the morning, a man in the building next to ours would expose himself to us behind the safety of his building's glass door, his face obscured by his sweatshirt. Once I even saw a rat as big as my lower arm race from a garbage bag dumped on the sidewalk back to the safety of a building. It was all part of the adventure, though I could have done without the flasher.

Some days, I'd head to the footpath along the Hudson River in the morning. I'd walk south, my legs moving briskly in the fresh morning breeze. I'd see the construction around Lincoln Center, the grittier buildings of Hell's Kitchen, the heliport around Thirtieth Street. I'd make my way all the way down to Chinatown, where I'd fight through the crowds on Canal Street and buy myself a steamed pork bun or a little paper cone filled with quarter–sized piping–hot egg cakes to eat on the side of the street. On the more secluded streets of the East Village, I'd hear birds chattering over the din of nearby traffic. I got to know all the city's farmers' markets and knew where to go for the best tomatoes and apples. In autumn, I clutched paper cups of hot tea on strolls through Central Park, where dried leaves in shades of rust and ochre gathered at the base of tree trunks. In spring, I saw New York City through that pure, shiny, clear light that filters down through the first tender green leaves.

And just like in Paris, whenever I needed some quiet time alone, I'd head to the grocery store. I'd buy cheap olive oil and imported rice at Fairway, browsing the dried beans and cereal aisle as I pushed my cart past neighbors. Fairway sold little tubs of Quark that made me think of Berlin, and jars of cornichons and plastic bags of sliced sourdough bread from the Poilâne bakery in Paris that made me think of Max. I went to Zabar's for pickled herring that I'd eat on matzo, like my father taught me to, and for wrinkly black olives and fat smooth green ones, my mother's favorites. Sometimes I'd go upstairs to the second floor and stare at the gleaming copper pots and pans and kitchen equipment for hours, losing myself between pastry bags and Microplane graters.

Back at the apartment, I'd dissolve a can of tuna in garlicky tomato sauce studded with capers and use it to dress pasta for dinner. I baked seeded loaves of bread that blistered in the oven. I once roasted a whole eggplant for baba ghanoush but forgot to pierce it with a fork beforehand, so it exploded all over the oven with a terrifying bang and the flesh instantly fused to the hot oven walls. I learned to make triple-layered devil's food cake that I toted to Central Park for birthdays and made gooey brownies for parties. I pored over the newspaper's food section every Wednesday, fantasizing about a life in which I'd cook things like Caramelized Onion Tart with Brown Butter Crust or Lady Baltimore Cake. And I clipped recipes like a woman possessed, adding them to the hand-written recipes from Paris, hoarding them in binders and in books, pasting them in carefully with rubber cement, and telling myself that one day I'd need them, these recipes for Roasted Striped Bass with Salsa de la Boca and Beef Stew with Prunes.

Like most young New Yorkers, my roommates didn't really cook so much as they shopped. Kirsten bought fudgy little blocks of Norwegian gjetost cheese that she sliced carefully and ate on whole wheat crackers. Julie, who replaced Kirsten when she moved out, subsisted mainly on a diet of Tasti D-Lite. Betsy once made a batch of her mother's whipped potatoes, thick with hot milk, butter, and chives, but for the most part I was the only one who cooked. And for a while we coexisted congenially in the kitchen. Until I discovered a recipe for braising chicken with tomatoes and white wine. That's when everything changed.

I'd been reading a funny little book called *Clementine in the Kitchen*, by an American artist named Samuel Chamberlain writing under the pen name of Phineas Beck. It described the life of an expat American family living in France before World War II with an intrepid Burgundian cook named Clementine. The book was full of simple little French recipes with lyrical names, although maybe that was just the way they sounded in French: *Côtelettes de Porc aux Navets, Foie de Veau Poêlé à la Bourgeoise, Langue de Boeuf en Gelée*. But what I got hung up on the most was the *Poulet Sauté à la Paysanne Provençale*.

It was a simple dish. You simply browned a bunch of chicken pieces in olive oil before adding white wine, shallots, and tomatoes to the pot and braising the browned chicken pieces in that gravy of sorts until the meat was tender and juicy and the tomatoes had broken down into stewy sweetness. Olives were thrown in at the end and the whole dish took only a little more than half an hour to get to the table. And, at least to a group of girls eating endless plates of spaghetti or soft-serve frozen dessert for dinner, it was an impressive payoff for very little work.

Betsy was the first one who paid attention when I started cooking the *Poulet*. She'd hear me setting up in the kitchen and would come and join me, shyly at first, looking over my shoulder as I rinsed the chicken and floured it. Then she grew bolder and started asking questions. "Why does the chicken have to be dried off?" "Why do you remove the chicken from the pot only to put it back in again later?" And "How do you know when it's done?" I told her what I knew, what I had learned by trial and error and endless nighttime reads in cookbooks over the years. You dry the chicken so that it fries up crisply instead of steaming. You take the chicken out while you cook the onions so that it doesn't overcook later. You know it's done with practice, practice, practice. So just keep cooking.

Soon Betsy was helping me to cut the tomatoes and slip the chicken pieces into the hot oil. One day, I came home to find her cooking it all by herself, olives pitted, shallot minced, wine poured. And after that, the lessons really began. I taught my roommates how to make spaghetti sauce and how to fry zucchini blossoms the way Pietro did in Italy, how to sauté clams with garlic and hot chiles, how to make a pot of fragrant meat ragù. And somewhere along the line, between the onion-flavored steam on the windows and the fairy-light-strung dinner parties, we cemented our friendship through cooking. Years later, long after we'd all moved out of that little apartment, Julie still called me from the farmers' market to ask if she should buy the zucchini

blossoms to fill and fry and Betsy rang from London
the evening she made our chicken for her future husband,
proposal was imminent.

I hadn't fully realized before that knowing how to cook was a spe૮
skill or something to be proud of. I'd always wondered if my mother
was right, that my obsession with cookbooks and clipping newspaper
recipes was a little weird. I didn't know anyone else who read cookbooks before bedtime and who sat down happily with the Wednesday
food section and a pair of scissors each week. But I knew no one else
my age who really cooked either. The look of joy on my friends' faces
when they made a real, from-scratch dinner for the first time was sort
of fantastic. It made me feel a lot better than any good day at the office.

And it wasn't too long before I figured out how to get that feeling
again and again.

Poulet Sauté à la Paysanne Provençale

SERVES 4

This is a rustic braised chicken dish that lends itself perfectly to weeknight
dinners because it's so quickly and easily made. Since it's a braise, the
chicken skin won't crisp up delectably like a roast. It'll be a little soggy and
limp. But the flavor of the onion and wine and tomatoes infuses the
chicken meat, making it toothsome and juicy. Serve with mashed potatoes
or steamed rice to soak up the delicious gravy.

> All-purpose flour, for coating
> 1 4-pound chicken, cut into 8 pieces (2 drumsticks, 2 thighs, and
>   2 bone-in breasts each cut in half crosswise; save the wings
>   and backbone for stock)
> Salt and freshly ground black pepper
> ¼ cup olive oil
> 1 shallot, minced

½ cup dry white wine

4 medium plum tomatoes, peeled, seeded, and coarsely chopped, or
    2 handfuls of cherry tomatoes, halved

1 small clove garlic, chopped and mashed

12 oil-cured olives, pitted

1 tablespoon finely minced flat-leaf parsley

1. Put the flour on a plate. Rinse the chicken pieces under cold water and wipe them dry. Season them liberally with salt and pepper, and then dip the chicken pieces lightly in the flour. Set aside.

2. Put the olive oil in a broad 3-quart sauté pan or 4-quart cast-iron pot over medium heat, and when the oil is shimmering, slip the pieces of floured chicken into the oil. Cook until golden brown on each side, about 15 minutes in total. Then put the browned chicken pieces on a clean plate and pour off all but 2 tablespoons of the pan drippings.

3. Add the minced shallot to the pan and let it cook over low heat until golden. Add the white wine, bring it to a simmer, and let it cook until it is reduced by half, 5 to 7 minutes.

4. Add the chopped tomatoes, garlic, and olives, and stir well; then slip the chicken pieces back into the pan. Cover and cook over low heat for another 15 to 20 minutes. Stir in the minced parsley a few minutes before the end. Then turn off the heat and let the chicken rest for a few minutes before serving.

11

The Wednesday Chef

I WAS AT THE OFFICE ONE DAY WHEN MY GIRLFRIEND BARBARA SENT ME an e-mail. "Have you heard about this girl named Julie Powell? She's cooking every single recipe in Julia Child's cookbook and writing about it on her blog. It made me think of you." I had a vague understanding of what blogs were, but the few I'd seen were written by tech nerds. That you could write a blog about cooking had never occurred to me. I clicked on the link in Barbara's e-mail and within minutes I was lost. Here was this girl, just a little older than me, and to distract herself from a job she didn't like, she was cooking dinner and writing about it online. It was spectacular. (And very funny to boot.)

I'd been lucky enough, after I'd moved on from being the publisher's assistant, to find a job as a scout for an agency representing foreign publishers. I got to read manuscripts and write book reports and travel to book fairs in Europe, and on the whole, I could scarcely believe I was being paid for things I would have been happy to do for free. But as the years passed and I got closer and closer to the metaphorical ceiling at the agency, I started to wonder what was next for me.

For months I read Julie's blog religiously, checking in every day to see if she'd posted something new, cheering her on when she mastered the complicated *Pâté de Canard en Croûte* or the *Charlotte Malakoff au Chocolat* and commiserating when she collapsed, exhausted, to a Tex-Mex meal that her husband prepared once a week so that they could have a reprieve from Julia Child's steady diet of meat, cream, and butter. There was something intoxicating about being invited in to Julie's world as a reader. In fact, it was better, more immediate, than all those cookbooks I'd read like novels over the years. There was a connection between the blog writer and her readers that felt intimate in the best possible way. I was invested in Julie's success just by virtue of reading her posts every day. By the time the year was over and the blog was supposed to end, I was as disconsolate as when I finished books in grade school. Whatever would I read next? Who would ever come as close to entertaining and moving me? Most important, what would it be like not to know what was happening in Julie's life every day?

I turned to Google and before long I had found new blogs to follow: *Chocolate & Zucchini* was one, written by a Parisian woman just a year younger than I who was learning how to cook. *The Amateur Gourmet*, written by a graduate student in Atlanta who was teaching himself to cook by following recipes and posting his results online, was another. There was an Italian man who loved to bake artisanal breads and a Singaporean banker who was obsessed with making Alice Medrich's low-fat cake recipes. Falling into a rabbit hole of like-minded people who wanted nothing more than to write about what they made for lunch (or dinner, or dessert) all day long was like discovering Plimoth Plantation as a child. I could scarcely believe my good fortune. I never wanted to leave this new and wondrous world.

My apartment share with Betsy and Julie had dissolved when Betsy moved to London and Julie finally got engaged to her longtime boyfriend, Mike. I was living in another apartment with roommates on Eighteenth Street in Chelsea when I started to wonder why I wasn't writing a blog too. After all, I sent my father e-mails about what I'd made for dinner all the time and I was feeling that old familiar itch to write. Some of my favorite books were about food, from Laurie Colwin's collection of columns on home cooking for *Gourmet* magazine to Ruth Reichl's memoirs about growing up and becoming a restaurant critic. Plus, I was drowning in recipe clippings, yet I wasn't actually *using* any of them. I was carefully building an ever larger and larger library of recipes to try someday, but that day never seemed to arrive. I couldn't help but wonder: what if that someday was now?

"I think you should do it," said Sam. We'd been dating for a few months. He lived just a few blocks away and came over for cozy dinners at my apartment most nights of the week. "It sounds neat. Besides, I get to eat everything you make, right?" He smiled. "You'd *have* to eat everything I make," I corrected. "How on earth would I get rid of all that food otherwise?" I didn't have a very big appetite, but Sam, at almost six foot five, had been known to eat an entire pound of spaghetti in one sitting. "It's a deal, Weezie. Just remember, no anchovies, no bacon." No one had called me Weezie since the fourth grade, when a teacher I didn't particularly like insisted on it. But Weezie sounded entirely different coming out of Sam's mouth. Besides, he gave everyone he loved a nickname.

There were a lot of little parallels between Sam's life and mine. Our parents were both divorced. Our fathers, both remarried, lived barely a mile apart in a suburb of Boston. Our mothers, never remarried, lived overseas. We'd even attended the same elementary school for a few overlapping months in seventh grade before I moved back to Berlin. When I met Sam, I decided that all these things were little signs pointing toward kismet. That and his easy laugh.

Easy seemed to define a lot about Sam. He didn't go in for any of the push-pull that so many of the men my girlfriends dated did—he was just there, available, from the start. And I liked the fact that he didn't expect much from me and never really got worked up about anything. I had found that love could be frightening, the way it swallowed you up, demanding sacrifices and hard decisions. It was safe, I decided, to be with someone who was just kind and funny, calling me every day, laughing at my jokes, making me feel adorable. Sam made me feel taken care of. Within a few months, I could barely remember a time when he hadn't been around.

The more I chewed on the idea of starting a blog, the more I thought it would need to have some kind of structure—a mission, for lack of a better word. I decided I would spend one year cooking my way through all my clipped newspaper recipes, reporting on whether they were good or not. In the process, I'd winnow my stack of clippings and keep an online journal of sorts. It would be useful to clean out the duds and it would be good practice, I figured, to force myself to write and to cook something other than the family recipes I could make with my eyes closed. In tribute to the newspaper food section's weekly publication day, I called the blog *The Wednesday Chef*.

On August 22, 2005, I wrote my first post. And for a while I'm pretty sure my father was the only one read who read my blog every day. He would send me encouraging one-line e-mails after each post.

Dear Luisa,
     Great post!
          Love, Papi

Dear Luisa,
     Those peppers sound delicious!
          Love, Papi

Dear Luisa,
     Your best post yet!!
          Love, Papi

If my father was my most loyal reader, then Sam was my most loyal eater. He ate everything I put in front of him (though I once found him picking minced bacon methodically out of a bowl of collard greens and lentils on New Year's Day), and I faithfully reported his opinions on chicken salad wrapped in naan bread or waffles made with buckwheat flour in my blog posts. Sam became the blog's hungry mascot, its second pillar. Without him eating, I could never have cooked as much as I did. I cooked for him and I wrote for my readers.

My readers, yes, because to my everlasting delight, click by click, people soon started to find my blog. First there were a handful and then a few dozen and then there were hundreds and thousands. I had an honest-to-goodness *audience*, a whole mass of people who liked what I wrote enough to keep coming back for more, who felt compelled to write comments and send me e-mails, and who laughed when I was being silly and told me they had tears in their eyes when I blogged between the lines about feeling blue. I hadn't ever thought I'd reach people like that. Or that their reactions would touch me as much as they did.

The initial premise, to work through my stack of recipes and evaluate them, fell away pretty quickly. I decided to keep cooking from my clippings, but it was clear that when I wrote about my everyday life, it resonated far more with my readers than any dry appraisal of a recipe. And it felt pretty good to me too, like a journal of sorts, a diary I wasn't embarrassed to share with perfect strangers. So I wrote about the first time I nervously cooked for Sam's mother, Evelyn (panfried trout, green beans in vinegar cream), and what it was like to spend Thanksgiving upstate with Sam's family (hashed Brussels sprouts, cranberry chutney). I wrote about feeling homesick (Spanish flan) and having a dinner party with friends (salmon rillettes).

And just like when I was teaching Betsy and Julie how to braise chicken and fry zucchini flowers, my greatest reward was the reaction of my readers, who cooked and ate alongside me, learning that when you melt anchovies in oil you get rich flavor in your dish but no fishiness, that putting red peppers in a hot oven for forty minutes is the only way to roast them into silky suppleness, or that tomato bread soup made at the height of summer is possibly the most delicious food in the world. I got bossy with my readers, telling them which recipes they had to laminate and rush home to make right away and which ones they could throw straight in the garbage can. I waxed rhapsodic about chicken cooked in crème fraîche and lemon zest and found a rapt audience, eager to make the same thing for dinner.

Although I had started the blog more as an exercise than anything else, I was delighted to discover that it was so much more than just a regular writing practice. Through the blog, I was finding new friends who felt the same way about food as I did, who loved being in the kitchen as much as I did, for whom food was a currency as potent and real as any dollar bill. In the middle of all that vastness, my blog was my little spot in the world and I was cheered on by every comment my readers left.

Tomato Bread Soup

SERVES 4

Sometimes I get asked what my favorite recipe on the blog is, which is a little bit like asking a mother who her favorite child is. I find it difficult to pick just one. However, if you really force me, like, really put a gun to my head, I'd have to point to this tomato soup thickened with cubes of bread. The recipe is adapted from Bill Telepan, a chef who owns the restaurant Telepan on Manhattan's Upper West Side. When the bread cubes hit the silky tomatoes, they go all custardy and soft. Basil and *ricotta salata* add perfume and flavor. It's simple to prepare, but absolutely exquisite. What's crucial is that it be made only, and I mean only, in months when tomatoes are at the height of ripeness at the farmers' market. You also need a source for good sourdough bread, but these days that's not so hard to find. If you don't have one, substitute rustic peasant bread or bake a loaf of Jim Lahey's brilliant No-Knead Bread (the recipe is on my blog, thewednesdaychef.com) and use that.

    3 pounds fresh, ripe plum tomatoes
    2 tablespoons extra-virgin olive oil
    1 small onion, minced
    3 cloves garlic
    Salt and freshly ground black pepper
    2 cups cubed, crustless sourdough or peasant bread
    ½ cup grated *ricotta salata*
    1 tablespoon minced fresh basil leaves

1. Core and quarter the plum tomatoes. Place the tomatoes and their juices in a food processor and pulse just a few times to chop them coarsely. You don't want a tomato purée.

2. Heat the oil in a 4-quart saucepan. Add the onion and garlic and sauté until soft but not browned. Add the tomatoes and their juices. Season with salt and pepper, bring to a slow simmer, and cook for 45 minutes, covered, stirring from time to time.

3. When the soup has simmered for 45 minutes, stir in the
and simmer for an additional 10 to 15 minutes. Check the se
discard the garlic cloves.

4. Serve slightly cooled or at room temperature, with grated *ricotta
salata* and minced basil strewn over each serving.

12

So Easy

BEFORE TOO LONG, THE BLOG HAD REORDERED MY LIFE, GIVING IT A NEW rhythm and schedule. My days went something like this: I woke up in the morning and got ready for work. Before leaving the house, I would go through my recipe clippings and my bookmarked recipes and choose something to make for dinner that night. A bean gratin, maybe, or a spiky mizuna salad topped with boiled eggs. At the office, I would do my duties as a foreign scout, calling editors and agents throughout Manhattan to talk about the manuscripts they were reading and excited about. I'd write e-mails to my clients overseas and put the finishing touches on a reader's report. But on my lunch break, I would leave that world and head out into the city, to the greenmarket at Union Square or Garden of Eden on Fourteenth Street, where I would gather my ingredients for the evening, sometimes rushing over to Curry Hill if I needed a bottle of ajowan and invariably ending up back at the office with something like dried Persian limes or fresh curry leaves to boot.

In the evening, after work, I headed home to cook and photograph what was happening on the stove before Sam came over for dinner. Sometimes I blogged right after dinner. Sometimes I got up extra early in the morning to cram a new post in before heading to the gym and to work. I'd never felt so productive, or creative, in my life. I loved how blog writing made me feel so loose and free: When cabbage leaves stuffed with lamb and braised in tomato sauce reminded me of my school lunches in Berlin, that's what I'd talk about when I wrote up the recipe for the blog. When thick rigatoni sauced with braised kale and fresh ricotta that I bought at an Italian wholesale market around the corner from my apartment made me think of my summers in Italy with my mother's family, that's the angle I took. The more I wrote, the easier it got. The more I wrote, the more I wanted to write. And I loved this new semisecret life I was leading, the world I was discovering on the other side of my computer screen. Sam helped out by doing the dishes without my ever having to ask and by eating almost everything I made with gusto.

By the time Sam and I had been together for a year, I'd met most of his family. They welcomed me with open arms, particularly his sister, Liza, who had a PhD in Italian history and who had instantly felt like a kindred spirit. I loved spending time with her and listening to her gentle voice. Soon, Sam and I were scheduling weekends upstate with Liza and her Spanish husband, Javier, and planning holidays together. I loved being a part of their family, cooking in the kitchen with Javier, hearing the din of voices spilling over from the next room, and sitting down at a crowded dinner table together. It felt cozy and warm and almost instantly familiar. And before too long, Liza started feeling like *my* sister too. "I'm so lucky I found you," I told Sam one weekend when we were all gathered upstate. "Nah, Weezie," he said with a smile, "I'm the lucky one."

So the last thing I wanted to do was push him into anything, even though after a couple of years passed I started to wonder why he never asked me what my plans were for the future. At his little brother's wedding, a well-meaning relative asked him why he wasn't married yet. "Don't you have a nice girlfriend?" she wondered, narrowing her eyes at him as they stood in line for the buffet dinner. He recounted the story to me later, back at our table, incredulous at her presumption and rudeness. I nodded my head sympathetically, but later I had to ask myself too: *After more than two years together, at the age of thirty, why have we never even had a conversation about our future?* I found myself wondering, for all the ease and simplicity of our relationship, if there wasn't something crucial missing, something deeper that would bind us together besides our good natures.

In the next moment, I told myself in exasperation that there was absolutely nothing to worry about. *Sam loves you very much. The whole point of this relationship is that it's relaxed and easy. Why muck up a good thing? Anyway, just because some nosy woman at a family wedding thinks it's weird does not in any way mean it's* actually *weird.*

Besides, most of the time, life was too hectic for me to spend much time worrying about Sam's intentions. I had accepted a new job as a cookbook editor at a small publishing house on Eighteenth Street, and carving out time for my blog before and after work was becoming harder than ever. With the time needed for shopping and preparing each meal, not to mention photographing the food and then actually writing each post, the blog had become a part-time job in terms of the time commitment. But it was still the best hobby I'd ever had, especially now that I could use my contacts in the online food world to help me find new books to publish at work.

Another year passed by and when our apartment leases came up for renewal, Sam and I decided to find a place together. Friends of ours lived out in Forest Hills, Queens, and told us about an apartment in their building that was up for rent. I liked the neighborhood, even if it was a little far away. There was an indie movie theater, a nice cheese shop that smelled agreeably funky, and a train that whisked its riders to Penn Station in fifteen minutes flat. And the apartment was huge by New York standards, full of light, and affordable. It even had a balcony. When I looked out from the balcony over the leafy trees and rooftops of the houses in Forest Hills, the view reminded me of Berlin. The decision was easy.

Sam and I moved in a few weeks later, his leather desk chair paired up with my bookshelves, his IKEA coffee table planted in front of my father's nubby cream sofa, his street hockey sticks stuck next to my suitcases in the closet. Once we were settled, we spent cozy winter afternoons together on the couch and whiled away warm weekend days on the balcony. When we had friends over for dinner parties, our living room was big enough that sometimes, if it got late enough and we gave them enough to drink, people danced on the shiny parquet floor. One day, Sam's mother, Evelyn, started referring to me as her daughter-in-law, even though Sam and I had still never spoken about marriage.

For our first vacation together, Sam and I rented a house on a remote part of Prince Edward Island and drove eight hundred miles from New York City to get there, up through Maine's regal forests, the comparatively bald-looking Canadian landscape, and over the long Confederation Bridge until we reached the soft red earth of Prince Edward Island at night. For our next trip, we flew to the South of France, renting a car and driving up hairpin roads in the mountains. After that, we went hiking in Rocky Mountain National Park with the intention of camping, but I lasted only two nights on a sleeping pad in a tent before I found myself begging Sam to stay in a motel instead.

Then all our friends started getting married. One year, we were invited to eight weddings, so we spent our vacation days and our budget on wedding gifts and hotel rooms. The year after that, we spent our vacation days on family trips, to see my family in Italy and his mother in Israel. The next winter, when I asked Sam if he wanted to try to schedule a trip just for the two of us that summer, he confessed that he wanted a break. He didn't really enjoy all the traveling we did. He hated having to crush his tall frame into a small airplane seat. He had a hard time with jet lag. And it was tough for him when we spent time in Italy or Berlin, because he didn't speak German or Italian and I couldn't be his constant interpreter. I found myself about to ask him why he hadn't tried learning either language, even cursorily, since meeting me, but I choked it back. *This isn't about you,* I tried to tell myself. *Don't turn this into something it isn't.*

Still, it was unnerving to find out so late in the game just how burdensome Sam found traveling. I couldn't ever allow myself to think about how annoying airports were, how expensive it was to go back and forth between Europe and the United States, or how exhausted it could make me. It was the only way I knew how to exist: a few times a year I had to get on an airplane to see the people I love. I had to go a little farther than a lot of people did. But that's just the way it was, and the way it always would be. I swallowed my concern and tried to think about other things.

But the concern, instead of fading away, started morphing into something else: the answer to a question I hadn't even known was nagging at me. A few months later, over breakfast one morning in May, I asked Sam if he could ever imagine living anywhere but the United States, if living in Europe would ever be an option for him. I think I knew the answer before he even opened his mouth, but I was surprised by how much his flat "No" affected me. "Do you want to move back?" he asked me, his fork in midair. "No . . . not, well, no, I don't, not right now. But I don't know, I don't not want to move back either. I mean, I don't know. I just, I guess I just need to know what you want." I was stammering and suddenly on the verge of tears. I had no idea they had been lurking.

That night, to try to fix things, I cooked chicken for dinner. It was Sam's favorite thing to eat. I bought chicken thighs and a piece of ginger and a shiny little jalapeño that felt like a green lipstick bullet in my hand, pacing the grocery store aisles to calm my nerves. At home I made a spicy, gingery paste out of the ginger and jalapeño and a few other spices lying around, slathering it thickly on the chicken thighs before roasting them in the oven. I'd learned the hard way that I had to use plastic gloves when I did this; a previous recipe for a chile paste—slathered chicken had me contemplating a visit to the emergency room as my hands glowed with pain.

The chicken thighs were really good—the meat was moist and tender, with just the right amount of heat—and Sam praised the dinner effusively as usual, but his smile was a little too wide and I found I didn't have much of an appetite. We both fell uncharacteristically silent as we ate, the spices tickling my mouth. I didn't know what was happening, why that one innocuous question, or answer, really, had made me so unhappy, why it felt as though the food was sticking in my throat. Not just the food, actually, but everything.

I suddenly thought of the night, twenty years earlier, when I had told my father that I wanted to go back to Berlin to live with my mother. I was terrified of his reaction, of hurting his feelings. But I didn't expect him to say no. When he did, the feeling I had—of suddenly falling down a long black hole, of wanting to scream but having no voice, the sickening sense that my life was not mine to control—was the very same one I had now, in Queens, with Sam chewing his chicken across the table from me.

I hadn't really known that there was a door to a different life in my head and that that door was still ajar. I was homesick for Berlin at times, it was true. But I'd always assumed that was just the way my life would always be, living in one place, missing another. I'd gotten really good at existing this way and had never allowed myself to contemplate leaving New York. What was in Berlin for me anyway? My friends, my career, Sam, they were all in New York. But Sam was making it clear that this door to my other life was not something that interested him. He wanted to close it firmly. Which made me realize that I wanted nothing more than to inch a little closer to the door, maybe even push it open, just to see what was on the other side.

Spicy Roasted Chicken Thighs

SERVES 4

These spicy chicken thighs are delicious both hot out of the oven and cold the next day (they make great picnic fare). You simply process a bunch of spicy, aromatic ingredients and smear the paste onto raw chicken thighs, then roast them until they're juicy and fragrant, and a gorgeous little gravy has formed at the bottom of the pan. The recipe is adapted from the Indian chef Suvir Saran and was first published in Mark Bittman's *New York Times* column in 2004. Take care, when working with the jalapeño, to wear rubber gloves. Serve with steamed rice or couscous.

8 chicken thighs, with skin, pierced all over with a small knife
5 cloves garlic
1 2-inch piece fresh ginger root, peeled
1 small jalapeño pepper, seeded
Juice and grated peel of 1 organic lemon
2 tablespoons tomato paste
½ teaspoon salt, or to taste

1 teaspoon ground cumin
1 teaspoon ground coriander
Vegetable oil

1. Heat the oven to 400 degrees. Put the chicken thighs in a bowl. Roughly chop the garlic, ginger, and jalapeño and put them in a small food processor with the lemon juice and zest, the tomato paste, salt, cumin, and coriander. Process to a paste.

2. Wearing gloves, rub the spice paste all over the chicken thighs.

3. Put the thighs, skin side up, in a roasting pan that you've rubbed with a drip of vegetable oil. Roast in the oven for 45 minutes. Serve hot or at room temperature.

13

A Divided Heart

I F YOU'VE EVER WONDERED WHAT WEST BERLIN LOOKED LIKE IN THE 1980s, there's no better movie to watch than Wim Wenders's *Wings of Desire*. It'll show you the vast empty field that was once Potsdamer Platz, the punky folks who flocked to loud, smoky concerts in dimly lit nightclubs, the drab rows of old apartment buildings, enlivened every now and then with a scribble of graffiti, a splash of color. Each time Film Forum screened the film I couldn't help but buy a ticket. Nestled in the dark theater, I was flooded with homesickness, my heart constricting at the sight of those familiar cobblestone sidewalks and Cassiel the angel sitting atop the gilded winged victory statue in the middle of the Tiergarten, where my mother and Joanie always went to the flea market. I strained to hear snippets of Berlin's funny dialect, thrilled every time I saw Peter Falk eating a Currywurst at the snack stand across the street from my mother's office. My heart tugged when I saw the landscape shots of the city, so lovely and unlovely alike. But my favorite part of the movie was Berlin's many voices filling the air as you were made to realize that the angels could hear the inner thoughts of every human being around them.

I always loved that idea, that angels are among us all the time, ready to hold us, wrap their arms around us, and love us despite our deepest, darkest thoughts. Because, truth be told, I was ashamed of my deepest, darkest thoughts. Despite all my success in New York, my life was feeling empty. Despite Sam's companionship and his shoes parked comfortably by the front door of our apartment, I had started to feel deeply alone. Despite the caring friendship of my girlfriends, I envied their uncomplicated certitude about where they belonged in the world. The division I'd always felt within me, between my American half and my European half, was growing more difficult to ignore.

Sometimes I would pass an apartment building in Manhattan at night and look into the warmly lit windows of a home, wondering if that was what my apartment looked like from the outside too, when on the inside it had started to feel so cold. No one I knew struggled with the same sense of division that I did. It seemed unbecoming to be a young woman in her late twenties who wanted nothing more than to move back home. So I tried my best to ignore it. But as these things usually go, pushing down what I felt in my heart of hearts didn't make it go away. It just made it get worse. I felt tugged eastward all the time.

On my way to meet my old friend Amy from Paris one afternoon, not long after my conversation with Sam, I passed the chunk of the Berlin Wall tucked away on Fifty-third Street between Fifth and Madison Avenues and I stared at it with sudden hot tears in my eyes, remembering what it was like to pass it all the time, with nary a second thought. Amy and I met at Café Sabarsky, the Viennese café on the first floor of the Neue Galerie on Eighty-eighth and Fifth. As she caught me up on the latest in her life—a new job, a feud with her boyfriend—I bit into a piece of yeasted plum cake with whipped cream and felt myself flooded with longing. Joanie made a big tray of plum cake every June for her birthday picnic. It was always my favorite thing to eat at the picnic. I'd hunker down in the tall grass of the park and chew my way through a square or two, the soft, sour, cinnamon-sprinkled plums sagging down into a yeasty, lemon-scented dough, wasps buzzing lazily overhead, Joanie's sons playing soccer in the field next to us.

Amy looked at me in puzzlement as my face fell. "Are you okay?" I swallowed and forced myself to smile. "Yes! Sorry. Just feeling a little homesick." I cleared my throat, looking around the wood-paneled room with its Thonet coatracks and strudel-filled vitrines. "Do you want to try a bite?" I asked, pushing my plate toward her, hoping she wouldn't probe further. "It's delicious. So what did he do after you told him to leave?"

I wasn't always sad. But the melancholy cropped up far more than I liked to admit. And nebulous questions floated in my mind constantly: *If I take that job offer, will it mean I can't move back to Berlin for another year or maybe two? If I move into that apartment with that lease, will it bind me even more?* And now, more insistently, *If I let things go forward with Sam, will he be the reason I never go back?* These questions weren't even articulated clearly in my mind at first. But they were there, the ghostly precursors to more treacherous thoughts later.

When I did go back to visit Berlin, always at Christmastime, the trips were too short and too rushed. I'd haunt old neighborhoods whose streets I knew as well as the back of my hand and go poking around curiously in new ones, marveling at how the city managed to be so familiar and so foreign to me at the same time. In one half of the city it sometimes felt like I had never left. In the other half a whole new world lay waiting to be discovered. The new Berlin, the one that had Mitte at its center and not Charlottenburg, was a place I didn't really know and certainly didn't recognize, its old apartment buildings sharing space with shiny new developments, fancy boutiques, and studiously hip coffee bars. It was strange to realize that there was a new generation of people in Berlin now whose concept of the city, their city, was entirely different than mine. I was relieved when I visited my mother and saw the newspaper stores, sausage stands, and Italian restaurants in her neighborhood that had never closed, had never been replaced by anything else. *But how long will it stay like this?* I wondered. *Like it's just waiting for me.* With each passing trip, I was reminded by my mother's ever-whitening hair and my ever-deepening connections to New York that a clock ticking deep within in me somewhere was running out of time.

I didn't know who to talk to about all this. Over the years, I'd done a very good job of neatly keeping my two worlds separate, much like Berlin had been for so long. My friends in New York knew only the American me. People in Berlin or my family in Italy saw only the European me. I'd be one version of myself and then I'd get in the airplane to go to the other place and up in the air somewhere, in a metal tube hurtling over the ocean, I'd turn into the other version. I hadn't ever realized before that this would turn into a problem one day or that I'd have to explain why I felt so terribly torn when I thought about where I should settle or where I belonged. Max had once asked me what it was like to have two separate identities, able to slip seamlessly from one world to another. I was so surprised by his question that I didn't know how to answer. No one had ever asked me that before. No one had ever figured that out about me.

But sometimes there were moments when my two worlds overlapped, like when I cooked stuffed cabbage for my blog and remembered my lunch trays at school in Berlin or when I spent an evening baking star-shaped hazelnut Christmas cookies, cinnamon perfuming every corner of the apartment, just like Joanie's. Those little moments soothed me, made me feel as if the huge expanse of ocean separating my two lives wasn't all that big after all. All I had to do, I decided, was get in the kitchen and bring Berlin to New York via the stove a little more often.

So I looked for home in kitchen. And I was careful to avoid the minefields in New York—that little chunk of the Wall on Fifty-third Street, the exhibit of German painters at the Museum of Modern Art that featured frame after frame of street scenes of Berlin. I hid my longing from my friends and from Sam, not wanting to burden him with something I realized he couldn't or wouldn't help me with anyway. I put on a brave face and I soldiered forward, trying to anchor myself in New York, never allowing myself to wonder what I would do if I were free to decide, all by myself.

The one place where I felt I could open up a little about how I was feeling was on my blog. I guess it was the sense of anonymity that the computer screen afforded me. I was oblique at times and a little shy. I didn't want to come right out and say how much I was struggling. But my readers listened, read between the lines, and held me up, silently and not so silently. I had never expected the blog, my imaginary fireside circle, to make me feel less alone in those strange, confusing months, but it did. It absolutely did.

Pflaumenkuchen (Yeasted Plum Cake)

MAKES ONE 9-INCH ROUND CAKE

A seasonal treat throughout Germany, *Pflaumenkuchen* is something I missed terribly when I lived in New York. The sweet yeasted dough base is covered with as many quartered Italian prune plums as you can fit on it—the more plums you can squeeze in, the better—and then topped with cinnamon sugar (you could also put slivered or sliced almonds or streusel on top). What results is a juicy, jammy, not too sweet cake best paired with a hot cup of tea or coffee and a generous scoop of freshly whipped cream alongside. Traditionally it's made in a half-sheet pan, so simply double the recipe below if you'd like to serve a crowd. *Pflaumenkuchen* is best eaten the day it's made.

Butter for the pan
1½ cups plus 2 tablespoons all-purpose flour, plus more, if needed
½ ounce fresh yeast
½ cup whole milk, lukewarm
6 tablespoons sugar
1 egg yolk
3 tablespoons (1½ ounces) unsalted butter, melted and cooled, plus 2
　　tablespoons unsalted butter, melted and cooled (keep separate)
Pinch of salt
Grated zest of ½ organic lemon
1¼ pounds Italian prune plums, pitted and quartered
2 teaspoons ground cinnamon
Unsweetened whipped cream, for serving

1. Butter the bottom and sides of a 9-inch springform pan. Set aside.
2. Pour the flour into a mixing bowl and make a well in the middle. Crumble the yeast into the well, and add half the milk and a pinch of the sugar. Using a fork, mix the yeast, milk, and sugar together, incorporating some of the flour, until the yeast has dissolved. Cover the bowl with a cotton towel and let it sit for 15 minutes, until foamy. Then, stirring, add the remaining milk, 3 tablespoons of the sugar, egg yolk, 3 tablespoons melted butter,

salt, and lemon zest. The dough will be a bit shaggy. Dump it out onto a floured work surface and knead for a few minutes until it is smooth. You might need to add a little more flour to keep it from sticking, but don't add too much—you want the dough to still be soft and slightly floppy. Form the dough into a ball and put it in the buttered pan. Cover with a dishtowel and put the bowl in a warm, draft-free place (like the oven, turned off) for an hour, or until the dough has doubled in bulk.

3. Heat the oven to 350 degrees. Using your fingertips, gently deflate the dough and push it out evenly to fit the pan, giving it 1-inch-high sides. You want the dough to be uniformly about ⅛-inch thick.

4. Starting at the edge, push the quartered plums into the dough at a 45-degree angle, making concentric circles and squeezing in as many quarters as you can. Combine the cinnamon and remaining sugar, and sprinkle evenly over the plums. Drizzle with the 2 tablespoons melted butter. Set aside, uncovered, for 20 minutes.

5. Put the pan in the oven and bake for 40 minutes, until the crust is golden brown and the plums are bubbling. Remove from the oven and set aside to cool until the fruit is no longer hot. Cut into wedges and serve with a dollop of unsweetened whipped cream.

14

Everything You Could
Ever Want

ALL ITALIANS HAVE THEIR OWN VERSION OF *RAGÙ*, A LONG-SIMMERED
meat sauce to be tossed with fresh pasta or layered in lasagna.
And all of them think their version is the best, the sauce to end all
sauces, the only one worth spending five hours in the kitchen for. Most
people have had their recipes passed down in the family from great-
grandmother to grandmother to mother and so on. But some, like me,
got their recipe through other means, like abject begging. One summer
evening in college, when I was beginning to assemble my recipe arsenal, I was visiting my grandfather's little village, where our close friend
Gabriella and her family live too. Gabriella's *ragù* had always been the
gold standard for me and on this visit, armed with a pencil and notebook, I sat next to her and took careful notes as she told me how to
make it. And then I went back to Boston and proceeded to make it—
over and over and over again—until I committed it to memory.

Gabriella is from Bologna and is, besides my Sicilian uncle, possibly
the best cook I know. She can take the lowly mackerel, fry it, and mari-
nate it into a lusty pickle. She can boil an enormous rubbery octopus
into velvety-soft submission and then cut it up into potato salad so
good it can make grown men grow misty-eyed after just one taste. She
can make a rather sad-looking paste of breadcrumbs and grated cheese
and an egg and then scrape it into boiling broth, and before we know

it we're eating the most ethereal *passatelli* the world has ever known. But her *ragù* is her crown jewel.

It's a pretty wonderful thing and very simple. There are no exotic spices or complicated base ingredients, just a simple *soffritto*, two kinds of meat, and good-quality canned tomatoes. The key, really, is to let the *ragù* cook as long as you possibly can: five hours at least and up to seven or eight, until it fairly quivers. It will be deeply savory and full of the essence of meat. It will taste like summers in Italy and Gabriella's kitchen, a blue-and-white-tiled paradise. Whenever I made it, my friends clamored for the recipe. It was one of the things I knew how to make that I was proudest of. And whenever I was feeling blue and out of sorts, like I didn't know where I belonged or if I even belonged anywhere at all, this *ragù* anchored me, reminded me who I was and where I came from. Which came in especially handy when I started to feel like I was drowning in someone else's version of my life.

After so many years of not talking about the future, now it seemed that it was all Sam and I did. Our conversation over breakfast in the spring had given way to a strange new existence in which we each tried to convince the other that our own basic needs and desires for the future were the ones that we, as a couple, should follow.

We spent months negotiating, hashing out possible vacation schedules with hypothetical children. Sam and I, it soon became clear, had fundamentally different ideas about what our future lives were supposed to look like. I wasn't sure yet where my place was in the world, but I did know that some part of my year had to be spent in Europe, and Sam was hesitant to agree. I couldn't entirely blame him—he didn't speak German or Italian and his family was firmly anchored in the United States—but it never occurred to me that I would end up with someone who would effectively make me choose.

All the little things that had felt like kismet to me once—Sam's mother abroad, his Spanish brother-in-law—turned out not to be the guarantee I thought they were that he would understand my divided heart. That I had once been naïve enough to think that those small details made him right for me when we were facing such an existential divide left me with a pit in my stomach.

When I asked Sam if it didn't seem strange to him that we were both so insistent on defending our territory and that neither one of us seemed able or interested in putting the other person's happiness ahead of their own, he told me evenly, "That's not the way real life works, Weezie. That's just a fantasy, like true love." My heart sank somewhere deep and unknowable when I heard those words. I stared at my plate.

He has no idea, I thought. And suddenly I was at the edge of a deep black canyon and the abyss below was dizzying, nearly making me sick. It was dawning on me that this story, this whole thing, was not going to end well. Our safe, loving home, our easy evenings, they were all in jeopardy. I could see them slipping out of my grasp even as I struggled to catch my breath.

Somewhere in the middle of all this, armed with good intentions and an engagement ring stashed in his bag, Sam flew out to California to meet me while I was traveling for work in September. He rented a car and drove us to a fancy hotel in Sonoma wine country, where we had our own little bungalow with a private yard. It was over the top, nothing like anything we'd ever done before, and he confessed, as we checked in, that his boss told him about the place. As Sam signed the check-in form, I found myself looking around the swanky lobby and feeling slightly shame-faced.

Sam proposed in a vineyard, hiding the box containing a slim diamond band behind his back. I didn't understand the timing of the proposal or even the proposal itself, not when we were clearly in the thick of hashing out whether we could even be together at all. But Sam had organized everything so nicely and so clearly believed that this would fix things. Also, I loved him. I didn't know how I could say no. So I said yes. I could feel myself flush when I realized that I didn't have a better reason to say yes. I hid my face in his shoulder as we embraced.

Late that night, in the hotel bed, I wanted to grab him by his T-shirt and shake him awake. *What are you thinking?* I wanted to yell. Or maybe it was me I wanted to shake. *What are we doing?* I was starting to wonder if

Sam thought that all I'd been waiting for was an engagement ring, a commitment. All the talk about homesickness and needing to spend more
time with my family in Europe was, to him, just a ruse, nothing serious.
Could it be that Sam didn't realize how deep my doubts went? My hands
trembled.

Two days later we flew back to New York on separate airplanes and
I stared at my ring in the dimmed light of the airplane cabin, trying to
imagine myself as Sam's wife, trying to imagine saying my vows to
him. I couldn't conjure up a thing. A deep, unflagging sense of terror
set into my gut.

What more do you want? I asked myself in solitary moments back
in New York when I was trying to get a grip on things. *You have everything you could ever want. You should feel grateful.* But as much as I loved Sam
and our cozy little apartment with the view that reminded me of Berlin, I was starting to realize that there was something profoundly
wrong with the equation I'd set up for myself over the years. I was
starting to realize that I didn't belong to that place or to that person, no
matter how much I may have beaten my brow and commanded myself
to feel grateful and happy and lucky. No matter how many good jobs
and sweet friends tethered me.

I wanted so much to believe that with Sam's marriage proposal
came an implicit agreement that we were in this together for the long
haul, that any struggles we had individually would now become part
of a collective effort. That I could trust him enough to show him all of
me, the girl from over there and the girl from right here. But it turned
out that he wasn't really interested in helping me navigate the thickets
of my divided heart. It was not out of ill will; he simply didn't know
how. If I needed to make my way through this particular struggle, I was
on my own. He made that clear, over and over again.

A few months after we'd started dating, Sam took me from Manhattan
up to Beacon in the Hudson Valley, the Metro-North train smelling
faintly of urine and deli sandwiches, leather seats blistered and crack-
ing. We walked from the Beacon train station, down by the river, to his

mother's house, a cozy Victorian perched on top of a little hill with a porch that wrapped nearly all the way around, an upstairs bathroom painted periwinkle, floral wallpaper in the hallway, and an Art Deco table in the living room. We spent a snowy weekend holed up in the house, cooking spaghetti for dinner and sleeping late, venturing outside only to take a hike up Mount Beacon, where we took pictures of each other, wrapped up warmly in scarves, thick coats, and hats, at the summit.

Over the next four years, Beacon became my home away from home. Javier and I cooked together in the wonky kitchen that Sam's mother always talked about renovating. Javi taught me about gastriques, reductions, and herb rubs while I made homey pots of meat sauce and vegetable stews. At night, I'd lie awake in the back bedroom and listen to the faraway whistles of trains chugging alongside the Hudson. I fell in love with Sam's family in that house, felt welcomed into their arms with a certitude I never questioned. I had always wanted a family like his and now, by some stroke of fortune, I had one. They loved me; I loved them. It was simple. Except of course it never really is.

Because there I was for Thanksgiving, newly engaged, four years after my first visit to Beacon, walking behind my future family as they strolled down Main Street, and I felt completely lost. I was on my cell phone talking with my mother, thousands of miles away, on the other side of the dark ocean that divides my life, and at the sound of her voice crackling through the phone line, tears welled in my eyes. I looked ahead at Sam and his mother, his sister and her husband and their baby boy, his little brother and his wife, and I saw a family, three families, really. So similar, despite their differences, so bound together. And as much as they had welcomed me into that family, as much as I was a part of it already, I was consumed by the fact that each step I took in their direction was a step that carried me further away from my own family.

"I miss you," I whispered into the phone, embarrassed by my tears. What thirty-year-old woman couldn't have a phone conversation with her mother without crying? "Be strong," she said to me in Italian. "I miss you too. And I wish I wasn't so far away." I heard her sigh, the breath coming from somewhere deep within. We had had the same conversation a dozen, a hundred times in my life.

"But we'll see each other soon. Eh, bella? Just six more weeks." I nodded, though she couldn't see me. I wondered what it was like for her, to hear my voice suffused with tears almost every time we spoke lately. "How is the baby? How is everybody?" My mother had met Javi and Liza's infant son on her last trip to New York. He had sat on her lap and gazed at her adoringly as she cooed at him in Italian. "They're fine. He's adorable. So chubby and sweet." I saw Javi turn around to look for me. I hastily wiped my eyes. "I should go," I said. "We're taking a walk. They're waiting for me." I took a deep breath. *Get a grip*, I said to myself. *You're a grown woman.*

"I love you, Mamma," I said.

"I love you too," she said gently. "I'll see you soon. Cheer up. Smile. Okay? Are you smiling?" I tried to smile into the phone.

Javi turned back and walked beside me, draping his arm across my shoulder. "You okay, Lu?" I nodded, suddenly exhausted. For months now, I'd slept only a few hours a night. Each night after Sam fell asleep, I lay sleepless next to him, remembering that strange feeling of loneliness I'd felt on the airplanes I took over the Atlantic as a child. My parents put me on those planes, trusting their obedient, well-behaved child not only to be responsible enough to travel back and forth, but also to survive the emotional seesawing. They had no idea how much it tested me. I long ago forgave them; I knew that they were doing the best they could. But now I was supposed to be getting married and my future husband didn't seem to have any understanding of what he was asking me to do.

Javi squeezed my shoulder and I composed myself. We caught up with the others and I slipped my hand into Sam's. He smiled down at me, so much taller than my five foot three inches. Sam still seemed convinced that our struggle was just a passing phase. He couldn't see that it had niggled its way into everything that I liked about my life and, worst of all, that it made me see past all that I loved about him— his ease, his confidence, and his sense of humor—to the darker depths within. In the meantime, I was beginning to realize that my happiness might just come at too high a cost for him, that what I needed from a husband simply might not be within his reach. It was devastating to understand that Sam's love for me wasn't big enough. I was starting to feel something in me fall apart, the resolve holding everything together beginning to crumble.

We walked down Main Street, stopping in at our favorite café for a double order of bread pudding with whiskey sauce and seven spoons, a yearly tradition. Then we went back home, past the glass factory and the tiny dog run, the baby asleep in Javi's arms.

At dinnertime, all of us sick of turkey, I lodged myself at the kitchen counter and slowly chopped onions and carrots into a fine dice, soothed by the simple movements and the familiar scent, sweet and biting. I cooked the chopped vegetables in oil and butter, then added ground meat, puréed tomatoes, and a splash of wine, and let it cook and cook and cook until Gabriella's unctuous, quivering *ragù* came together, filling the house with its richness.

We ate it for dinner slicked onto spaghetti that we dug out of the back recesses of the kitchen cupboards, and I felt a tiny nugget of satisfaction that the flavors of my childhood, my world, were at the table in Beacon.

Ragù alla Bolognese (Beef Ragù)

SERVES 8 TO 10

This recipe is deceptively simple, but don't be fooled: the ingredients are not to be messed with. Don't follow the urge to add celery, a bay leaf, or a dash of cinnamon. You'll be rewarded for your obedient focus with a meat sauce that truly tastes of Italy. Layer the *ragù* into lasagne or slick it onto spaghetti or, better yet, homemade tagliatelle. It is a classic and no kitchen should be without it (it doubles *and* freezes very well). And I really do mean it when I say "finely" minced carrots and onions—what you're aiming for are bits that are, in size, almost indistinguishable from the ground once the sauce has finished cooking. If you've got good knife skills, do the mincing by hand. Otherwise use a food processor (but take care not to let the onions or carrots turn to mush). Okay, enough bossing: get cooking!

1 tablespoon olive oil
1 tablespoon butter
1 large yellow onion, finely minced
2 large carrots, finely minced (you want roughly equal amounts of minced onion and carrot)
1 pound ground beef
1 pound ground pork
½ cup red wine (open a fresh bottle and drink the rest with dinner)
1 28-ounce can peeled San Marzano tomatoes, puréed
1 teaspoon salt, plus more to taste

1. Put the oil and butter in a large cast-iron pot over medium heat, to melt the butter. Add the onion and cook, stirring often, for about 7 minutes, until the onion is well cooked. Do not let it take on any color. Add the minced carrots and cook for another 2 to 3 minutes, stirring now and then.

2. Add the ground meat to the pot, and using a wooden spoon, stir and chop up the meat so that it cooks and breaks down into uniformly tiny pieces. Raise the heat to medium-high or even high as you do this. It takes a good amount of elbow grease and a little bit of time. Continue to stir and cook until the meat is no longer pink (at no point, however, should the meat be browning). There will be liquid at the bottom of the pan. Continue to cook until that liquid has mostly evaporated, 8 to 10 minutes.

3. Add the wine and stir well to combine. Simmer until the wine has mostly evaporated, 2 to 3 minutes.

4. Add the puréed tomatoes and the salt, and stir well to combine. The sauce will come to a simmer almost instantly. Lower the heat to the lowest possible setting, put the lid on the pot, and let the sauce simmer for as long as you possibly can, stirring it occasionally. Seven hours would be wonderful, 5 hours is pretty good, but any less than 3 and you're really

missing out. The longer you cook the sauce, the richer and more flavorful it will get. At some point in the cooking process, the fat will separate from the sauce and float at the top, so just give the sauce a good stir every so often to reincorporate the fat.

5. At the end of the cooking time, taste for seasoning and add more salt, if needed. Then serve tossed with pasta or use in a classic lasagne (this recipe makes enough for a 9 x 13-inch pan). If you plan on freezing the sauce, let it cool completely before putting it into freezer bags or other plastic containers.

15

It Shook Me Awake

I T WASN'T HARD, FOR A WHILE, TO AVOID SAM. HE WORKED LONG HOURS now, often coming home after dinner, and was gone for long stretches of time on the weekend, tied up with commitments in the city. Alone in the apartment, I watched all the old movies that he never wanted to see, choked down cereal for dinner, and spent night after night online. It was easy to while away the hours engrossed in other people's stories. When we did spend time together, it was strained and unhappy. Every conversation we had deteriorated into an argument about the same old things, the two of us trying to hash it out just one more time, hoping that *this* time would be the time the other one would finally get it. It never was.

The kitchen—my refuge—became a place I no longer wanted to go to. I was losing my appetite, and fast. None of the dishes that usually comforted me worked now, and neither did cooking, which had always been supremely soothing. I felt stifled and nauseated by whatever I tried—homemade pickles, lamb stew, even plain old buckwheat pancakes. I tried to write about my predicament on the blog, but I was muzzled by the little I felt I could share. Some well-intentioned readers wrote me concerned e-mails to recommend their favorite brands of antidepressants. I wished there was a pill I could have swallowed that would have made everything go away: the heartache, the dull, persistent nausea, the homesickness, the sleeplessness. But when I spoke to a therapist, wondering if medication would indeed solve my problem, she smiled at me sympathetically and told me gently that I wasn't depressed. Instead she recommended couples' therapy.

One weekend, to escape, I flew to Puerto Rico to see Joanie and Dietrich, who were at their family's house for their annual winter visit. I hadn't been to Puerto Rico since they'd brought me there as a toddler while my parents were divorcing. Joanie engulfed me in a hug at the airport, her grip around me as strong as ever. I had to swallow hard not to show my tears.

I spent three days in the sunshine with them, picking grapefruits off the tree in the garden with a homemade, long-handled picker, going for a hike in the junglelike ferns surrounding their house, making *requesòn* out of milk and bitter orange juice. We ate it for breakfast along with rosy slices of guava paste and whole grain bread that Joanie made with homemade sourdough, fed up with the white bread filling the island's grocery stores. At night, with the *coquì* frogs singing outside my window, I lay in bed and tried to figure out what I wanted.

The night before I left, I finally fell into a deep sleep and found myself dreaming about an apartment in Berlin, near the Winterfeldtplatz greenmarket where my mother and I used to go to buy organic milk and smooth brown eggs so many years ago. The apartment, at the top of an old building, had long plank flooring and a bookshelf in the living room that covered most of the wall. A long hallway led from the front door past all the other rooms of the house. A rice paper lamp hung in each room. In my dream, I stood in the living room and looked out the window at the cars on the street below. It was gray and wet outside, but the room was warm and well lit. No one was there with me and nothing was happening, but it was home and it was mine. When I woke up and the dream evaporated, I felt bereft.

Back in New York, I tried to summon the apartment again when I turned off the lights at bedtime. But it wouldn't come. I ran the images in my head over and over, wondering what the dream was trying to tell me.

Sam and I tried for a long time to hold on to our relationship even as we could see it sliding away right in front of us. I no longer knew if I was holding on because I didn't want to lose Sam or because I'd come too far to give up. It was hard not to see the end stages of our relationship as a battle, a thin–lipped Western shootout of sorts, both of us too scared to give even a single inch or simply to walk away. Since I didn't want to give up on us, stubbornly wouldn't allow myself to imagine a future without Sam, I could no longer imagine the future at all. I started to wish that I would not grow old. Those were horrifying days. I lay awake at night, loneliness, rage, desperation, and fear coursing through me like poison. I felt so far gone, so helpless.

It was only then, after all the struggle and misery of the past year, that I understood that I was on the verge of losing everything, not just Sam and our fantasies for our life together. That was when I realized my life needed saving.

But first I had to fly to Paris.

The trip to Paris had been planned months earlier. My old roommate Betsy and our friend Teri had decided to go to Paris for a few days after the London Book Fair in the spring. Our other friend Jenny was heading there at the same time to meet her husband, who'd been traveling in Germany. The three of them were making plans to spend to a few days together in Paris when Betsy—these things usually were her idea—called to tell me I should buy a ticket too. "Tickets are cheap," she said over the phone from London. "You need to come."

Betsy was always very good at coming up with plans like that and even better at getting me to go along with them. Everyone needs someone like Betsy in their lives: advocate, enabler, agent, big sister. She could hear the despair in my voice every time she called me. She was worried. And she knew I needed an escape. I said yes immediately. Four days away from New York and the misery lurking in our apartment would do me a lot of good. Four days in Paris in April with my best friends would be the perfect medicine.

At the time my friends and I hatched the Paris plan, I didn't know just how desperately I needed to get away. By the time the flight rolled around, things had gotten so bad that Sam had moved back into his old apartment and I spent my days wondering which one of us was going to be brave enough to pull the cord. I was so fragile I teetered on the edge of tears every hour, every day. I needed some magic, preferably on an IV.

The magic started right away. As soon as Jenny and I got on the RER train to Paris from the airport, two men carrying huge bunches of lilacs got on and sat next to us, their chapped hands clutching the ragged branches. I peered at Jenny through the thicket of tiny blossoms that waved between us as the train jiggled forward. New York had been cold and gray when we'd left the night before and here we were, the air perfumed with lilacs, sun streaming through the window. It was hard not to feel bewitched.

We walked around the city for hours that afternoon, waiting for Teri and Betsy to arrive from London. We walked down rue Bonaparte, where I'd lived ten years earlier, realizing the limits of my own independence, and I saw my old apartment door, still painted peacock blue, shining in the afternoon light. We went to the Jardin du Luxembourg and luxuriated in the sunshine, eyes red-rimmed from the overnight flight and from life lately. Jenny and her husband had been trying for over a year to get pregnant, but things weren't working and they were scared of what lay ahead.

And as we walked, we talked. When I asked Jenny, for the umpteenth time, what she thought I should do about Sam, a pigeon flew straight toward me, seemingly out of nowhere, and then dipped down to flap one wing, very clearly, against my scalp. In a flash it was gone, but its touch came just as I had finished my question. "What was *that*?" we squealed in disgust, but deep down I wondered. I was a full head shorter than Jenny. Why had it picked me? Frankly, that pigeon looked distinctly like it was aiming for me.

We went to eat a chocolate éclair in a café on the place de la Contrescarpe, where fruit trees in bloom framed the sky, and we talked about friends who'd struggled to have children and others who'd gotten pregnant without even trying. It all seemed so arbitrary. It was so hard to see Jenny, normally so upbeat and funny, hurting. When the sun started to set, we set off for our hotel, Jenny obliging me with a dramatic pose every time I stopped to take a photo until we got back to the Hotel Verneuil. Then we headed out for dinner with Betsy and Teri at Astier, where the waiter winked at us as he set the enormous cheese tray down on the table after dinner and motioned for us to help ourselves.

We were lucky with the weather on that trip: we had a few of those perfectly moody spring days, when the sky is a soft shade of gray and the light falls just so and it never quite rains, but sometimes the bright, brilliant sun emerged and the beauty all around us left me dumbfounded. I started to feel my heart crack open again after feeling so shriveled and sick during that long, hard winter. I started feeling alive again.

I spent most of the trip head turned upward in wonder all over again at the streets of Paris named after grammarians and revolutionaries and mathematicians. *This* was the way I wanted to see Paris, not the way I had when I'd lived there. We watched little boys play a fierce game of soccer on the place des Vosges and went shopping in the Marais. We shared a pot of hot chocolate at Angelina, rich and thick and topped with spoonfuls of whipped cream. We saw a flower-printed dress on a mannequin in the window of a pretty boutique and made Jenny, tall and slim, go in and try it on. Jenny twirled in front of the mirror, the skirt flaring out, looking happy. The four of us crowded into a tiny sandal boutique and tried on sandals for hours. With the day drawing to a close, the salesmen eventually closed the store for us. One of them, a handsome, slightly consumptive-looking man, flirted with me as I dithered between two pairs of sandals. When I put on a pair of gleaming red patent leather gladiator sandals, he stopped me. "Doz." He pointed at my feet as I stood in front of the mirror and looked at him. "Doz make my 'eart go 'boom'." And with that, he pounded his chest and looked deep into my eyes. We howled with laughter and it was all I could do to keep from falling around his neck.

We met friends for dinner at a bistro in the 11th arrondissement and tucked into scallops served on their magnificent shells and thick cuts of veal napped in cream sauce. I tried morels for the first time, my teeth sinking into their firm, textured flesh. As my friends talked, I watched a beautiful older woman drinking wine at a table near ours as she chatted with her companion. She seemed so at ease with herself, so wise and calm and sexy still. She even managed to keep her haughty elegance as she ate a palm-sized pink macaron filled with tiny *fraises des bois* for dessert. I wondered if she'd ever had a crisis in her life. I wondered what she would tell me to do. When her eyes flickered over to meet mine, I looked away, embarrassed.

We were all in crisis those days. Betsy and her husband were also desperately trying to get pregnant and failing, and Teri was just emerging from a scathing divorce. Months later, we would laugh about the weekend, at how each of us dissolved into tears at least once during the trip. But while we were there, we struggled to put one step in front of the other, learning to be patient or strong or brave.

I was, as my friends reminded me, the only one of them who could force action at this point in my crisis. Teri had already been strong enough to leave her marriage; now she had to deal with the aftermath and the scorched earth left behind. Jenny and Betsy were in a holding pattern, at the mercy of modern medicine and the vagaries of the human body. They had to have patience and faith and not much else. I, however, could *do* something. I could free myself. All I had to do was be brave enough.

When you spend your whole life doing what people tell you, being obedient, and swallowing your protests when other people's lives move forward at your expense, you're bound to burst at some point. Something about that weekend in Paris, something about being with my girlfriends, feeling held in their arms and strengthened by their company, something about the life-affirming quality that Paris has, the rich meals we shared, and the long strolls we took along all those beautiful, familiar streets finally shook me out of the sad, desperate pit I found myself trapped in.

Something happened in Paris that weekend. Sometimes I think it's when my obedient childhood finally ended. When I finally understood that I had to stop worrying about how anything I did affected the people I loved. When I finally found the strength to see that it was time to choose the life I wanted over the one that was causing my soul to dwindle before my very eyes. It was in Paris that I started to realize that I was worth saving, even if it meant losing Sam, that easiness and a sense of humor wouldn't make up for the deeper, harder, more necessary things that were missing. In Paris, it finally happened, something finally pushed me to snap out of that dangerous fog, to wake up and take my life into my own hands before it was too late.

In those strange, clear days in late spring in Paris, I remember finally realizing with earthshaking certainty this simple yet essential fact: You, and only you, determine your own fate. You get only one chance at this life. *Do* something with your life; open your heart to risk. At some point, enough is enough and you must think of the biggest leap you can fathom and then take it.

Now bear with me, dear reader. What I'm about to tell you might possibly make you think I've lost my mind, convince you that you're dealing with an unreliable narrator or, possibly even worse, a hippie. But what I'm going to tell you really happened. I promise it did.

You see, for months I'd been praying to God, the universe, or whoever might be listening, to help me find a way out of my mess. I was raised without religion and wasn't really in the habit of praying, but these were desperate times. And desperate times, as you well know, call for desperate measures. Besides, I would have asked the homeless man on Seventeenth Street who ate Skittles for breakfast and wore a snowsuit in August for advice if I'd had the nerve. At night, in our bed in Queens, I silently begged and I prayed for an answer, for clarity, for permission even. Anything. A sign. An answer. I got nothing, nothing but the deafening sound of silence in my own head.

Until, that is, I went to Paris. There I got my answer, at last. A slightly confusing, veiled, pigeony answer, but an answer nevertheless.

The day after that first pigeon tap—you know, the one where I felt like the pigeon was aiming directly toward me—the four of us were in the Jardin du Luxembourg. I was supposed to take portraits of my friends and we whiled away the hours on a few park chairs, posing and having fun. Before leaving, I went to find the restroom, tucked in a subterranean part of the park. As I bounded down the deserted stairs to the public toilets, I found them all empty. I could not have spent more than a minute in the facilities, but as was my wont those days, in any solitary moment I found I was consumed with thoughts of hard decisions and Sam. Heaviness settled over my heart as I washed my hands.

As I turned and started walking up the stairs, back to the park and to my girlfriends, I found the staircase covered with pigeons. There were fifty of them or more. I stared in disbelief. Where had they all come from in the past sixty seconds? I hadn't heard a peep or a flutter of wings. I started walking up the stairs, bracing myself for the flaps of their wings as they flew away, fearful of their germs and ratty feathers. But instead of flying away as I neared them, these pigeons turned and flew *toward* me, one after the other, in a huge pulsating swarm. They weren't particularly menacing, I didn't feel like I was Tippi Hedren or anything. But there was something urgent in their movement, as if they were trying to alert me to something. As I neared the top of the stairs and the pigeons kept flying at me, I started to wonder. What was going on here?

The next day, our last one in Paris, Teri, Betsy, and Jenny all had different appointments for work and I was left to my own devices. I went for a long stroll across the river to the Right Bank. At a little market just behind the place de la Madeleine, I saw rust-colored rascasses piled high on ice. You can't find them in the United States, but I always read about them in recipes for bouillabaisse, that thick, spicy fish soup from Marseille. There were big bowls full of olives so pungent I could smell them from four stands away. One stand sold handfuls of bright yellow ranunculus for just three euros, clustered next to those roasted beets I used to buy, all those years earlier, cooled for shoppers to take home. I could feel my stomach rumble faintly. We'd had a late dinner the night before, with sparkling wine and perfect *pommes frites* and, for dessert, tiny strawberries swimming in a pool of mint syrup. The waiters had let us sit at our table long after all the other guests had left, laughing and taking photos of one another until the chef came out of the kitchen and posed with us for silly snapshots. Back at the hotel at bedtime, I'd clicked through the images, stopping at a photo of Betsy and me smiling into the camera. I'd forgotten what I looked like when I was happy.

As I walked and thought about how funny it was that this time I wanted nothing more than to simply stay in Paris, where the biggest concrete thing I had to decide was whether to order cheese or dessert after dinner, I got to thinking about those pigeons. What had it all been about? Was it just a silly coincidence? Or was the universe trying to communicate with me after hearing me beg, night after night, for some kind of answer or sign?

At that moment, as I began crossing the place de la Concorde, one of my least favorite places in Paris, so formal and cold, I came under a small copse of trees. Lost in thought about pigeons, marriage, and what I was slowly realizing I wanted my life to look like, I found myself coming into a sort of clarity, the kind I'd been desperate for for nearly a year. Maybe it was because I was far away from New York, maybe it had been the time with my girls, all of us struggling, maybe it had just been some of that old Parisian magic. But as I walked and thought, I realized quite clearly what I needed to do. It all became crystal clear.

And in that moment, I swear to you, a pigeon shit on my shoulder. If that's not a sign from the universe, what on earth is?

"Who was it?" Teri asked, wide-eyed. "Was it your grandmother, do you think? Your Italian one?" "I don't know!" I was out of breath. I'd doubled back to the hotel room immediately after it happened, taking the stairs two at a time, and burst into the room to tell my friends about the pigeon and show them the bird dropping on my shoulder, a fetid badge of honor. We stared at each other. I didn't really believe in an afterlife, or in dead grandmothers speaking to me from the beyond through pigeons. But Jenny and Teri were more sanguine about it; while my mother prayed at the altar of news journalism and science, their mothers regularly went to see astrologers and psychics. It seemed natural to them that the universe or God or a dead Italian relative might be trying to communicate with me via a flock of Parisian pigeons. And honestly, I was relieved that they didn't think I'd lost my mind. I'd never been so desperately in need of help. If this was how the universe was going to help me, it was fine by me.

I went back outside for fresh air and clarity and one last walk on the narrow sidewalks under the cool gray sky. I went down to the Seine and stood on the Pont Neuf, a bridge I hardly knew. I looked down the river to the Ile de la Cité, where I'd realized, all those years ago, that I was falling in love with Max. I thought about my life in New York and about the fact that Sam was waiting for me at home. I thought about Nini and how much my grandfather had adored her, and about my parents' failed marriage and my own desperate homesickness. And then I closed my eyes and tried to be as still as I possibly could.

What do you want from this life? I asked myself. *What will make you happy, you and you alone? How do you want to live? What kind of love do you need?* With my eyes closed, I saw the lilacs on the RER and felt the insistent flap of pigeon wings, and then I felt Paris shaking me—gently at first and then harder, with urgency. *Open your eyes*, it seemed to be saying. *There's no time to waste anymore.*

The answer is right in front of you.

A week later, it was all over. I told Sam I couldn't keep going anymore and he moved out for good. My mother flew to New York to keep me company in those strange days when I alternated between unbearable pain and sadness and a strange lightness in my heart, something that felt remarkably like a sense of peace. One particularly difficult night, I asked her why it was so hard, after all those months of struggle, to let go. "Because you thought you were going to spend the rest of your life with him," she said quietly. Then she added, "And you fought harder for this than you have for anything else in your life." She waited as big, heaving sobs went through me, the ugliest cry of all. And then her voice grew firmer. "But you did all you could. You hear me? You did everything you could." She shook my knee. "Look at me, Luisa. It's done. It's finally done. And now you have to leave it behind you."

The next day it was warm enough to wear my new red sandals to work. And at the office my Irish friend, Dervla, told me that pigeons— and doves—are the symbol of homecoming.

16

Eating for Heartbreak

THE TRULY LOVELORN WILL LOOK AT THIS TITLE AND SCOFF, FEELING that familiar, slightly sickening ache that's taken up residence in their gut. After all, nothing kills an appetite faster than heartbreak, as I'm sure you know. And there's little you can do about it—heartbreak, that is. It has to run its course in its own time, a little parasite ravaging the host from within.

However, as black as your days may be—and black they are, that I'll say—life does, amazingly, go on. As must you, one foot placed in front of the other, one tedious morning after another. And the thing is, you've *got* to eat. You can't simply drop out of life. The trick is to find the right thing, the thing that won't turn your stomach, won't make you want to push your plate away while you feel yourself start to sob with despair. The trick is to be kind to yourself—always a good thing, it's true, but imperative in times of heartbreak.

First of all, allow yourself a few indulgences. For example, if you, under normal circumstances, do not allow yourself such abominations as processed salami sticks or salt-and-vinegar–flavored potato chips, out of consideration for your health and your waistline, now is the time to cast away your good sense. You need small indulgences to heal your heart. This has been scientifically proven. Anything else is self-cruelty.

Second of all, salad can count as dinner. Now, I'm not talking about big leafy green salads. Those won't do for heartbreak. What I find to be

116

a very reliable meal in times of misery involves a little bowl of what some people might call an abbreviated version of Greek salad. What's important is that you find yourself a snappy little cucumber without any give (I like seedless Kirbys or Persian cucumbers), a handful of cherry tomatoes that actually taste like something, mercifully available all year long now, a small slab of feta cheese (Greek or French, it doesn't really matter as long as it's fresh), and dried oregano (Greek or Italian, please).

Don't bother peeling the cucumber, but slice it in half lengthwise and then in little half-moons. Cut the tomatoes into halves or quarters and the feta into small cubes. Combine all of this in a bowl and sprinkle judiciously with the oregano, plus a good pinch of flaky salt. Don't skimp on the salt just because of the feta. Trust me, it's a mistake. Your body needs the salt; haven't you been crying your eyes out? Replenish. Then add a good glug of olive oil and the smallest drip of vinegar (I use white wine vinegar, but you could use Champagne, I suppose, or sherry vinegar; whatever you do, no balsamic, I beg of you), and toss the whole thing together until the tomatoes glisten with olive oil, the herbs are dispersed, and the feta is starting to break down, ever so slightly, at the edges.

Now, if it's summer, and I hope it is because at least then you've got a leg up on the poor winter heartbroken who definitely have the rawer end of the deal, go out onto your balcony, your backyard, or, all else failing, your front stoop. I find it rather important to eat this little salad, which might be all you can stomach in a day, in the setting sun. As you crunch your way carefully through your bowl, the sun makes you squint and warms your hair, and the soft evening breeze will feel like a caress, which I think you need almost as much as you need the salad.

As your fork spears ever more hungrily, you can start to daydream about that trip to Greece you'd like to think about taking, where you can eat feta and tomatoes all day long every day, and great big olives too, and nice warm bread, and there will be a few handsome waiters winking at you as you sit by the bar with your glass of retsina and your sun-kissed tourist glow. Suddenly, you'll find yourself scraping the bottom of your bowl rather lustily and you might feel sheepish, or at least a little guilty, for enjoying that simple meal so much when you thought you might never eat again.

Don't worry, the heartbreak's not entirely gone, and it won't be until it skulks away of its own accord. But in the meantime, you snuck a meal past its shadowy figure and are feeling rather good, like you wouldn't mind another one of those, or at least a spoon to get at the dregs of the dressing at the bottom of the bowl. Here's a little tip from me to you: no one, but no one, will notice if you raise the bowl to your lips and tip it back, letting the herbed oil and vinegar, flecked with bits of feta and tomato seeds, pour down your throat. You might cough a bit if it's too sharp, and you might feel just a little bit greedy. But it's worth it, I think, to feel your appetite and your lust for life come back to life, one cherry tomato at a time.

Part 3

17

A Solemn Oath

CONVENTIONAL WISDOM SAYS THAT AFTER A BIG BREAKUP OR A DI-vorce, you're to make no other big decisions for quite some time. I guess the theory goes that you're all decisioned out. You've used up your last brain cells to figure out what's right for you and now you have to give them a little break. Get a massage! Take a walk! Meet your girlfriends! But for goodness' sake, don't contemplate anything heavier than whether to buy those suede-and-patent pumps with vertiginous heels that you have no real excuse for wearing but can't stop thinking about all the same.

This philosophy sounded good to me. I treated myself to theater tickets. I drank hot chocolate for breakfast. I bought myself those suede-and-patent pumps if only because they made my legs look nice. I even found an excuse to fly out to Los Angeles for a business trip. Perhaps it was proof of how far gone I was that I found driving my boxy red rental car all over the city the most thrilling thing to happen to me in months. Los Angeles was sunny and warm and everywhere I went there were delicious things to eat: transcendent hole-in-the-wall tacos, fat huckleberries in my author's backyard, a six-course Korean dinner at a restaurant so off the beaten path that we were the only non-Asians in the whole place. When I got lost on the highway back to the airport and almost missed my flight I was uncharacteristically unperturbed.

I figured that if Los Angeles and its kumquat trees and bougainvilleas wanted to keep me, they could. I didn't have anyone waiting for me at home anymore. I didn't have to take anyone else into consideration anymore. My life was wide open. This thought was thrilling beyond belief.

Back home, I steered clear of the kitchen entirely. It didn't hold much for me besides cereal and milk and a steady supply of cherry tomatoes that I ate by the handful if I was home for dinner. I apologized to my blog readers, blaming my silence on my travel, then headed out with friends for pizza after work or bought myself Vietnamese or Cambodian sandwiches that I ate perched on bar stools, my eyes watering from the slices of chiles tucked in among the roast pork and saucy meatballs. I figured I'd cook again when I could. For now, I was going to let the city feed me. I knew that nothing could heal a broken heart like New York City could.

And then, as if the universe was just waiting to mess with my head, I was offered a job as the editorial director of a publishing company in San Francisco. It was the kind of job offer you really can't turn down. The kind you have to take very seriously even if conventional wisdom is practically shrieking at you to take a seat and let this one go on by. *Pish posh*, I said to myself. *I'm perfectly capable of entertaining this job possibility* and *the prospect of a cross-country move to northern California. Why wouldn't I be? I just had a rough year. My faculties are still perfectly functional.*

My gut seemed to have other ideas entirely. When I flew out to San Francisco to see my prospective employer and meet the members of the team I'd be working with, I couldn't shake its disapproving, downright worried voice. *Why*, it scowled at me, *are you even* thinking *about this? You are so not in the right place to be making decisions like this. Get a grip, woman. Go home. Get another massage. And put this foolishness right out of your mind.*

But I didn't listen, as I imagine you might have gathered by now. It was the perfect next step, really, if I wanted my career to keep moving forward. And it was flattering; I'll admit that too. In fact, everyone I told about the offer seemed to be urging me to accept. You must go! You have to take it. What an incredible opportunity, they said. I know! I would respond. How could I not? Only one person, my former boss from my scouting days, cocked her head at me when I told her about the offer and raised one eyebrow skeptically. "If you're going to go anywhere," she said, "shouldn't you be going in the other direction?"

In San Francisco, old family friends took me to their favorite farmers' market and out to dinner at Zuni Café, where I ate ethereal ricotta gnocchi. I saw the Golden Gate Bridge at sunset. I strolled through the city's greenmarkets, marveling at the mounds of tomatoes, artichokes, avocados, and nutmeg-scented doughnut muffins. I bought a Mission burrito, which I couldn't get even close to finishing, I rode the Muni a few times, and I tried my best to imagine myself in the city.

But I couldn't. It was like a brick wall, every time I tried. The city was nice enough, but I didn't really *get* it somehow. I found myself missing New York, even wishing the job offer had come from a company in Los Angeles. It was sort of strange, really.

Despite this, though, and the fact that at one point near the end of my visit, when the job offer was made even more irresistible, my gut fairly yelled that my former boss was right, if I were going to contemplate moving anywhere, it should be in the other direction, across the Atlantic and back to Berlin, I accepted the job, not even a few weeks after my breakup with Sam. I accepted the job, I quit my position as cookbook editor, and then I wept all the way home.

And that's where I got a little confused. Because, you see, once I started crying, I couldn't seem to stop. I cried in my office. I cried on the walk to the train. I cried on the train. I cried when I got home and told my friends on the ninth floor the good news (their dinner guests looked at me with alarm). I cried before I got into bed and I cried as I was falling asleep. I had just accepted the job of my dreams and I couldn't stop crying. It was so weird.

Somehow I managed to sleep fitfully but woke up the next morning at 6:00 like a bullet shot out of a gun. I'm not really exaggerating either. One moment I was asleep in my bedroom, the next I was standing in the living room and I couldn't breathe. Then my knees gave out and I found myself crumpled on the floor. *What have I done?* Not being able to breathe seemed to be making a bad situation worse. I tried to steady myself, but I was shaking all over. What was even more troubling was the crystal clear knowledge in my heart, my brain, and every other organ in my body that I had made a terrible mistake accepting. Epic. Huge. (My gut, as you can imagine, had a snide grin on its face. I wanted very much to punch it where it hurts, but I resisted.)

It wasn't until I called my father, the only person awake at this time of the morning, and he explained to me in a level, calm tone that I *did* have a way, one way, out of this mess—this embarrassing, disastrous mountain of a mess—that I started to have feeling in my hands and feet again.

"The same thing happened to me, you know," he said. "It was when we were leaving Berlin. I'd been offered two jobs, in Boston and in Baton Rouge." I know this story, I thought. The way I'd always heard it, my father couldn't imagine raising me in the South, which was why we went to Boston. "The job in Baton Rouge was the better one, really," he continued. "So I accepted the job, even though I really liked Boston. I turned down the job there, because I thought I was making the right decision for my career. But overnight, I realized I'd made a terrible mistake. That I couldn't live in Baton Rouge and, more important, that I couldn't raise you there, either. The next morning, I called up the people in Boston who'd made me the offer and I asked them to reconsider. They did so right away. And then I called Baton Rouge and told them I was terribly sorry, but that I'd changed my mind. And, you know, that was it. I've never looked back."

I swallowed hard. "You can do this too, Luisa, you can. But you have to do it now, this morning. The window of time is pretty small. Call your boss and tell her what happened. Just be honest. She'll understand, I'm sure she will. And then call San Francisco and tell them you've made a mistake."

I made a small, strangled noise. "Pops, I'm so embarrassed." He laughed. "Just think of it as a grand family tradition, like dropping out of graduate school was. Go on, call her. Then call me back and tell me what happened."

To make a long story short, I did exactly as my father told me and the disaster was sorted out by 10:00 A.M. By 11:00, I'd taken a solemn oath never to disregard my gut again. My poor, maligned gut who wanted nothing but the best for me, who had been sounding the alarm bells all along. Suddenly everything was so clear! Why did I ever even contemplate the new job?

That evening, for the first time in weeks, I cooked myself dinner. I didn't know quite what I wanted to eat when I left the office, but I knew that I wanted to be back in the kitchen again, feeling the weight of the knife handle in my hand as I chopped, watching olive oil go squiggly in the hot pan, making my own dinner for once instead of going out and buying it. I went to the grocery store and strolled the aisles for inspiration, filling my cart with sensible stuff: yogurt, broccoli, a sack of organic lemons. It wasn't until I turned the corner into the bean aisle and saw the rows of neatly stacked cans that it occurred to me what I was really hungry for. I was starving, actually, for the baked beans my father used to make for dinner every week when I was a kid, served with a bunch of boiled broccoli. Suddenly I couldn't wait to spoon up the sweet, vinegar gravy and feel the velvety beans sticking gently in my teeth again.

At home, I warmed up the beans on the stove and steamed a bunch of broccoli that I dressed with grassy-green olive oil and lemon juice. I ate with long-lost gusto, mopping up the sticky-sweet bean sauce and lemony olive oil with bread until my plate was almost entirely clean. Then I leaned back in my chair and looked out the window, over the rooftops of Queens, so happy to be right there and nowhere else.

Fake Baked Beans

SERVES 4

Canned baked beans are just fine in times of need, but the truth is that you can get far more delicious beans by doctoring up a few cans of pinto beans with ketchup, molasses, mustard powder, and a few other seasonings. The idea originally came from Melissa Clark's "A Good Appetite" column in the

New York Times. She goes the slow food route by having you soak dried white beans before cooking them in seasoned broth and then adding the other ingredients that make fake baked beans taste, well, like the real thing. But I've found that using canned pinto beans most closely imitates the canned version of baked beans I grew up loving, without the cloying sweetness that the industrial brands inevitably bring to the table. And frankly, it's quicker than using dry beans. Instead of Clark's addition of bacon, I use a pinch of smoked Spanish paprika for smoky flavor and depth. But really, just a pinch. You don't want the smokiness to overpower the beans. I like to eat these beans with steamed broccoli for nostalgia's sake, but you may, of course, go the more traditional route and serve them with corn bread or steamed Boston brown bread. Either way, I promise that eating these beans will make you feel better, no matter what ails you.

    3 15-ounce cans pinto beans
    ¼ cup ketchup
    ¼ cup molasses
    3 tablespoons apple cider vinegar
    1 ½ teaspoons mustard powder
    ¼ teaspoon Tabasco sauce, or to taste
    ¼ teaspoon freshly ground black pepper
    1 pinch smoked Spanish paprika, or to taste
    Salt to taste

1. Dump the canned beans into a pot along with their liquid. Add the ketchup, molasses, vinegar, mustard powder, Tabasco sauce, pepper, and smoked paprika, and mix well.

2. Bring the beans to a simmer and let cook over low heat, covered, until the liquid has thickened, 30 to 45 minutes. Season with salt if needed.

18

I Believe It Now

I N JUNE, TWO MONTHS AFTER I TURNED MY LIFE UPSIDE DOWN—OR RIGHT side up, depending on how you see it—I went back to Berlin for my first summer visit in ten years. It was cold and rainy when I arrived and I was wholly unprepared, having left New York in the middle of an early heat wave. I had to dig out my mother's winter jacket to wear with a wool scarf looped around my neck. I didn't mind, though, because, despite the cold, Berlin was in full bloom and the air smelled loamy and fresh. It was a treat to see the sky stay eerily pale long after dinner was over. And I could sit outside at a café, drinking something warm, wrapped cozily in my scarf. Back in New York, I knew that the sidewalks were steaming in the summer sun.

It was the week of Joanie's birthday and she celebrated, as she did every year, with a big, sprawling picnic under an oak tree in a sloping park at the very edge of Berlin. The bridge to Potsdam, where spies were swapped during the Cold War, was barely a mile away. The grass in the park hadn't been cut in a while and was knee high and damp, but Joanie didn't let that deter her. She and Dietrich brought huge plastic tarps and plenty of good food, so my mother and I dressed warmly, put on our rubber boots, and trekked off to join them.

Although the adults all had gray hair now and us kids were grown up and there were even babies—Joanie's grandchildren—toddling about, nothing about the picnic or the park had changed since I was a child. There were still the same plaid blankets layered over the tarps and the same colorful little plastic cups for us to drink out of. I found myself a little spot on a red plaid blanket and there, nestled down among the tall stalks of grass, with all my old friends and my mother nearby, I felt safe. The heartache of the past months was being replaced with something more buoyant, something powerful and strong. I had leapt forward out of the sadness. I had listened to my intuition. I had saved my own life.

We filled our plates with marble–sized Sicilian meatballs in a sticky, rust–colored sauce, tomato paste—stained bulgur salad, and potatoes and Romano beans soaked in a mustardy vinaigrette. There was a smoky herb dip that we scooped up with wedges of toasted pita and deep purple olives bobbing in a spicy brine. There were squares upon squares of my old favorite, plum cake sprinkled with almonds and cinnamon, and we dipped into a big basket of freshly picked strawberries until the straw and our fingers were stained red. There were thermoses of iced tea and wine for the grown–ups, and Kim's wife even made a big bowl of wiggling green Jell-O for the kids. But by the end of the picnic, they weren't the only ones eating it. Everything tasted so good and the flavors were big and juicy. It had been a long while since I'd felt this hungry.

That buoyancy and hunger were still in me when I decided to see Max, who lived in Berlin again, not far from my mother's apartment. The first years after we'd broken up, I couldn't see him without going weak in the knees. I'd never known anyone to have such an effect on me and I'd rebuffed his attempts at reaching out over e-mail during the past five years, too afraid of being sucked back into the intensity of his orbit again to allow any kind of friendship to develop. But in my new-found role as Superwoman, Determiner of Her Own Life, there was no room for any of that fear anymore. So when I found myself wondering how he was doing, this time I was the one to get in touch. To my delight, he sounded happy to hear from me and even happier that I was in Berlin.

Max suggested we go for a walk in the gardens of Sanssouci, Friedrich the Great's summer palace in Potsdam. My mother and Florian had dragged me along on many a walk through Sanssouci as a kid, me re-luctantly dragging my feet through the gravel as I walked behind them, but now the idea of a park walk sounded just right. I picked Max up in my mother's old jalopy and we drove out to Potsdam together. We chattered excitedly, trying to fit five years of stories into a half-hour drive, and I found it hard not to keep turning my head to look at him. I couldn't believe he was sitting right there, next to me.

The weather had mercifully warmed up and there were big cotton-candy clouds puffed throughout the blue sky. We strolled along the manicured pathways, past marble statues and fountains and espaliered fruit trees, until we found a bench where we could sit and sun our-selves, eyes closed, in companionable silence. Sometimes I stole a peek at Max, head thrown back against the park bench, his blond hair lighter at the temples and the tips. His smile hadn't changed, but his eyes had grown even kinder.

There was much more to catch up on, of course, than we were able to cram into the drive over, so after we'd had enough of the sun, we headed to an outdoor café in Potsdam and settled down for a snack. Max ate a flaky slice of apple strudel doused in a puddle of yellow cream and I ordered a wedge of Quark cheesecake, lemony and slightly grainy. Unlike American cheesecake, which was always too rich and heavy for my taste, my slice of *Käsekuchen* tasted light and whole-some. Steam rose off our teacups as I told him about Sam, the San Francisco job fiasco, and my family. He listened carefully, watching me. What I didn't tell him was how homesick I'd been. How much I'd longed to be back in Berlin.

What was unnerving and lovely at the same time was the feeling that no time at all had passed between us. Though that wasn't entirely it. On the one hand, no time had passed. On the other, so much had changed. For one thing, we were older—I had found my first gray hairs and Max's voice, his carriage, had softened and mellowed. I found my-self thinking about how much calmer he had become and then real-ized all that I had gained in wisdom too in the years since we'd parted ways. Yet, despite all this, we were still recognizable to each other. Far more than we were the last time we saw each other, when I was leaving him behind. That was ancient history now.

The last time I had seen Max, he was a university student in a small Bavarian town. Now he was a lecturer at the university in Potsdam and was working toward his PhD. He had been back in Berlin for five years, living around the corner from where I grew up. "Sometimes I think I might run into your mother buying groceries," he said. "But I never do." Max and my mother had always gotten along well. They'd stayed in touch after I'd ended things with Max, until I'd asked her to stop, surprised by my jealousy.

When we finished our cakes and started walking back to the car, he stopped me in the middle of the sidewalk. "Would you mind if I gave you a hug? I just kind of have this urge. Is that okay?" He stood there squinting at me in the sun. I held out my arms. I couldn't see why not. It felt kind of good to say yes, actually. He held me very tight for a few long moments and then released me, with a sheepish look on his face. We spent the drive home discussing cheesecake. (Baked with a crust or without, that was the question; apparently it was a hotly debated subject among *Käsekuchen* lovers.)

As I slowed the car to drop him off at his apartment, I realized I didn't want the afternoon to end. I swallowed hard and ginned up my courage: "This was so nice. And look, I'm here for the whole week. Do you want to do this again before I go?" He laughed. "Of course I do."

So we prowled around an exhibit of sand sculptures in a vacant lot near Berlin's Hauptbahnhof and got caught in a flash rainstorm that vanished as soon as it appeared. We took walks on shaded sidewalks, past corner bars with illuminated Berliner Kindl or Schultheiss beer signs hanging out front, and drank cups of afternoon tea in cafés all over the city. We ate cheap Thai food down the street from the apartment I dreamed of all those months ago, back in Puerto Rico, and we stayed up too late drinking wine at a cheap bar in what was once East Berlin.

We swapped rueful war stories about all that had happened over the past few years. It almost felt, at moments, like we could see one another's wounds. Everything was so different from how it had been. We were gentler, both with ourselves and with each other. Everything I told him, he understood. There was never any incomprehension in his eyes, never a sense that he wasn't really listening or that he didn't fully understand what I was trying to say. All of him was right there, fully present. He listened, he *saw* me, in a way no one else ever had. And now I understood what a gift that was.

Still, I wasn't looking for anything. I was just happy to be spending time with Max, feeling so at home again on streets shadowed by fragrant, arching linden trees. We were having a good time. We were easy breezy, as my friends would say, old friends reconnecting after a long time apart.

Everything changed the night Max invited me back to his apartment. That evening, we had spent six hours in a café talking. At 4:00 in the morning I started to feel that nervous belly that I always used to feel when I spent time with him, a combination of joy and adrenaline. It was all I could do to keep from reaching out and touching his angular face. But I kept my hands folded in my lap. It was late and we were tired and, finally, neither one of us could bear to order anything else to drink. I was hoping my mother wouldn't wake up and wonder where I was, when Max suddenly asked me if I wanted to see his apartment.

We drove to his street and parked in front of a dark green door almost at the end of the cul–de–sac. The street was silent; our footsteps were the only ones reverberating on the sidewalk. We walked through the courtyard, quiet and dark, into the back apartment building that smelled of a mixture of coal smoke and laundry detergent, the inimitable smells of Berlin. My heart tugged in my chest and out of nowhere I heard a very firm voice, so firm it startled me: *This. This smell. I want this smell around me all the time.* What?

We walked up the stairs on our tiptoes, careful not to wake the neighbors, and at his apartment door Max pulled out an old iron key, three inches long, and fit it carefully into the lock. It looked just like the key to my mother's old apartment on Bamberger Strasse. That key used to sort of squeak and scrape as it went into the lock and when the door swung open and I stepped over the threshold, one wooden floorboard would always creak the exact same way, like it was greeting me. I was filled with a terrible longing. And I heard that same firm voice again: *I never want to leave this place. I am here now, finally, and I never want to leave.*

We walked into the apartment's dark foyer. Max turned the lights on and one by one opened the doors to the kitchen, the living room, and the bedroom. And that was when my heart felt like it was going to burst.

On Max's kitchen wall, next to the map of the Paris subway and a few postcards from friends, I saw a print of culinary plants and mushrooms framed in glass. It was a visceral thing, the immediacy of seeing it. I *knew* this print, the way it was framed slightly off center, even the tiny metal clips stuck on the side of the frame; its image had been imprinted in my brain long ago. I stared at it for a moment—searching, searching—and then I remembered. It had hung in my mother's kitchen all those years ago. All the way back, before my father and I left for Boston, on the wall next to the stove. I used to look at it when I sat in a high chair, and later too, when I graduated to a proper chair. Every day I would run my eyes along the swooping old German script, trying to memorize the names of the plants and their corresponding characteristics: the furled blue petals of flax, the plant with the funny name, *Lungenkraut*, the moody black berries of salsify. I was mesmerized by the division of the mushrooms, carefully colored and labeled, into edible and poisonous, even when I went through a brief but intensely weird phase of being terrified of poison, convinced it was everywhere.

The print was always there, a part of my everyday landscape. But then one day it vanished, sometime after I had moved to Boston. I hadn't seen it since. I'd forgotten it existed. And now it was here, in Max's kitchen.

We moved silently to the living room, and there I saw the little fat-bellied red reading lamp that had sat on Florian's side of the bed in my mother's bedroom during the many years they were together. Florian and my mother broke up when I was eighteen years old and shortly thereafter my mother left Berlin for work and we lost our beloved apartment. I realized I hadn't seen the lamp since we were all still living in that apartment together.

And in the bedroom I saw the rug that had lain in my parents' living room while they were still married. It was in almost every photograph taken of me at home as a baby and a toddler, its brown and green and yellow design blurred in the background. I hadn't seen it since the divorce, when my mother packed it away, but I'd looked through those photographs a thousand times, rifling through my mother's desk to get at them, to see what it used to look like, our old life, when we were all still together. And now that rug, as familiar as anything, was here. It turned out that, years earlier, after our breakup, after Max moved to Berlin, my mother had loaned him these things to furnish his new apartment. All of them were here now, the physical objects of my whole childhood in Berlin assembled in the home of this person whom I had loved and lost and who was now standing in front of me again, as if it were the most natural thing in the world.

Later, much later, I would wonder if Max's invitation to come up and see his apartment wasn't some sort of cosmic intervention. It was hard to imagine that it was all just a coincidence, all these talismans from my life here in Max's home, when it felt more like Providence nudging me along, saying in an urgent whisper, *"See, woman? It was here all along. All you had to do was wake up and* listen."

I drove back to my mother's a little later, after having stood next to Max, hip to hip, in the kitchen papered with maps of Paris and Berlin, until the daylight started dyeing the edges of the sky a pale, pale blue. I felt like I was a high school kid coming home past her curfew and I was filled with a delirious, stomach-roiling fever.

I flew back to New York a few days later, loath to leave behind the linden-scented city and everything I'd just discovered, but leaving Berlin felt different this time. For the first time in my life it wasn't sad and final. I had just peeked behind that door I had been wondering about for a long time, and as I flew up over the red-roofed city I realized I still had so much more I wanted to see. And back in New York, I started to contemplate what would have been inconceivable even just a week earlier.

Käsekuchen (**Quark Cheesecake**)

MAKES ONE 9-INCH ROUND CAKE

German *Käsekuchen* is vastly different from American cheesecake because it's made with lean Quark instead of cream cheese, producing a far lighter cake. This particular *Käsekuchen* makes things even simpler by eschewing a crust, since there's farina for ballast in the batter along with lemon peel and vanilla (use regular Cream of Wheat, not the quick-cooking kind). There's no need to fuss with a water bath—*Käsekuchen* is a rustic cake that's supposed to have wrinkles and fissures. The top will look dark when you remove it from the oven, but don't panic: that's the way it's supposed to be. The cake tastes wonderful the day it's made, but I like it best after a night in the fridge. The cold compacts the cake a little and what you get the next day is these deliciously creamy slices of cold, slightly sour cheesecake that you could eat out of hand standing up at the counter. It's pretty great stuff.

Butter and farina for the pan
2 pounds Quark (see page 23 for sources)
⅔ cup sugar
1 tablespoon vanilla extract
4 large eggs
3 tablespoons cornstarch
8 tablespoons (4 ounces) unsalted butter, melted and cooled
2 tablespoons farina
2 teaspoons baking powder
Grated peel and juice of 1 lemon

1. Heat the oven to 375 degrees and put the oven rack in the lower third of the oven. Butter the bottom and sides of a 9-inch springform pan and sprinkle in enough farina to lightly to coat the pan.

2. In a large bowl, beat together the Quark, sugar, vanilla, eggs, cornstarch, butter, farina, baking powder, and lemon peel and juice until the batter is smooth and creamy.

3. Pour the batter into the prepared pan and smooth the top. Bake for 45 minutes, rotating the cake pan halfway through. The top will be quite dark by the end.

4. Remove the cake from the oven and place the pan on a cooling rack. As it cools, the cake will slump down, losing its height. Let the cake cool entirely before removing the sides of the pan. It keeps well in the fridge covered for a few days.

19

Leap and the Net Will Appear

I AM WHAT YOU WOULD CALL A RESPONSIBLE PERSON, POSSIBLY EVEN A square. I always eat my vegetables. I never have that third glass of wine (in fact, rarely even that second one). I get palpitations if I'm not punctual. And I tell my parents everything. Sometimes I think this stodgy obedience is the honorary German in me, the stuff that rubbed off on me by osmosis. I may not have German blood in my veins, but the joy I get from being on time must be far more than coincidental.

So it was a little out of character when, a few weeks after returning to New York from Berlin, my head still spinning with thoughts of the week and Max and the way it seemed that the whole world I had lost when I left Berlin as a child was gathered in his apartment waiting for me to return, I decided on a whim to book a flight back again. Just for three days. It was even odder that I didn't tell anyone, not my parents or my friends. The thing is, for once I didn't want anyone to interfere with what felt right. I'd had enough of not listening to my gut, of doing what was expected of me. Now my gut was telling me to go see about a life that might possibly be waiting for me after all the unhappiness, confusion, and sadness of the past year. I was damned if I didn't listen.

"What would you say if I told you I wanted to come back to see you?" I wrote to Max. "Like, soon? Just for a few days."

"I'd think you were nuts," he responded. "But in the best possible way." And then, "I can't wait." I booked my flight online, my hands trembling with anticipation as I clicked the purchase button.

But the night before my flight, I was suddenly wracked with fear. *What are you doing?* I wondered, as I lay sleepless again. *You're going to Berlin for a weekend after having spent a few afternoons and evenings just talking to the guy again? It's going to be a disaster. What exactly do you think will happen?* I was panicked, almost frantic with worry. This was not what a responsible woman would do, just pick up and fly across the ocean for a weekend on a whim. But I couldn't bring myself to cancel my ticket either. I tossed and turned and berated myself until, finally, I realized that if the weekend went horribly wrong, I had the keys to my mother's apartment. She was in Italy. I could always escape. With that consolation, I somehow managed to sleep fitfully.

The next day, before my flight, I was a mess of nerves. Max called to wish me a good flight and I almost snapped. *This was the worst idea ever,* I thought. *I can't believe I was so naïve.* At the last minute, terrified that precisely because I had told no one that I was flying to Berlin the plane would go down and no one would know that I was on it, I wrote my mother to tell her where I was going. (Told you I was a square.) Convinced she would tell me I was crazy and counsel me not to go, not with the steam still rising off my breakup, I practically had to close my eyes with shame as I typed. Instead, she responded with this:

"My love, have a safe flight. I love you. You are a wonderful person and I say that not because I am your mother, but because it is true. Mamma."

Propelled by this and by some kind of stubborn, scared–stiff bravery that I found buried deep within me, I put one foot in front of the other until I got to the airport and then on the airplane and before I knew it we were airborne and then, if I can admit it, I was actually kind of excited. I stayed awake through the night, drinking tomato juice that I doctored with lots of salt and pepper, wondering what lay ahead, too nervous even to read.

When we landed in Berlin early the next morning and I walked out of the gate at Tegel airport and saw Max standing there, leaning against the wall with one leg crossed over the other, all my remaining worries evaporated. I was filled with a delicious sense of adventure and thrill and not a little bit of relief too. It *was* the right decision to come. I could just tell. And in that moment I saw myself in my black leggings and long chambray shirt, pulling a little rolling suitcase as I moved forward, and I thought in wonder, *That is me.* I would have hardly recognized myself a few months earlier. *That is me, following my heart. Who knew I had it in me?* It was a wondrously powerful feeling.

Max took me into his arms and we looked at each other for what felt like a long time before he smoothed my hair and we kissed. Then he took my bag and we walked out of the airport and settled into the bus that would take us back to his apartment. The weather had much improved in the few weeks since I was last in Berlin, and as we sat side by side in the bus, the sun beating through the windows, the air was heavy and warm but not entirely unpleasant. I could feel Max's warmth radiating through his white T-shirt next to me. The bus took a route I didn't know and we rolled along streets I hadn't seen in a long time, but everything looked so perfectly familiar and unchanged. Like it had been waiting for me. Like I was home.

The bus passed the grand Charlottenburg Palace, where I had to go on so many walks as a child, dawdling behind my mother and Florian in the manicured palace park. We passed the intersection of Adenauer Platz and the Kurfürstendamm, West Berlin's famous old shopping mile, where, clad in baggy jeans and a long flannel shirt, I bought my first pair of Doc Martens in high school. Then we got off the bus and walked down Fasanenstrasse, past the stately Villa Grisebach auction house, until we ended up back at Max's apartment. This time, daylight streamed through the windows, illuminating the thick wooden floorboards.

The thing I would come back to again and again, even months later, is how much his apartment smelled like home. It was a mixture of laundry detergent and wood and fresh Berlin air, and something else, something ineffable and impossible to locate. And yet it anchored me. The long floorboards creaked just the way they were supposed to, and when I ran my fingers along his walls, covered in the standard-issue bumpy white wallpaper of all Berlin apartments, I remembered how I did the same thing as a child, lying awake in my enormous bedroom with the printed curtains. I would touch the wall to steady myself.

Max and I spent the next three days walking around Berlin. On Friday, we went to the East Side Gallery, a huge open-air mural that runs along the Spree River, and walked over the Oberbaumbrücke, the bridge that used to separate East Berlin from West Berlin. We joined a crowd of people clustered around a couple dancing the tango under the bridge and Max put his arms around me as we stood and watched. I could feel his chest rise and fall as he breathed. I closed my eyes in the sun and leaned back against him. Afterward, we sat outdoors eating grilled squid for lunch, salty and tender, at a Spanish restaurant on a leafy church square in Kreuzberg, and when the bells of the red-brick church next to our restaurant pealed they were loud enough that we had to stop talking and listen.

On Saturday, we walked through my old neigborhood, stopping in front of the apartment building I used to live in as I craned my neck and looked up at the bay windows of what used to be my room. The building was no longer pea green, but had been painted a pale petal pink. It was funny to be back again, being able to walk right up to the front door. After that, we made our way to the greenmarket on Winterfeldplatz, holding hands shyly at first, then slinging our arms around each other as we strolled. We gathered ingredients for dinner: a few tomatoes, a big ball of mozzarella, and some plums. Back at Max's apartment, I decided to bake pizza from scratch, stirring together flour and olive oil and yeast and warm water in a big plastic Tupperware in lieu of a bowl. I showed Max how to knead the shaggy dough into supple smoothness, and later, when it had risen and we'd patted it out to fit the edges of his baking tray, we covered the dough with a few spoonfuls of puréed tomatoes, several fat anchovies that we both loved to eat, and shreds of mozzarella that we pulled apart, our fingers milky and cold. We ate squares of the pizza, yeasty, salty, and delicious, by candlelight on the balcony with cold bottles of bitter Berlin pilsner to wash it down.

On Sunday afternoon, we settled on an outdoor café in Kreuzberg, swinging on an old recliner, drinking apple sodas and watching the families around us in amiable silence. As we pushed our feet into the dusty ground to keep the swing going, Max said, "No one makes me feel the way you do." I looked down at our interlaced fingers. "When you're with me, I don't need anything else. It sounds like such a cliché, but these past five years I kept waiting for someone who made me feel like you did to come along again. And it never happened." I squeezed his hand and said, "It just feels right, doesn't it?" He nodded. I felt so alive, so happy in that moment. Like I'd arrived some place incredibly important. "Let's not ruin this again," I said. He squeezed my hand back.

In the evening, we went to a party and Max's old friends clustered around to greet me. The next morning, I woke up before he did and looked out the balcony window to the house across the courtyard. It was so quiet that I could hear the birds chirping in the trees below and nothing else. I felt such a sense of peace. When Max awoke, we ate breakfast on the balcony in our thin cotton pajamas, spreading slices of dark bread with butter, waxy and cold, and when it was time for me to leave, I was already calculating in my head when I could return.

Back at my desk in New York the next day, I read an e-mail from him. "I'm still transfixed by the days we just spent together. I'm still processing how lovely every moment was. Everything just felt so right. But best of all was seeing you so happy and relaxed, so able to enjoy the time you had here with me. Thank you for taking that leap."

A few weeks later, I came back for another secret weekend, and then Max came to New York to see me, and at the end of the summer we met in Italy at my mother's house. I was spending the only disposable income I had on airplane flights, but I didn't care in the least. The words that echoed in my ear in Paris only a few months earlier were in my head all the time: *Open your eyes. There's no time to waste anymore. The answer is right in front of you.* And so I listened.

In the end, the thing I continued to return to with stunning clarity was how long it had taken me to realize that going my own way was within my reach. I had to trust that when I leapt, the earth could rise up to catch me. And that is just what happened. Within a matter of

months, I went from feeling lost and hopeless, powerless and depressed, to feeling free and strong, like I could climb a mountain in
flip–flops. Happy too, because I was finally brave enough to follow my
heart and go after what I really wanted.

Pizza Napoletana

SERVES 3 TO 4

I've tried many pizza doughs at home over the years, but this one, adapted
from a recipe by Jamie Oliver, has to be my favorite. It comes together in a
flash and bakes up beautifully into a bubbly, burnished crust. I am a purist
when it comes to pizza toppings, and a minimalist too. I like using only the
very basic trinity of tomatoes, mozzarella, and anchovies (though you, of
course, are free to top away to your heart's content), and I use them spar-
ingly, so that the crust isn't overwhelmed with juice and moisture and gets
nice and crisp.

3½ cups all-purpose or Italian "00" flour, plus more, if needed
1 teaspoon instant yeast
Pinch of sugar
1¼ cups lukewarm water
2 teaspoons salt, plus more to taste
2 tablespoons olive oil, plus more for the bowl
1 14-ounce can good-quality peeled plum tomatoes
2 teaspoons dried Italian or Greek oregano
8 anchovy fillets, or more to taste
1 ball fresh mozzarella (not buffalo mozzarella), thinly sliced and
    shredded

1. Put the flour in a mixing bowl and make a well in the middle. Put the
yeast and sugar in the middle of the well, then pour in the water. Using a
fork, draw the flour in gradually as you mix the ingredients together,

sprinkling in 2 teaspoons salt and 2 tablespoons olive oil as you go. Work the dough in the bowl with your hands; then knead it on a lightly floured work surface until the dough is smooth and springy. Shape it into a ball.

2. Wash out the mixing bowl, dry it, and oil it lightly. Put the ball of dough in the bowl and turn to coat it with the oil. Cover the bowl with a damp dishcloth and let it sit in a warm room or oven (turned off) for about 1 hour or until the dough has doubled in size.

3. Gently deflate the dough with your hands and divide it in two equal pieces. Line a baking sheet with parchment paper. Roll out one piece of the dough until it's as thin as can be, then transfer it gently to the baking sheet. Cover the second piece of dough with the damp dishcloth and set aside.

4. Heat the oven as high as it will go. Drain off half the juice from the can of tomatoes and then, using your hands, shred half of the remaining contents of the can and distribute onto the round of dough. Salt the tomato layer to taste and sprinkle with half the oregano. Distribute half the anchovy fillets over the pizza and then top with half the shredded mozzarella. Drizzle with a bit more olive oil.

5. Slide the baking sheet into the very hot oven and cook until the pizza is crisp and bubbling, about 8 to 10 minutes (depending on your oven). Remove from the oven, slice into wedges, and serve immediately. Then repeat with the second round of dough and remaining toppings.

20

A Chorus of Thousands

T HAT SUMMER I FELT LIKE I WAS LIVING IN A DREAM. ALL THE PUZZLE pieces of my life were sliding into place. I'd been given a fresh start, a chance to fix things, but, most important, a chance to be happy. Somewhere in the middle of all those transatlantic flights and jet-lagged nights I realized that I was making some kind of a decision. And in the end it came rather quickly. After so many years of wondering where I belonged, I was surprised by how swiftly I decided that what I wanted was to be in Berlin. I'd never felt so certain about anything in my life. It was hard to second-guess that kind of certitude. It was what helped me move forward. I felt weightless with relief.

You already know about Max's cheekbones and his kind smile and that when I first met him in Paris I knew we belonged to each other in some cosmic way. It turned out that we had a lot of growing up to do before we could figure out a way to make each other happy. And along the way we came close to leading entirely different lives. But maybe that was exactly why, when we did find our way back to one another, it felt like such a gift.

This time I decided to give it everything I had. Because after all that had happened, Max was right there, holding out his hand and willing me to jump. All I had to do was take hold and do it. Part of me was terrified: I still had a few voices in my head that I could listen to, the same ones that told me to be careful a decade ago. But being scared of things hadn't ever helped me. And besides, the voices in my head were no match for the chorus of thousands in my gut. I'd come out of the biggest struggle of my life and the universe was telling me in no uncertain terms that I was being given a second chance. When do you ever get a second chance?

I expected there to be more inner turmoil or fear about the unknown when I realized that I needed to leave New York. But there wasn't any. There was only a quiet within me, not an eerie quiet, but a simple, placid quiet. *Yes*, the quiet seemed to be saying, *this is exactly what you're supposed to be doing. I was just waiting for you to figure it out on your own.*

Leaving New York, giving up my job, my whole career in fact, was a huge thing to do. But what I wanted more than anything was to go home again and I wanted it more than any job. After years of being sensible and responsible and mature and doing what was expected of me, I very much simply wanted to follow my heart. I wanted to love Max, whose face was etched with my future, more than I wanted to stay in New York. For once, finally, I realized that that was enough.

I broke the news to my friends and family, who seemed to have been expecting it. All that was left now was for me to jump, to take a big running leap out of the life I knew into one that I thought, I hoped, could be my future. But one more thing I had discovered during this magical, charmed summer was that since I'd been given the chance to change my life, really change it, I had to go for it, dig deep into my belly, or maybe my soul, and see where it wanted to go. I had to think big, take a huge leap, be fearless. Who else was going to fight for my happiness besides me?

So I put my ear down to the ground to hear what the universe was trying to tell me and I decided to do one more big, big thing. I'd need a job when I got to Berlin—after all, that had been part of the problem the last time. Love was all well and good, but once everyday life set in, a girl had to have to something to *do* all day long. I thought about looking for a job in publishing or maybe teaching English—safe, predictable ways to make a living—but I couldn't figure out why I wasn't aiming a little higher. *I'm already making the biggest jump of my life*, I thought. *Why don't I just go for broke?* I thought of my blog and my readers, who had cheered me on and followed me through highs and lows. And I thought of how I dreamed as a child of being a writer one day. *Be brave, Luisa,* I told myself. *Follow your heart.* And I decided to take a stab at writing a book.

I joked about it with my friends, how everything good seemed to be falling into place, how I was just daring the universe to say no. And I worked on a book idea, over and over again, until it was just right. Still, when my agent, a good friend, and I sent out the proposal to ten editors, I wasn't overly optimistic about what would happen. I had spent too many years on the other side of the fence as an editor and knew that lots of good ideas went nowhere. But I figured I had nothing to lose. My one-way ticket to Berlin was already purchased.

So I was all the more floored when, a day after sending it out, an editor at Viking called my agent and told her she wanted to make a deal. I closed my office door when my agent called to tell me and I cried. But for once, in that strange, brilliant year, they weren't tears of sadness. I was crying with joy. Was it really possible that all these good things were happening? To *me*? I couldn't believe it. When I called to tell Max, I found myself stammering into the phone. My parents whooped and hollered when I told them the news, my father beside himself with pride. The road to Berlin was wide open now.

In the final months before I left New York, Max sent me countless letters and postcards and e-mails. He knew what I was giving up to come back and he knew to keep holding his hand out, a lifeline. When he came to New York to visit me, he charmed me by being as smitten with the city as I was. He bubbled with excitement whenever I met him on my lunch break and after work. "This city is so amazing! You won't believe what I saw an hour ago." We spent hours sitting in the shadow of the Brooklyn Bridge, watching the boats pass us by in the harbor as the sun set. I took him to my favorite dumpling shop in Chinatown and watched him, wide-eyed with pleasure, eat twenty-four dumplings in one sitting, doused in black vinegar and chile sauce. We went to Central Park to see the dancing roller skaters on the weekend, and when Max saw tears form in my eyes as we watched them wiggle and jump to the beat of the loud music coming from the boom box, he put his arm around me and squeezed hard. "We'll come back all the time," he whispered. "Don't worry."

Knowing that he loved New York made it easier to leave. Knowing that he knew how much *I* loved New York made it easier too.

And when I flew back to Berlin for one last weekend in October before the move two months later, Max surprised me by making a huge pot of silky pea soup studded with pink rounds of *Würstchen* and inviting all his friends over for Sunday lunch. He got the recipe from his mother, who also lent him a pot big enough to cook for a crowd. The apartment smelled sweet and smoky from the sautéing onion and bits of smoked ham in the soup, and when his friends and their children arrived we all sat perched on the kitchen counters and on the floor, big bowls of soup on our laps. We spooned up the rib-sticking soup and chased the dregs in our bowls with pieces of crusty bread. The soup tasted like Berlin in a bowl, all salty and porky and earthy and simple, welcoming me back home again.

I knew what Max was trying to tell me, with his pot of pea soup and the cozy afternoon with friends: that as hard as it was going to be to leave one place behind, there was a new life for me waiting in this place, new friends to be made, new traditions to cement. And no matter what happened, I wouldn't be alone. He'd be there, by my side, to help me find my way, with a bowl of pea soup to keep me warm.

Erbsensuppe (German Pea Soup)

SERVES 4

Thick and warming, this stick-to-your-ribs soup is a staple in German households and canteens all over the country. While it's certainly possible to make it vegetarian-friendly by leaving out the smoked bacon and hot dogs, I think the added flavor they give is essential. Plus, it's fun to fish around for the pink rounds of sausage in the soup as you eat. Serve with a few slices of German rye bread to wipe the bowl.

3 tablespoons olive oil

1 medium yellow onion, minced

⅓ cup minced Speck or lean bacon

1 leek, white and pale green part only, cut in half lengthwise, well
    rinsed, and then sliced into half-moons

1 medium carrot, diced

½ small celery root, diced

1 tablespoon fresh marjoram, minced

Salt

1½ cups dried split green or yellow peas

5 to 6 cups chicken or vegetable broth

3 medium Yukon Gold potatoes, peeled and diced

Freshly ground black pepper

4 *Wiener Würstchen* or hot dogs

1. Heat the olive oil in a 4-quart pot. Add the minced onion and bacon. Cook over medium-high heat for about 5 minutes; then add the sliced leek and stir well. Cook for another 7 minutes. Add the carrot and celery root and stir well. Cook for a few minutes. Add the minced marjoram and a pinch of salt, and stir well.

2. Pour in the dried peas and the broth. Stir well and cover. Bring to a boil and then lower the heat to a simmer. Cook for 20 minutes.

3. Add the diced potatoes and stir well. Cook for another 20 minutes. Taste for salt and add freshly ground black pepper to taste.

4. Cut the *Würstchen* or hot dogs into bite-sized rounds and add to the pot. Warm through (don't let the soup boil once you add the *Würstchen*) and serve immediately.

21

Crossroads of the World

W HEN I WAS ABOUT NINE YEARS OLD, I HAD A SERIOUS CASE OF
what I call Peter Pan Syndrome. Here's how it went: I would
sneeze, say. Or tie my shoelaces. Maybe even just toss my hair. And then
it would hit me. *That is the last time I will ever sneeze at exactly that moment.* Or in a slightly more emotional tone: *That is the only time I will ever tie
my shoelaces at this precise moment in time, the only time I'll ever toss my hair that exact way again.* And with that, the earth would fall away from under my feet.

The day before I turned ten was a disaster. I sat weeping at my desk,
inconsolable. "I will never be nine again," I wailed, as my father sat on
the bed next to me in perplexed silence. I was in mourning. My ninth
year was gone forever. Was this how all of life was going to be? I wasn't
sure I could stand it.

My father fought back a smile as he sat there patiently, patting my
head. He told me solemnly that everything would be okay. "But I don't
want to grow up," I hiccupped. "I want to be little forever!" "Well, you'll
always be my little girl," he answered hopefully. Which made me cry
even harder for my poor, deluded father, who clearly had no understanding of the cruel passage of time.

The embarrassing thing was, ever since I decided to leave New York,
I found myself doing a similar kind of countdown. It was totally maddening and kind of made me want to smack myself gently in the face to
snap out of it, but I couldn't seem to help it. I'd be standing somewhere,

not even somewhere special, maybe just on the corner of Seventh Avenue and Twenty-eighth Street, which is sort of Nowheresville compared to other glimmering parts of this city, but who cares, I happened to love it. Anyway, I'd be standing there on the corner of Seventh and Twenty-eighth and the light would be falling just so while the strangest accumulation of beautiful creatures in vertiginous heels and tight pants emerged from the subway moving like jungle cats and some cab driver would be screaming epithets from three lanes away while leaning on his horn and the other cars would be moving along gracefully in this perfect symphony and a homeless dude would smile at me sweetly and I'd see the Rafiqi's lunch cart guy pulling into his regular space and the wind would whip through my hair and suddenly I would lose my breath, it would get caught in my throat and my heart would stop and I would find myself thinking, *This is it, this is the last time I'll ever be on the corner of Seventh Avenue and Twenty-eighth Street when the light falls just so with that crazy cabbie yelling over the din and the Rafiqi's guy setting up his cart, the Very Last Time. Oh, my holy hell. I must be crazy if I think I can leave, how on earth can I ever leave?*

And because I am a sentimental sap, this happened to me on almost every street corner, at almost every moment.

It was all pretty ridiculous, of course. No one was *making* me leave New York. I was doing it of my own free will and I was thrilled about what lay ahead. In fact, most mornings I woke up with a disbelieving grin on my face at all my good fortune. Also, and this helped when I found myself on one of those street corners with a clenched heart: New York wasn't exactly going anywhere. As most kind people told me in those days, I could always come back. And although New York was without a doubt the Greatest City in the World, fully deserving of every tear I shed for its wondrous, sparkling, incredible self, I think it's fair to say that I tended toward the slightly hysterical when it came to saying goodbye, no matter where I was. Let's be honest.

To take leave of the city properly, my way, I did everything I'd ever loved in New York. I wandered the small streets of Chinatown, past blinking electronics, past ladies selling lotus-leaf-wrapped sticky rice on the sidewalks, and into fragrant grocery stores. I went to the Cloisters to see the medieval tapestries one last time and to look at the New

Jersey Palisades across the Hudson River, resplendent in their fiery autumn colors. I walked over the Brooklyn Bridge one last time and took myself out to dinner at my favorite Cambodian sandwich shop, perched at the counter, mouth on fire.

When I met Jenny for pizza at Franny's in Park Slope one day at lunchtime, we ordered a plate of roasted Brussels sprouts that were so good—spicy and charred and with a haunting background flavor that neither of us could place—that I begged the waiter to give me the recipe. I had never asked a waiter for a recipe before, never in my life, but those Brussels sprouts were a different story. It was something I desperately wanted in my recipe arsenal so I could pull it out whenever I needed to remember New York in Berlin. I was thinking ahead here, anticipating what would cure my future-imagined longing for New York. But the waiter wouldn't tell me a thing.

After I said goodbye to Jenny, I wandered down Flatbush Avenue until I got to the Brooklyn Bridge at sunset and watched a bride and groom have their pictures taken against the backdrop of Lower Manhattan, the bride's full skirt dragging behind her lazily. I saw the hole on the horizon where the Twin Towers used to stand and I remembered the morning I got stuck on the Manhattan Bridge on my way to work, three days after September 11, and how the entire train car went silent, like we were holding our breath collectively, willing ourselves not to look out the window at the smoking pile. There were hundreds of people in that car and you could hear a pin drop. Nine years had passed since then, which was hard to believe. Sometimes it felt like it had just happened.

In my final days in New York, I gave daily thanks for jaywalking, a serious no-no in Berlin, good bagels, yellow cabs, and my daily glimpses of the Chrysler Building. I marveled at all that had happened to me here, at the woman New York helped me become. I sat at dinner with my friends and watched them as they talked and ate and I thought that my heart would burst I loved them so much. I didn't know how I would have survived the year without them. And now I was leaving them behind. What would I do without them?

I'll admit that this part of leaving New York scared me a little. The stable job, the city I knew inside and out, I was ready to leave those behind. But my girls were a different story. I had needed them so much this year; how did I know I wouldn't still need them for what came next? A whole new life awaited me on the other side, and it was still nebulous and unknown. I wanted them near me to hold my hand. But their lives were moving forward too.

In those moments, I tried to remind myself that any fear I did have was lodged only in my head, not in my heart. When, at random moments, I considered simply not showing up at the airport or wrapping my arms around a particularly lovely lamppost and never letting go, no matter how many sensible policemen tried to pull my deranged self off, I did my best to pat myself on the shoulder and be understanding, like I would be with a good friend. *You're going to be fine, you hear? This is all going to work out. Just you wait.* Trust *me.*

So I emptied my apartment, selling my favorite tapestry to a friend and my lamps and empty bookshelves to an Indian couple from down the road. I brought books by the boxful to the Strand, finally separating myself from those cookbooks I never used and the galleys I once toted home gleefully by the dozen. I hugged my friends goodbye with a quivering lip, promising to be back soon, and I took a hundred last longing looks at the New York skyline. *I'll be back soon, I promise,* I whispered to the city as I walked the streets in those final days. But I was no longer sure if I was speaking to the city or to myself.

Then, on a crisp December day, I was gone, my one-way ticket to Berlin stashed in my back pocket, my fists clenched with panic and exhilaration, my heart beating for everything that awaited me. Now all I had to do was think of that face on the other side of the arrival gate, smiling at me when I walked through the glass door.

Roasted Brussels Sprouts with *Colatura* and Chiles

SERVES 4 AS A SIDE DISH

I first ate a dish similar to these spicy, salty, deeply addictive sprouts at Franny's, a pizza restaurant on Brooklyn's Flatbush Avenue. There the sprouts were roasted in the fiercely hot wood-burning oven along with slivers of chile and had a wonderfully blistery, smoky flavor. Through a lot of trial and error, I figured out how to make a similar dish at home. What gives these oven-roasted sprouts richness and depth is *colatura*, the Sicilian version of Vietnamese fish sauce, pungent and stinky. If you're an anchovy-hater, do not fear: the *colatura* doesn't make the sprouts fishy, but simply gives the dish a special zip. You can find *colatura* online at gustiamo.com or zingermans.com.

2 pounds Brussels sprouts
3 to 4 tablespoons best-quality olive oil
2 dried Italian chiles, crumbled, or 1 to 2 teaspoons hot red pepper flakes
3 plump cloves garlic, lightly crushed and halved
Grated peel of ¼ organic lemon
Juice of ½ lemon
1 to 2 tablespoons *colatura*

1. Heat the oven to 400 degrees. Wash and trim the Brussels sprouts, and cut them in half.

2. Toss the sprouts with 3 tablespoons of the olive oil and the crumbled chiles, and place on a baking sheet.

3. Roast the sprouts in the oven for 18 to 20 minutes, stirring the sprouts halfway through so that they brown evenly.

4. Meanwhile, combine the garlic, lemon peel, juice, and 1 tablespoon of the *colatura* in a small bowl.

5. When the sprouts have blistered and browned, take the baking sheet out of the oven and immediately pour the *colatura* mixture over the sprouts, mixing well. Taste a sprout: if you'd like a stronger-tasting dish, add up to another tablespoon of *colatura*. Mix well to combine, and then scrape the dressed sprouts into a serving bowl or dish. If you'd like, drizzle in a bit more olive oil. Serve immediately.

Part 4

22

Not for the Faint of Heart

ONE DAY I WAS SAYING GOODBYE TO NEW YORK, GIVING ONE LAST backward glance at the glittering city receding under a bright blue sky as my train to JFK shuddered forward over the tracks, the wheels keeping time (ba–*bump* ba–*bump*) with the thudding I felt in my chest. And the next day I was standing next to two enormous suitcases in the swirling snow in Berlin, a thick cloud cover overhead.

I don't know if I was expecting the heavens to crack open or for the conductor on the Long Island Rail Road train to look at my one-way peak ticket and beg me to stay, but the departure from New York was more uneventful than I had expected. Before I knew it, I was sitting in the airplane, willing myself not to look out the window as we lifted up over Jamaica Bay. Then, after dinner and two movies, we landed in Berlin. It was early morning and it was pitch black outside. I peered out the window and saw nothing but a flurry of snowflakes in the darkness, drifts already gathering on the runway.

By the time we disembarked and made it through baggage claim, day was breaking and a cold, metallic light was seeping weakly through the thick clouds. As I walked through the arrival hall toward Max, bundled up in his warmest jacket and waving at me through the throngs of people, I could feel a fresh page of my life opening as I moved forward, pulling my heavy suitcases behind me. *I have made this happen*, I thought. *I am walking here right now because of my decisions, not because of anyone else's.*

155

It was, I realized, the first time in my life that I could say this unequivo-cally, and the realization made me feel ten feet tall. I also wondered, *How long will it snow for?*

It turned out, a very long time. That first winter back in Berlin was the coldest, snowiest winter on record since 1946 turned into 1947, when several hundred thousand Germans, weakened by hunger, homelessness, and other ravages of their terrible war, died from the consequences of unforgiving cold. When the Baltic Sea froze solid for twenty-one miles off the coast and sheet ice formed on the walls of homes around the country.

Our winter was, of course, nowhere near that bad and I didn't struggle with hunger or homelessness, but the weather was far worse than anything I'd ever experienced, even when I lived in Boston. There were long stretches of days (up to sixteen, at one point; I was counting) in which the sun didn't shine at all, and the lack of it was profoundly unnerving. There was so much unrelenting snowfall that the authori-ties stopped plowing nonessential streets and the city ran out of salt and gravel. The snow had been festive and clean at first, but soon it piled up in massive drifts and, without any sun to warm the air, com-pacted to solid, impenetrable ice. Cars shivered loosely down the streets; old men and women were sequestered in their homes, terrified of breaking a hip outside. My mother's car froze to the pavement and we spent an afternoon with shovels and a box of coarse Italian sea salt trying to liberate it, to no avail. Meteorologists on the radio alter-nated between blaming Arctic winds and Siberian winds for the terri-ble cold.

But I had not exactly given up my whole entire life in New York to be intimidated by one bad winter. Oh, ho, *no*. Not after how hard I'd worked to get here. So I wrapped myself in three layers of sweaters and thermal socks, turned up the heat in Max's apartment with its ten-foot ceilings (though I admit that the warmth mostly just rose up to the beautifully ornate ceiling moldings while I sat, shivering, below), and started to bake. I baked to stay warm. I baked to find control. I baked because it was Christmastime in Germany and in this new life I was, at last, a full-time food writer.

I made chewy little squares of gingerbread studded with candied citrus and snow-white anise-flavored domed cookies that disappeared with a quick crunch. Meringue-topped hazelnut stars that crackled lightly under our teeth, nuggets of almond paste adorned with peeled almonds and baked until glazed and toothsome and snappy, spiced butter cookies shaped into narrow rectangles and decorated with a scatter of slivered almonds. Not to mention rich, winey fruit bread, damp, dark, and mysterious, and dense, buttery Stollen coated in a thick layer of powdered sugar. I went through gallons of honey, pounds of nuts and flour, countless packets of baking powder and hartshorn salt, a hill of sticky candied citron and orange peel, and small mountains of ground ginger, cinnamon, mace, and cloves. I mixed and rolled and chilled and glazed and frosted and printed and decorated.

German Christmas baking is the stuff of legends, and with good reason. There are no simple drop cookies to be found in this cold, dark place (well, there might be a few, but those are for weaklings), and there is nothing about traditional German Christmas baking that is easy. These doughs were muscle-busting affairs, leaden with molten honey, chopped nuts, and heady spices. I watched Dietrich retrofit an industrial-strength drill machine with a dough hook to mix his mother's recipe for East Prussian gingerbread dough that would later be rolled out thinly and cut into angel- and deer-shaped cookies. The baker has to have not only strength and fortitude, but patience too. Some cookie doughs were even prepared in November to ripen on the balcony until the time came to shape and bake the dough in December. And I shaped Springerle cookies in antique molds for hours at Joanie's dimly lit work table, brushing flour into the crevices of the hand-cut wooden molds, tapping the dough into the molds gently and then unmolding each cookie onto an anise-seed-strewn cookie sheet. I soaked fruit in hot tea and brandy overnight and baked fruit bread, fragrant and moist, that tasted best after days of ripening.

They weren't for the faint of heart, German Christmas cookies. Neither was moving across continents in search of happiness. Both required elbow grease and determination and commitment and then weeks, even months, of mellowing. And one had to learn to look past their hard, beautiful exterior to see the warm, homey things that they were on the inside.

When you spend most of your life longing to go back to a place that seems out of reach and then one day you actually do return, chances are your ideas about what life will be like there will have not much to do with the reality of life on the ground. I thought taking leave of my life in New York was the hardest part about leaving, but the real work didn't start until I got to Berlin.

Deep down, I thought I would just walk out of the airport into my old life, like a chair moved from one room to another. The decision to move back was made on such a visceral, gut level that I didn't allow myself to spend too much time thinking about it, that it might be hard or that I might struggle to find my footing. I *knew* Berlin, I thought, even though the last time I'd lived here was fifteen years earlier, in high school. It was where I was meant to be. It was going to be easy, I was sure of it. And then it wasn't.

I'd spent ten years in New York walking around with a heart-shaped piece of Berlin within me, always wondering if I'd ever make it back again. Now that I was in Berlin, I was carrying New York with me.

In those first few weeks, I spent a lot of time alone while Max was working and found myself, at times, second-guessing my move. Berlin's hatchet-faced bus drivers and postal workers intimidated me, and I longed for the ease and friendliness of the New Yorkers I'd left behind. Everything in Berlin was so much rougher, more raw around the edges than I'd remembered. People were blunt and less polite. Even something as mundane as where to eat lunch had me entirely stumped. I had no idea where to go for a bowl of noodle soup or a good sandwich. In fact, I didn't even know if either of those things existed in Berlin.

And though I had worried about losing touch with my friends in New York, in Berlin, even more, I worried about whether I would ever make any new ones. I started to feel cowed. "Be patient," Max urged me when he came home one night and found me in tears on his couch.

"No one ever said this was going to be easy. I know the people here can be a tough crowd. Laugh at them and their rules. You're here with me. That's all that matters. Give yourself some time to adjust. Don't expect to be settled in a week or two."

So I barreled through the Christmas baking, keeping my head down and my teeth clenched, until all the tins and boxes I had collected at the thrift store were filled up, each cookie type divided from the next with a layer of thin paper that crackled agreeably every time the box was opened. Sometimes I brought the cookies as offerings to new friends. Sometimes I just stared at them, all glazed and nut-spangled and fragrant, a physical testament to the strange, hard test I was being put through as I started to readjust to life in Berlin.

And, with one frozen foot in front of the other, I learned to snarl back at the old ladies who reprimanded me for crossing an empty street at a red light. I stumbled across a noodle shop where a Chinese cook in a white cap nonchalantly flung soup noodles in the storefront. I rediscovered the glory of German bakeries, and although their identical sandwiches—crisp white roll, single slice of cheese or salami, limp leaf of lettuce, possible slice of egg for garnish—were forgettable, there were mysteriously dark loaves of whole grain breads to try, sweet streusel-topped rolls, slices of damp poppy seed cake, and marzipan-stuffed braided pastry. I took the subway—clean, punctual—all over town, and thrilled each time the U2 line emerged from the tunnel into blinding daylight as it ran from the west to the east of the city. From the bridge along which the train ran, I could look down onto a colony of Berlin's allotment gardens, their little wooden huts guarded by garden gnomes. Slowly I started to recognize the city again.

And when I got back home in the dark afternoons in those first few weeks, I ate scores of Christmas cookies, softened in hot tea and chewed on the couch, my feet curled up under me for warmth. Biting into a chewy, fragrant *Basler Leckerli*, I tasted my childhood, a hundred cookies munched by a candlelit tree, and I tasted the longing for home I had felt each time the cookie-baking season rolled around in New York. I tasted the struggle of sky-high expectations. And I tasted a little bit of triumph too, because at the end of the day, I was home.

Basler Leckerli

MAKES ABOUT 40 1-INCH SQUARES

These little cookies pack a wallop of spicy flavor. The recipe comes from Switzerland and roughly translates means "little delights from Basel." The candied citrus peel is crucial; you want those little pockets of bitter-sweet citrus flavor to counterbalance the honeyed dough. The honey makes the dough quite stiff, so if you find you're having a hard time stirring it, enlist the help of a strapping young man. And watch your timing: the sugar glaze and the cookie base must both be hot when you ice the *Leckerli*.

¾ cup honey
⅓ cup plus 1 tablespoon granulated sugar
¼ teaspoon salt
2½ cups all-purpose flour
2 teaspoons baking powder
1 large egg, beaten
Grated peel of 1 organic orange
Grated peel of 1 organic lemon
⅛ teaspoon freshly grated nutmeg
⅛ teaspoon ground cloves
1½ teaspoons ground cinnamon
Scant ⅔ cup blanched almonds, finely chopped
¾ cup candied orange peel, finely chopped
¾ cup candied citron, finely chopped
¼ cup powdered sugar

1. Melt the honey, sugar, and salt together in a pot over medium heat, and pour into a mixing bowl. Let cool to lukewarm.

2. Heat the oven to 375 degrees. Sift the flour and baking powder together.

3. Stir the beaten egg, the lemon and orange peels, nutmeg, cloves, cinnamon, and two-thirds of the flour into the honey mixture. Beat in the

almonds and the candied orange peel and citron. Add the remaining flour and stir to combine.

4. Line a baking sheet with parchment paper. Butter your hands and press the dough out on the parchment paper until it's ⅛-inch thick.

5. Put the baking sheet in the oven and bake for 15 minutes. Then turn the heat down to 350 degrees and bake for another 10 minutes, until the *Leckerli* are golden brown and slightly puffy. Don't let them burn.

6. While the *Leckerli* are in the oven, make the glaze by combining the powdered sugar and 2 tablespoons water in a small pan over medium-high heat. Cook until the water has mostly evaporated and the glaze is thick with big bubbles. Remove from the heat and use it right away to glaze the hot pan of *Leckerli* with a brush.

7. Cut the hot *Leckerli* into squares immediately, leaving them in the pan, and then let them cool to room temperature. At that point, you can break the *Leckerli* into squares and put them away in boxes. A slice of apple in the cookie box will keep the *Leckerli* fresh and chewy. The *Leckerli* will keep for at least 2 months.

Früchtebrot (Fruit Bread)

MAKES FOUR 8-INCH LOAVES

This fruit bread is a wonderful thing, consisting mostly of dried fruit that has been plumped in rum. The recipe comes from my Viennese friend and baker extraordinaire, Christine Aigner. It keeps for weeks and, sliced thinly, is a pretty fantastic counterbalance to all those spiced gingerbread cookies and German Christmas confections made out of marzipan and dark chocolate. I love how it looks too, all moody and dark, with a rich, winey flavor that will make you lick your fingers and go for another slice.

> 1½ pounds pitted dried dates
> 10 ounces dried figs
> 1 cup raisins

1 cup blanched almonds, chopped

2 cups powdered sugar

½ cup good-quality dark rum

2¼ cups all-purpose flour

4 large eggs

1. Cut the dates and figs into ¼-inch pieces and put them in a large bowl along with the raisins. Chop the almonds in a food processor until rough and pebbly. They should not be powdered. Add the chopped almonds and powdered sugar to the dried fruit. Pour the rum over the fruit-sugar mixture and mix until well combined. There should be no more streaks of powdered sugar left. Cover with a towel and let sit for 8 hours or overnight.

2. When ready to bake, heat the oven to 350 degrees. Uncover the fruit mixture and add the flour in four parts, alternating with the eggs, mixing well with a wooden spoon after each egg. The dough will be stiff and unwieldy, but do your best. (Don't use an electric mixer—the stiff dough will fry the motor.) After you've added all the flour and eggs, use your hands to knead the dough—it will be quite sticky—making sure that the flour and eggs are well mixed into the dough.

3. Line a baking sheet with parchment paper. Wet your hands with cold water and form the very sticky dough into 4 equal-sized loaves. Place them on the baking sheet.

4. Bake for 35 minutes, or until the loaves are golden brown. Remove and let cool on a rack. The loaves will keep, well wrapped, for 2 weeks. Before serving, slice thinly (⅛-inch-thick slices) with a very sharp or serrated knife.

23

Light and Sparkle

I'M NOT BIG ON NEW YEAR'S EVE. I'M HAPPY TO HAVE AN EXCUSE TO DRINK Champagne and it's fun to yell down the countdown to midnight together, but I've never really felt like I needed to have a big party to transition from one year to the next or that if I found myself in pajamas in front of the television on December 31 I'd somehow failed as a human being.

But in Berlin, New Year's is a *big* deal. Fireworks are legal and in the days leading up to New Year's Eve, you'll often hear the crack and pop of small ones being lit and tossed by overeager teenage boys. On New Year's Eve itself, the whole city gets involved. People tumble out of their apartments and houses onto streets and balconies, launching Roman candles into the sky from empty Champagne bottles for all the neighborhood children to marvel at. And at midnight, the whole city truly explodes. (Depending on what neighborhood you're in, this can be rather thrilling or a terror trip. Ten years ago, on the way to a party in Kreuzberg, I had to dodge firecrackers being tossed at me from balconies above.) If you like the idea of celebrating New Year's Eve like it's the universe's last chance at a party, come to Berlin.

Besides the insane displays of personal firework know-how, the Germans have a lot of other traditions for welcoming the New Year. They melt lead over an open flame in small metal spoons and then toss the molten lead into a bowl of cold water, where it seizes up instantly, forming gorgeously twisted tiny sculptures that forecast your fortune for the coming year. A shoe, and you'll have happiness. A ship, and you've got a journey to look forward to. An apple, and you'll be blessed with friendship. A bird, and you'll get unexpectedly lucky.

Another New Year's Eve tradition is the *Feuerzangenbowle*, a potent brew of wine and rum and caramelized sugar that is concocted in a Rube Goldberg–like setup. You place a sugar pyramid on wire mesh balanced over a pot of spiced red wine. You soak the sugar pyramid with dribble after dribble of rum and then you light it on fire. The rum–soaked cone of sugar slowly caramelizes, melting and dripping into the wine below, which is then portioned out to the guests. This is considered an integral part of the festivities.

Germans like to poach carp for New Year's Eve, pulling apart these great quivering fish at the dinner table. And they serve big trays filled with jam–filled doughnuts with one dud filled with mustard nestled in among all the delicious jam–filled ones. The person who gets the mustard doughnut exclaims aloud in surprise and disappointment, which leads all the children at the party to fall over themselves with delight and laughter. Then general merriment ensues. Hopefully.

Thirty–something years ago, only a few years after my parents arrived in Berlin, they were at a New Year's party at Joanie and Dietrich's house. No one had ever explained the tradition of the mustard–filled doughnut to my mother, so when the doughnuts were handed out and people sank their teeth into the pillowy crumb and my mother ended up with a mouthful of mustard, she didn't say a peep.

These crazy Germans, she thought, as she winced and swallowed. *This thing is* disgusting. Joanie's children ran around the living room, peering intently at all the guests as they ate, hardly able to disguise their glee. But as the plate holding the doughnuts emptied and people finished their doughnuts, licked their fingers, and no one said anything at all about having pulled the mustard doughnut, the kids' faces fell. "Who got the mustard doughnut, people?" Joanie finally had to ask. "Well, I did!" my mother said, as everyone stared. "For crumb's sake,"

Joanie said, "why didn't you say anything?" My mother, red-faced, answered plaintively, "I didn't know I was supposed to!"

On my first New Year's Eve back in Berlin, Max and I were in our car driving from one party to another, hoping to meet friends before midnight, when we realized or, actually, admitted to one another that instead of being at yet another loud, anonymous party we both just really wanted to be at home instead. We pulled into a parking spot on the side of the street. "What do you think? Can we ditch the party?" I asked. Max nodded. "We sure can." And just like that, he made a gentle U-turn on the snow-covered street and slowly drove home. It was 11:50 P.M., and then 11:55, and then suddenly, as we found ourselves in the narrow, residential streets of leafy Wilmersdorf, almost at home, it was midnight.

At that moment, the streets, so dark and quiet and empty moments before, exploded in light and sparkle. People flooded the sidewalks, setting up empty Champagne bottles to launch their fireworks, striking matches, preparing the show. As we drove, gliding almost, on the thick ice layer that carpeted the streets, our car barely made a sound. Street after street, we saw children's beaming faces staring upward into the black night, fireworks gleaming in their eyes. We saw their parents and other adults dancing on the sidewalks, with the night sky lit up, the colorful explosions reflected in the snow. And I sat in the passenger seat, mouth agape, looking out at Berlin transformed into a pink! gold! silver! green! blue! movie set, watching in slow motion as 2009—as painful and as joyous a year as I've ever known—ended, and 2010 opened its first pages.

It was a stunning couple of minutes. I felt so lucky to have had them. They were like a gift, like someone drawing open a heavy velvet curtain on the secret machinery of humanity and letting me have a few minutes to watch it all unfold. *Thank you*, I thought, sending my gratitude upward and outward to whoever was responsible for all that had happened to me in that impossibly hard and wonderful year. I could see all of it now, the heartbreak included, as part of a continuum.

If 2009 was the year my life was saved, 2010 would be a year full of learning experiences. I had to learn how to make new friends and how to stay close to my friends so far away. I had to learn to function out-side of my comfort zone, become my own boss, and I had to learn how to be confronted, again and again, with the funny fact that life can be glorious and infuriating at the same time.

But in those first hours of 2010, all that was still to come as our car glided silently onto our street. We parked as best we could on the inches-thick ice and made our way upstairs to the apartment, holding on to each other and trying to not to laugh as we slipped this way and that on the ice. As we got to the door of the apartment, we saw that my mother had left us a small fluted paper tray holding two plump dough-nuts filled with plum jam and covered in sugar that sparkled in the lamplight on the doormat. We took them inside and made ourselves some tea and sat at the kitchen table, carefully eating our doughnuts, nary a smear of mustard in sight, licking our sugar-spangled fingers, and making plans for the year ahead.

Pfannkuchen (Jam Doughnuts)

MAKES ABOUT 14 *PFANNKUCHEN*

Doughnuts are a cinch to make—the most complicated thing about mak-ing them is calibrating the heat of the oil. Too high and you'll burn the doughnuts in a flash. Too low and they'll get soaked with oil. But if you keep the oil at just the right temperature, you'll end up with a platter of greaseless doughnuts that are pillowy on the inside and golden brown on the outside. You'll also need a piping bag with a metal tip to fill the dough-nuts. You can use whatever jam (or mustard!) you like, but I'm partial to the traditional *Pflaumenmus* filling.

Contrary to what you might have been told, when John F. Kennedy stood in front of West Berlin's City Hall in 1963 and said "*Ich bin ein Ber-liner,*" he was not, in fact, calling himself a jelly doughnut. In Berlin, jelly doughnuts are called *Pfannkuchen*, while the rest of Germany calls them *Berliner.* So it was always crystal clear to Berliners that Kennedy was align-ing himself with the citizens of the beleaguered city, and if you hear the roar (the clip is on YouTube) that went up from the crowd when he said those words, no doubt will remain that the people he meant it for understood exactly what he was trying to say.

1 cup whole milk
3½ cups all-purpose flour, plus more for kneading
1 ounce fresh yeast
3½ tablespoons sugar
3 large egg yolks, room temperature
7 tablespoons (3½ ounces) unsalted butter, melted and cooled
1½ teaspoons salt
4½ cups neutral-tasting vegetable oil
1 to 1½ cup *Pflaumenmus* (Spiced Plum Butter; see page 237)
Sugar or cinnamon sugar, for coating

1. Pour the milk into a small pot and heat it on the stove for just for a minute, until it is lukewarm. Don't let it get hot.

2. Pour the flour into a mixing bowl and make a well in the middle. Crumble the fresh yeast into the well. Sprinkle a tablespoon of the sugar over the yeast and pour in the milk, mixing and dissolving the yeast and incorporating a bit of the flour from the sides of the well. Then cover the bowl with a dishtowel and let it sit for 15 minutes, until foamy.

3. Mix together the foamy yeast with the remaining flour, sugar, egg yolks, melted butter, and salt. Then knead the dough on a lightly floured surface until it is smooth and satiny, about 5 to 7 minutes. Put the ball of dough in a clean bowl that's been rubbed with a drip of the vegetable oil, and cover with the dishtowel. Set aside for 1 hour, or until the dough has doubled in volume.

4. Gently knock down the risen dough once or twice, and then gently roll it out on a floured work surface to about ½-inch thickness. Cut out 2½-inch rounds from the dough using a biscuit cutter or a drinking glass. Transfer the rounds of dough to a parchment-lined baking sheet. The remaining dough can be cut into pieces and twisted, sort of like a free-form cruller. Add them to the baking sheet and then cover the doughnuts with a dishtowel. Let them rest for 30 minutes.

5. Pour the oil into a heavy pot and heat over medium-high heat to 330 degrees. You must use a thermometer for this. It is essential to keep the oil at this temperature throughout the frying process. If you notice the temperature rising over 340 degrees at any point, take the pot off the stove until the oil cools a little.

6. When the oil is the right temperature, gently slip a few doughnuts at a time into the hot oil, puffy side down. Fry until golden brown on one side, about 3 minutes, and then, using a slotted spoon with care, flip the doughnuts to fry on the other side for another 2 to 3 minutes. When they are nutty brown all around, remove to a cooling rack set over a sheet pan. Repeat with the remaining doughnuts.

7. Fill a pastry bag fitted with a small metal tip with the *Pflaumenmus*. Stick the metal tip into the side of a doughnut and gently squeeze some jam into the doughnut. When you feel the doughnut start to swell in your hand, you've filled it enough. Roll the filled doughnut in the sugar or cin-namon sugar, and put it on a serving plate. Repeat with the remaining doughnuts.

8. *Pfannkuchen* are best eaten warm, but you can serve them at room temperature too. Don't bother keeping them overnight, though. They go stale remarkably quickly.

24

That Sacred Space

FOR THE FIRST TWO MONTHS AFTER I ARRIVED IN BERLIN, I COMMUTED between my mother's and Max's apartments, separated by a ten-minute walk down the same street I used to take to get to school every morning. My forty boxes of belongings had made their way from New York to Berlin on a freighter (they held, among other things, my books, my beloved pans and knives, four bentwood chairs that my mother had sent over from Berlin years earlier, and the nubby cream-colored couch that I had inherited from my father), but until I found my own place to live I had to stash them in my mother's vast, cold dining room. She kept the door closed.

Max kindly made room for my things in his closet, but I was never quite able to put a little suitcase of mine away. I hid it behind his living-room door. It held heavy woolen socks, thermal underwear, and turtlenecks galore, along with a pair of bright orange lounge pants with a huge dragon intricately embroidered on the back of one leg. I had bought the pants at Filene's Basement on Seventy-ninth Street years earlier on a whim and even though the top button was missing and my mother always said that the pants made me look a little crazy, they were very comfortable. And comforting. I wore them almost every day as I padded around the apartment while Max was at work, trying to make sense of my new life.

In order to anchor myself and find a new daily routine, I busied myself cooking at my mother's apartment and at Max's. But it felt like I had two left hands, like I was eating dinner at a table five inches too high. Everything was a little bit off. When I tried to bake a coffee cake, it turned out limp and flat. Poached chicken breasts were as dry as old bread. Dressing for a salad came out so sharp it made me gasp. Before long, I realized that my cooking mojo was more than just off; it seemed to have abandoned me completely.

I fled to the things I knew were foolproof: spaghetti with tomato sauce, fennel salad, and liverwurst sandwiches on dark German bread. But none of those things felt like real cooking. I'd lie awake at night wondering what could be wrong. Was it the recipes I was choosing? Was I having a fluke run of kitchen disasters? It could be possible, I supposed, like the inverse of winning the lottery. Perhaps it was the German ingredients. The butter here was higher in fat than in the United States, so perhaps their chicken was leaner and their vinegar sharper too. But that couldn't be the whole story. I sighed in dejection and Max, next to me, sighed sympathetically in his sleep.

The most likely explanation, I knew, was that I wasn't really here yet. I was a nomad living between two apartments, never really feeling like I was in my own space. I found myself thinking about the phantom apartment I'd dreamed about in Puerto Rico: the wall of books, the long hallway, the view of the gray, wet city street. As much as I loved Max's apartment, it wasn't really my place, or ours. It was his. So after another particularly inedible meal, it was decided: I would have to find my own apartment, and fast.

Hunting for an apartment in Berlin was nothing like what I'd come to expect in New York. There, a few weeks before the end of a lease, you would troll Craigslist and send out mass e-mails to friends. You would line up a bunch of viewings in a matter of days and head out after work, teeth gritted, to see some spectacularly awful places. Because it was New York and because almost everything affordable was pretty terrible, you'd be prepared for the grimy staircase and the deafening noise from the air-conditioning units on the apartment building across the way. The "cozy" apartment you'd hoped would be a hidden gem would turn out to be one room with roach traps in the corner, an airshaft across from the one window, and a price tag that would make your mother blanch. You, however, had been in New York long enough to consider it a steal. Even if it was three long avenue blocks from the closest subway station.

In Berlin, apartment hunting was much more civilized. Real estate agents were, like Germans in most regards, refreshingly honest about everything, including whether they thought something was overpriced or in need of renovation. There was no wide-eyed, breathless enthusiasm about "charm," "coziness," or anything being a "bargain." Yet the apartments were far larger, brighter, and cleaner than anything available in New York for the same price. Perhaps precisely because of this bounty, I found myself becoming a far pickier hunter.

A four-room apartment with a balcony, a kitchen large enough for a table with chairs, and two bathrooms? I found myself thinking, *Oh, I dunno, the balcony faces west instead of south and I want to grow tomatoes, soo . . . no.* A three-room apartment with pine floorboards, the original stucco, and a pantry, for Pete's sake, also had bedroom windows that looked out over a parking lot. *Sorry, but I can't take it.* The oddest part of the search was that the brokers were always very understanding when I turned up my nose, sometimes even pointed out the "flaws" before I saw them myself.

Max and I had agreed, just a few months earlier, when I was still in New York, not to live together during my first year back in Berlin. "We need to get used to being in the same city," I said. "Sure," he said. "You need to find your own footing first, then we can see about living together." I was so grateful that he understood, that he agreed. It was all so sensible. But now that I was in Berlin, camping at his apartment with my little suitcase stashed behind the living-room door and cooking dinner with him every night (he was a good sport for choking it all down those first few months), it seemed a little absurd to move out to my own place. In fact, it didn't make any sense at all, to either of us. "I don't want to live apart from you anymore," Max said quietly one night. "Why don't we find a place together?" The next day, I started looking for bigger apartments.

We saw an apartment in a neighborhood we loved. It had three

enormous rooms, a beautiful corner balcony with wrought–iron balus-
trades, gleaming parquet floors, western and southern exposures, and
the original stucco, but its bathroom was tiny. There was no bathtub, no
window, and no room to turn around in. Max vetoed it the moment he
saw it and the real estate agent nodded sympathetically. He wouldn't
take the apartment either. "That bathroom! It's a disgrace." I had the distinct impression that I could see his lip curl. "There is no way we're going
to be able to rent out the apartment," the agent said conspiratorially.
"The management will have to renovate it and knock down a wall to
fuse the kitchen and bathroom together. Otherwise, it's just not livable!"
As I walked down the stairs away from that gem, my protestations about
the beauty of the place falling on deaf ears, it was some consolation
imagining those two sissies on their first apartment hunt in New York.

We saw another place tucked in the courtyard of a building on the
Kurfürstendamm. It was on the far end of the long street, away from the
crowds, and had a charming spiral staircase winding up to the front
door. Inside, we found gleaming wood floors, exquisite molding, plenty
of light, and storage space to boot. But the kitchen was entirely empty.
We would need to provide our own kitchen cabinets and drawers,
countertops, and appliances. This was standard practice in Berlin (you
take the kitchen with you when you move), but it required technical
expertise and a willingness to invest in an entire kitchen, dismantling
and reinstalling it with each move. I couldn't muster the enthusiasm.

We saw apartments to renovate and apartments that were overpriced and apartments that simply didn't feel like home. We walked up
dozens of staircases a week, thick jute carpeting underfoot, rang door-
bells, stepped on a hundred creaky floorboards. As we looked and
looked and as the weeks went by, I started to lose steam. It was only
when I found myself missing the New York apartment hunt that I realized how dejected I was. After all, that had always made me question
the meaning of life.

The day I saw the apartment we ended up taking, it was yet another gray day in a very long string of gray days in February and I was
nearing the end of my rope. It was on the top floor of an old building

near Schloss Charlottenburg, in a leafy, sleepy part of the old West where old Turkish ladies in black coats shared the sidewalks with young German families. When the Wall was still up, Charlottenburg was considered the center of the city, but since the city's reunification and the emergence of the eastern neighborhoods as the new city center, Charlottenburg and its palace felt further and further away from the "new" Berlin. Which is precisely what made the neighborhood appeal to me. Given that I'd partly moved back to Berlin to reclaim my childhood, I wanted nothing more than to be in the part of the city that felt like it had never changed.

The apartment itself, on an unassuming little street tucked behind a contemporary art museum, had been carved out of an old attic in 1991, so it didn't have any of the old-world charm I'd been hoping for. But when I walked inside, I realized very quickly that what it did have was light, in short supply in many Berlin apartments. Thin and milky on that February day, it streamed through the windows in every room. There was a small balcony wedged into the side of the house overlooking the courtyard and a majestic chestnut tree, a foyer big enough to be a room of its own, and a full kitchen, cabinets and all. The apartment had a direct view of the palace across the street and of waving trees and sky. Its living room was big enough to double as the living room and dining room *and* it had a long hallway and two bedrooms. All for the price of the studio apartment I'd rented in Forest Hills.

A few days after that first visit, I made Max come back to look at it with me. His reaction was instantaneous. "Let's take it! It's perfect." I needed a few more trips to convince me, ever indecisive, but I didn't dare draw out the decision for too long. During my last visit, a young family had been prowling around the empty rooms with me. I called the landlord an hour later and a few weeks after that we signed the lease and moved in.

First I unpacked my forty boxes, emptying my mother's dining room, and put away my cookbooks, my knives, and my pots and pans. All my old friends—the six-inch chef's knife, the dark green cast-iron pot, and the many hundreds of clipped recipes—were gathered back together again. Then Max's couch joined mine in the living room and his books lined up next to mine on the bookshelves that we bought and carefully put together. For the finishing touches, we hung paint- ings on the walls and put fresh towels in the bathroom. Once every- thing was in its place and the boxes were all emptied and packed away in the basement, I could relax. I loved sitting in the quiet, peaceful kitchen. Sometimes I could hear traffic a few streets away, but mostly there was just the sound of little birds chirping in the eaves outside the window.

Max and I were a little on edge, thrilled to be living in the same space on equal footing and a little nervous to have moved so deci- sively onto the next chapter of our life together. We stepped gingerly around each other at first, tangling over small household details, his Faith No More poster and drum set fighting for space with my cooking equipment and New York talismans. As long as I'd been staying in his apartment, we'd had nary a disagreement. But now that we were creating a home together, opportunity to bicker lurked around every corner.

I didn't understand our first few fights. In fact, they scared me. We were supposed to be so happy, serene, and unperturbed after having found each other again after so long. But each conflict shook me. I'd left so much behind—my work and my friends and my independent life— that I couldn't help but ask myself, *If this big gamble in Berlin doesn't work out, where will I be left? What will I do?*

This line of thinking, of course, didn't take the pressure off our ar- guments. Instead, it heightened them. Before too long, I was jumpy and sensitive to each perceived criticism and Max felt like he was walking on eggshells, that I was parsing every word he said.

"We're supposed to be a fairy-tale couple, a dream come true," I wailed each time we made up. "Why are we fighting so much?" "Well," Max replied, "we've never spent this much time together before, with- out the threat of one of us leaving. I think we probably just need to get used to each other." *We should remember how lucky we are,* we told each other earnestly in the happy, relieved moments after making up. *Nothing this silly is worth fighting about.* Until, of course, the next time we found ourselves at each other's throats over a stack of dishes in the sink.

I guess, dear reader, I want to tell you that even when you have found *your* person in this world, the person who you know, deep down in your mitochondrial DNA, is meant to be by your side in this life, it is no guarantee that this person will not also drive you completely bat-shit insane at some moments along the way. It is unfair to expect your sweetheart to be a perfect person or to consider yourself above re-proach just because you love each other. Even if you have found your one true love, you will still have exact ideas about how to clean a floor, whether your family is nuts or simply lovable, and just what, exactly, are the requirements for being a good driver. But I knew we were on the right path when we managed to agree on potato salad.

There were, as I saw it, two camps of potato salad eaters. Either you were in the camp that bound their potato salad with mayonnaise to make it rich and creamy or you were from the faction that used a hot vinegar dressing for a light and sour salad. Though I had heard that there were some strange creatures on this great Earth who professed to loving both equally, for the rest of us, the lines were clearly drawn. Whether you put sliced cucumbers in your potato salad or bits of ba-con, celery crescents or rounds of scallions, was beside the point. The crux was the dressing.

I'd always been solidly in the hot vinegar dressing camp, having spent most of my life convinced that mayonnaise was an absolute abomination. I loathed its eggy scent, the way it quivered on the blade of a knife, and how it turned perfectly nice sandwiches into wet sponges. But one day I realized that I knew absolutely nothing about the way Max liked his potato salad.

It was a few weeks after we'd emptied the last boxes. We'd hung lamps in the hallways that day and agreed on where to put the coat rack, and now it was time for dinner. Since moving in, we'd eaten our weight in quick pots of pasta and the thought of another plate of spa-ghetti was enough to kill my appetite entirely. "What do you feel like eating?" I asked Max. "Don't say pasta, whatever you do." He hardly missed a beat. "Potato salad. And my mother's *Buletten*. But I want to cook with you. Let's do it together. You always disappear into the kitchen by yourself and this time I want to help." I was about to open my mouth and explain the potato salad faction situation when he added, "But no mayonnaise, okay? Just a nice vinegary dressing." My heart practically burst with joy and relief at that moment. The sun might have even shone a little more brightly right then and there.

We ran to the store before it closed and bought a sack of waxy potatoes ("Good for salad!" their label proclaimed). They were almost sunflower yellow and earthily fragrant. I boiled and peeled them still hot from the pot and then mixed together boiling beef broth, vinegar, minced onions, and mustard. This pungent mixture was poured over the still-warm potatoes and then mixed, and mixed, and mixed again, until each potato slice absorbed the dressing and the potato edges started to get ever so gently fuzzy.

Meanwhile, Max stood over the stove authoritatively, frying up *Buletten*, plum-sized pork-and-beef meatballs plumped up with chopped onion and milk-softened bread, in several batches. And I, so long accustomed to being the only cook in the kitchen, found to my surprise that I was happy to move aside and let him brandish the spatula. *I could get used to this*, I thought, as he brought a platter of *Buletten*, a pot of spicy mustard, and the bowl of potato salad to the dining table.

The potato salad was sharp and zingy but still soft around the edges and awfully addictive. The onions had mellowed in the vinegar bath but still had some snap and bite to them, and the mustard in the dressing was barely perceptible but added an extra layer of flavor to each waxy slice of potato. We ate big platefuls of the salad, Max scraping the bowl at the end, and promised to make it for each other every week until the end of time.

And slowly, as weeks went by and meals were cooked and we sat down at the dinner table each evening to eat and talk, we grew to know each other again. All we needed to stop fighting was a little patience and a little time. Though of course I like to think that the potato salad helped things along too.

Kartoffelsalat (Potato Salad)

SERVES 4

Germans boil their potatoes for salad the day before serving, believing that the overnight rest makes the potatoes hold their shape better when peeled and sliced. I've found, however, that using the potatoes the day you boil them is just fine too. The dressing is a hot marinade of beef broth, vinegar, mustard, and onions, among other things. The heat of the dressing helps it penetrate the potatoes, imbuing each one with a wallop of zesty flavor. At first, it will seem like there's far too much dressing for the potatoes, but as you mix the two together, the potatoes agreeably soak up all of it. If you can find the time, the salad is best if dressed a few hours before serving. But it's also delicious eaten right away, when it's still slightly warm.

> 2 pounds Yukon Gold or other waxy potatoes
> 3½ tablespoons unsalted butter
> 2 yellow onions, finely chopped
> ⅓ cup white wine vinegar
> ⅔ cup beef or chicken broth
> 1 tablespoon Dijon mustard
> 3 tablespoons olive or sunflower oil
> 1 teaspoon salt
> Freshly ground black pepper
> ⅔ cup loosely packed flat-leaf parsley, minced

1. Wash the potatoes and put them in a pot with cold salted water just to cover. Bring to a boil with the lid on; then reduce the heat to medium and cook the potatoes until they are just tender. Depending on their size, this should take between 20 and 30 minutes. Drain the potatoes and let them cool for at least an hour or two and up to overnight.

2. Peel the potatoes and cut them into very thin slices, about ⅛-inch thick. Put the potato slices into a serving bowl.

3. Melt the butter in a 10-inch sauté pan and add the onions. Mix well and cook for 3 minutes over medium heat. Pour in the vinegar and the

broth. Add the mustard and stir well. Let the mixture simmer over low heat for an additional 3 minutes.

4. Carefully whisk in the oil, and then pour the hot marinade over the sliced potatoes and mix well. The potatoes will take a few minutes to absorb all the dressing. Add the salt and as much freshly ground pepper as you'd like.

5. Just before serving, add the minced parsley to the bowl and mix well. Taste for seasoning and serve.

VARIATIONS

If you'd like bits of bacon or Speck in your salad, dice up 3½ ounces and fry the bacon or Speck in the butter for a few minutes before adding the chopped onions (reduce the amount of butter by a tablespoon).

Or add ⅓ cup of diced French cornichons to the finished salad to bump up the sour, crunchy factor.

25

Bitter Greens

HEN I LEFT NEW YORK, I THOUGHT I KNEW WHAT I'D MISS. MY friends, naturally, and the masses of people around me at all times, the way it sometimes felt like I was levitating when I sat in the back of a yellow cab as it bumped and jumped up over a pothole, and watching the golden gleam of the sun against the water towers around Union Square at the end of a workday. I was sure I'd miss the handsome face of the sandy-haired farmer who had his stand on the northwest corner of the greenmarket on Mondays and how his eyes crinkled when he smiled and handed me my bag of little Juliet tomatoes. I knew I'd miss heading downtown after work for a cheap dinner of fried dumplings and beer. And I'd miss feeling like I was at the center of the world.

Those were all the obvious things. So I thought I was being smart to acknowledge them in advance. But what I was not prepared for, what I had never thought to contemplate—naïve fool that I was—was just how much I'd miss dark green leafy vegetables. Nope, that one caught me entirely by surprise. Almost knocked me off my feet, really. In New York, after all, dark green leafy vegetables were everywhere. You couldn't pass a Korean grocer without seeing several bundles of broccoli rabe, escarole, mustard greens, and bok choy stacked together tightly over crushed ice. Collard greens and dandelion greens, frisée lettuce and Swiss chard (two kinds, in fact) abounded at the grocery stores. Spinach—fresh spinach!—was stocked in every store. It never occurred to me that it was something special. Something I wouldn't be able to find easily in Berlin.

My mother says that when she and my father first got to Berlin in 1971, the only place you could buy zucchini or a head of broccoli was at KaDeWe, West Berlin's fanciest department store. KaDeWe, which is short for *Kaufhaus des Westens*, or Department Store of the West, had the biggest food department of any store in Europe and it still does today. Up on the sixth floor, its shelves are stocked with jars of tiny French pickled quail eggs, fresh tamarind from Thailand, strudel dough from Austria, chocolate bars from around the world, foot-long rolls of Griebenschmalz, Russian sour cream, and Italian chestnut flour, not to mention cured hams from every region of Germany, oysters from Scotland, Canada, and France, Colombian cocoa pods, American cake mixes and jars of relish, and pastries from Paris. And in the mid 1970s, if you wanted to know where an Italian woman craving vegetables other than cabbage, potatoes, or carrots was shopping, KaDeWe was where you'd find her.

So I guess things are better now than they were then. These days, zucchini and broccoli are stocked at even the smallest grocery stores in Berlin. I should be grateful for this, I know. Much like I am grateful for the fact that Berliners are a lot friendlier than they used to be and that the city has become more diverse in the twenty years since the Wall fell. But the thing is, I had taken those greens for granted in New York and now I missed them terribly. What's worse, missing them made me a little resentful. Okay, a lot resentful, if I'm honest.

I resented vendors at the city's greenmarkets for not knowing what the vegetables were when I asked them if they ever sold them. I resented my friends who looked at me quizzically when I complained about this problem, and the garden show in the south of Berlin that had gorgeous lacinato kale plants growing as part of a landscape display. (I briefly contemplated returning after dark and ripping them out at the root for dinner.) I even resented the regional farmers who insisted on planting nothing but curly kale, which is scientifically proven to be the world's least delicious variety of kale.

But most of all I resented myself for getting hung up on something as superficial and silly as bitter greens. I knew deep down that the bitter greens weren't really what was bugging me (though I did miss their mustardy bite). I knew, in a way, that it was a relief to have found something tangible to be frustrated at. The lack of bitter greens was an easy target, easier than frustration with my daily life, so I chewed around on that until it resembled wallpaper paste.

I felt like I was walking around in a swamp of my own making. Things with Max were fine, great, even. It was thrilling to go to sleep each night and see him there next to me, knowing that he'd be there every evening, day after day, week after week. But a couple of months had passed since I'd arrived in Berlin and although I had a deadline and an editor waiting for book material from me, I simply could not bring myself to write a single word. It's not that I didn't have any inspiration, it was more that I felt, most days, like I was still in a state of shock.

I woke up each morning a little surprised not to be in New York anymore, in my old routine, with the things I'd grown so accustomed to over the past decade. And that made me feel foolish. I hadn't expected my adjustment to Berlin to take so long and as long as I was struggling with that I couldn't discipline myself to write. The words just wouldn't come. I felt like an utter failure.

Max urged me to get out of the house, to construct a routine for myself, no matter how small. So I made myself go for long walks, trying to find the beauty in the small details of Berlin that I saw each day. I tried being gentle with myself. Forgiving. Patient. And I tried to override the voice inside me that battered me every day with blame for feeling so overwhelmed. For not being happy every minute of the day. That voice was so scornful of my frustration. *You don't deserve to complain,* it said, *not after everything that's happened, all the good fortune that's come your way. You are lucky, don't you know it? You should just be quiet already.* And some days, most days really, I agreed with that voice. I felt so low.

On my daily walks through Berlin's icy streets I realized that all those things I was sure I'd miss about New York didn't really figure in my mind anymore. In fact, I didn't miss them at all. I'd focused on the wrong things before leaving and hadn't realized that once I was in Berlin what I'd miss would be something much deeper. I missed feeling useful, knowing what my everyday path in life was. I missed my routine and the comfort of having a busy life far more than I missed the farmer's face or the light on the water towers. I had convinced myself so well in those final years in New York that I didn't belong there that I hadn't really noticed that I'd long become a part of the city, internalizing the unrelenting work ethic and pace of the city that never sleeps. And I'd been so caught up in the hustle and energy of New York that I hadn't realized that learning to live without it would be my biggest challenge.

In Berlin, things were more languid and simple. People didn't live for their jobs the way they did in New York. Plenty of people hardly worked at all. Everyday life was slower and more contemplative than it was in New York. But I'd only ever been an adult in the city that mercilessly pounded forward, pulsing with ambition and big hopes and dreams. As I slowly emerged from the fog of the first few weeks and months in Berlin, I realized I simply did not know how to be in Berlin. I was still applying New York life lessons to a city diametrically opposed to it. No wonder I was resentful. No wonder I couldn't write a word to save my life. No wonder I was so hung up on bitter leafy greens.

I needed to change my attitude. So I swallowed my craving for rich, dark greens and cooked a lot of zucchini instead. I forced myself to shower every morning and get dressed as if I were going to the office, even if I just ended up on the couch with my laptop and a blank page in front of me. In lieu of boiled bitter greens, I made industrial-sized quantities of cucumber salads flecked with chopped parsley and made myself take the subway east to the side of the city I hardly knew. I boiled potatoes until the cows came home. I forced myself to drive to the neighborhoods I didn't know to learn the streets. I stewed frozen peas with mint and onion, which always tasted good, and sautéed great mounds of shredded cabbage with chile paste, enough to make our eyes sting. I walked for miles and miles through Berlin, carpeted in ice and snow, its bare tree branches snaking into the sky. I also braised a lot of leeks.

I used to think that leeks were nothing more than overgrown scallions (I also used to think that you got to heaven by climbing a winding spiral staircase that had a landing and a door at the top, so bear with me). Since I didn't much like scallions, or onions or garlic, for that matter, by association, I decided I didn't like leeks either. This was compounded by the fact that a well-meaning friend had once served me a salad composed of raw sliced leeks and dried fruit plumped in brandy. It was rather pretty, I suppose, with its pale green half-moons and winey-dark fruits. But it tasted so awful, so sharp and piercing and wrong, that I put down my fork after one bite and actually contemplated going to the powder room to wash out my mouth. I thought I might never recover.

But by some stroke of luck, I found myself at lunch with my father a few years later at a bistro in Paris where there was no menu, just a set meal of three courses that came when you sat down. That day, the appetizer consisted of a plate of smallish leeks steamed to softness, dressed with a sharp little vinaigrette. *Here we go,* I thought, as the waiter put the plate down in front me. But I couldn't exactly ask for something else, and anyway, these leeks looked quite different from that miserable salad that haunted my nightmares. So I picked up my fork and dug in. The tines sank into the flesh of the leek rather agreeably. When I put a piece in my mouth, I tasted a juicy sweetness, the acid in the vinegar pulling out all the leek's sugars, its slippery layers sort of melting in my mouth. It took some restraint not to eat the leeks off my father's plate too.

Since then, I've come around considerably to leeks. Cooking a leek mellows its oniony flavor and renders its fibers soft as silk. For someone who finds most members of the allium family overpowering, leeks stand apart. I like to steam them and sauté them, toss them with roasted chestnuts and cream until they collapse into a savory heap, whizz them with boiled potatoes into a velvety soup, or wrap them in ham and a soft cloak of béchamel and bake them in the oven until the béchamel bubbles and blisters. And in winter, when I want nothing more than a warm oven going for hours and a gentle, comforting meal that makes me feel centered and whole, I braise them. There's nothing like a panful of golden, tender braised leeks to make a house smell like home. And miraculously, these braised leeks let me forget about my craving for dark, bitter greens and my struggle with this new place I found myself in that was both familiar and entirely strange.

Slowly I started to figure things out in Berlin. Turkish greengrocers were where to go to find exotica like canned chickpeas and broccoli rabe (though they labeled it *cime di rape*, as the Italians do), alongside fresh baby amaranth leaves and tiny green *padrón* peppers. A chic little vegetable boutique on a fancy shopping street in Wilmersdorf reliably stocked crisp heads of frisée lettuce even if they cost almost as much as a new designer bag. A brand of frozen spinach at my local grocery store turned out to taste almost as good as fresh, the leaves still whole and intact.

And on my hunt for green vegetables and a routine in those snowy months, I started to find my own path through Berlin again. Slowly, slowly, I let go of New York, carefully peeling its grip off me. I found a yoga studio in an old post office with soaring ceilings. I discovered a good Japanese restaurant so Max and I could finally avoid all the Vietnamese joints selling cut-rate sushi. I stumbled across Berlin's very first whole grain bakery that had opened the year I was born, just steps from our front door. And I told that mean little voice within to leave me alone. I was doing just fine, going right at my own pace.

One day, I passed the Tiergarten, covered in snow, thick with impassive trees. Though the trees looked like they'd been there for hundreds of years, the entire Tiergarten had been razed for firewood just before the end of World War II. The majestic old park that had once been the hunting grounds of Friedrich I had been reduced to nothing by starving, desperate Berliners. The wise old trees I saw that day, bewhiskered and standing like sentries in the midst of Berlin, so silent in the swirling snow, had been there for only about sixty years. So much of Berlin was like that, a jumble of devastation and regrowth, buildings still scarred with mortar holes with creamily painted, pristinely restored apartments alongside them. Among all the wreckage still so visible to the naked eye, there was perseverance and bravery and stubborn determination too. There was nothing like it. And that's when I felt that longed-for thrill within me again, so happy that I was back in my old divided city, gilded and sooty alike. I didn't want to be anywhere else. I felt right at home. Right where I was supposed to be.

Braised Leeks

SERVES 4 AS A SIDE DISH

While bitter greens are not easy to find in Berlin, leeks are everywhere you look. This recipe is adapted from Suzanne Goin's *Sunday Suppers at Lucques* and, as with many of Suzanne's recipes, elevates a humble vegetable from the soup pot to the unrivaled star of the dinner table.

6 large leeks
Kosher salt and freshly ground black pepper
½ cup olive oil
1 cup sliced shallots
1 tablespoon fresh thyme leaves
½ cup dry white wine
1½ to 2 cups chicken broth

1. Heat the oven to 400 degrees.
2. Peel the top layer off each leek and trim the roots, leaving the root end intact. Trim off the tops, leaving about 2 inches of green. Cut each leek in half lengthwise. Rinse carefully to remove any grit between the layers. Pat dry and season with salt and pepper.
3. Heat a large sauté pan over medium-high heat. Pour in half the olive oil and then place the leeks, cut side down, into the pan without crowding (you may have to do this in batches). Sear the leeks for 4 to 5 minutes, until golden brown. Then turn them over to cook the other side for 3 or 4 minutes. Transfer them, cut sides up, to a gratin dish.

4. Pour the remaining oil into the sauté pan and set over medium heat. Add the shallots, thyme, ¼ teaspoon salt, and a pinch of pepper. Cook for about 5 minutes, until the shallots are just beginning to color. Add the wine and reduce by half. Add the broth and bring to a boil over high heat. Pour this mixture over the leeks.

5. Put the gratin dish in the oven and bake for 30 minutes, until the leeks are tender.

26

Breaking the Spell

B ERLIN, ON THE SAME LATITUDE AS LABRADOR, IS A COLD, DARK PLACE in winter. The sky is cloaked in clouds for days on end, and daylight seeps through weakly for only a few hours each day. Winter can be unrelenting in Berlin, a far cry from the sun–kissed, frigid winter days one gets accustomed to in New York. The difference is that New York's winter never quite feels inhospitable to human life, even on the days when a foot of snow curbs subway service and ankle–deep puddles of gray–green slush form on the corner of every block. During a Berlin winter, though, when a bitter cold reigns and weeks can pass without a single ray of sunshine, you can get the distinct impression that the city is doing its very best to try to get you to leave.

However, if you manage to get through it, padding yourself with enough cookies and hot tea, cozy cashmere throws, and sheepskin–lined boots, and taking brisk walks up Berlin's only mountain, the man–made Teufelsberg, while a desolate wind whistles around your ears, you will be richly rewarded. For spring in Berlin is one of life's loveliest pleasures.

When the days start to lengthen and the trees bloom and the air fills with the scent of linden blossoms, warming earth, and budding leaves, it comes as such a relief, such a much–deserved reward for having survived another bone–cold winter, that one could almost believe that Berlin was an equatorial paradise. Spring is what keeps people here year after year, miserable winter after miserable winter.

In Berlin, spring gives you a little time to unclench your shoulders from the cold of the past months, unlike in New York, when it often feels like winter goes directly into summer, somehow cheating us of those fresh, hope-filled days in which we can still remember the cold but haven't begun lamenting the humid sidewalks, overstuffed subway cars, and that inimitable summer stench of garbage and tar melting in the blistering sunshine. In Berlin, spring allows you to marvel at the surreal scene of a field of crocuses popping up where a week before there was a carpet of snow. It finds you rather desperately gulping in the floral air, so sweet and soft, like the scent of a lover long gone and then unexpectedly, blessedly, found again. The lengthening days of spring are like a tonic for your cold, hunched shoulders and your runny nose. Best of all, you can even bottle spring here.

Once the snow melts and the days warm up, elderflower bushes flower all over Berlin: on the back paths of the park around the Schloss Charlottenburg, along a little footpath leading to a canal in Steglitz, bordering the Jewish cemetery in Weissensee. The bushes produce fragrant, gossamer white blossoms that furl out from their towering bushes like lacy little UFOs. By midsummer, the bushes are hung with sprays of almost-black berries. Many a German gathers the berries to cook into jellies or bottles of juice, though I don't particularly like their oddly meaty flavor. But elderflowers are another thing entirely. They *taste* like spring.

The first time I tried elderflower syrup, I was still living in New York and had flown back to Berlin for the Christmas holidays. I was in a terrible state in those days, when my relationship with Sam was unraveling at an unnerving pace. When I found myself back in Berlin for a fortnight, it was all I could do to keep myself from digging in my heels and never leaving again.

One evening, before a long dinner at Joanie's, she asked me if I wanted something cool to drink, a break from all the long-brewed hot teas usually proffered in those cold, dark days around Christmas. We were standing in her kitchen, where she'd cooked me so many lunch-time meals all those years ago.

Joanie pulled out a bottle of golden liquid and cocked her head at me. "What do you say, monkey?"

I wasn't sure I wanted to try it, actually, because all I knew about elderflowers had to do with their berries. But I said I'd try a little glass, just to be polite. Joanie filled a glass with cool tap water and then poured in a finger or two of that golden liquid. I could see it swirling down into the glass, almost oily. I reached for the glass and took a sip. And. Well. Yes. Let me try to explain what happened next.

Suddenly, as though by a gentle thunderclap or a small fissure in the space-time continuum, I was transported. Spring, Berlin's spring, was in my mouth! How very odd. I stood quite solidly in Joanie's cozy kitchen, the wintry scent of cinnamon hanging in the air, candles aglow in the next room and darkness all around outside, and yet I was sure I could now also hear birds chirping and feel a warm breeze blow across my neck. It felt as though everything missing in my life was concentrated in that small, cool glass. If I could just stand very still in Joanie's kitchen, sipping away, I might find myself again and leave all the sadness and despair behind.

I don't know when the first seeds of leaving New York and moving back to Berlin were set in me, when the tiniest kernel of possibility implanted itself into my brain (or was it perhaps my heart?). But I do sometimes think that that glass of elderflower syrup drunk in Joanie's kitchen might have been the thing that broke the spell for me. Maybe that golden potion was what awakened me to what was still possible. It helped pave the way to my return home.

Now, as our long hard Berlin winter slowly came to an end, the gutters filling with rivers of melting snow, the sidewalks clearing to reveal the detritus from New Year's Eve that had been hidden under a foot of snow for months, Joanie took me on an elderflower-gathering mission in the park across from her apartment. We had baskets lined with paper towels and scissors in our hands and warm, tentative sunshine on our heads.

It didn't take long before we found a trove of elderflower bushes, fully in bloom and heavy with dustings of pollen. We held out our paper-lined baskets and carefully snipped each hand-sized cluster of blossoms into the basket, taking care not to lose any pollen, which is where all the delicious magic lies. We filled our baskets until tiny blossoms dropped from them left and right.

Back in Joanie's kitchen, where it always smelled good and the same blue-and-white pottery that had always been there lined the shelves, she had a clean earthenware crock at the ready, along with a vial of citric acid purchased for a pittance at the pharmacy and a small mountain of organic lemons sliced paper-thin. Holding each spray of elderflowers over the mouth of the crock, we snipped off the tiny blossoms and let them fall into the crock below, followed by a shower of pollen. Then we made a simple sugar syrup that she poured over the blossoms, the lemons, and the citric acid. After a few days of rest, the crock would be filled with a fragrant, lemony liquid that Joanie would strain into bottles and store for the year to come. I liked to drink my syrup mixed with sparkling water, tap water, or Champagne.

If you drink your elderflower syrup right away, that is, in the middle of a sweet Berlin spring, you'll be quite pleased with what you've made. It will taste good and refreshing and you'll be tickled by the fact that you just went foraging in the middle of a big city. If, however, you still have a stash of it left in winter, especially during a Berlin winter with what looks like permafrost on the sidewalks, I do believe your reaction will be entirely different. You'll take great gulps of it, as if it held all the promise of rebirth and regeneration, infused with the promise of spring and happiness. You might taste relief in it and even a little bit of joy. It's quite a potion.

Elderflower Syrup

MAKES APPROXIMATELY TWO 1-LITER BOTTLES

Your biggest challenge when making this syrup will be sourcing the elderflowers. Although they grow all over northern Europe, and in the Pacific Northwest and the mid-Atlantic region, they can be difficult to find elsewhere. Your best bet is to look for them in the wild. Elderflower syrup is delicious simply mixed with cool tap or sparkling water, but you can also mix it with Prosecco or Champagne for a refreshing cocktail. My favorite summer drink, the Hugo, combines elderflower syrup, Prosecco, muddled mint, a bit of soda water, and a squeeze of lemon. Find citric acid at Indian grocery stores (labeled as "lemon salt" or "sour salt") or online at amazon .com or lepicerie.com.

20 to 25 large elderflower sprays
3 or 4 organic lemons, washed and sliced paper-thin (seeds removed)
3½ tablespoons citric acid
3 pounds plus 6 ounces sugar

1. Carefully wash and dry an earthenware crock that can hold about 5 quarts.

2. Holding each elderflower spray over the crock, snip the tiny blossoms and let them fall into the crock, taking care not to lose any of the pale yellow pollen. Add the sliced lemons to the crock and sprinkle in the citric acid.

3. In a medium pot over medium heat, combine the sugar and 1½ quarts of water. Stirring occasionally, melt the sugar and bring the mixture to a boil. Then remove it from the heat and let the syrup sit until lukewarm.

4. Pour the syrup over the lemon and elderflowers and mix well. Cover the crock with plastic wrap and let it stand in a cool corner of your home for 3 days, stirring it once a day.

5. On the final day, uncover the crock and pour the liquid through a fine-mesh strainer into clean glass bottles. Discard the lemon slices and elderflowers. Store in the refrigerator or in a cool, dark cellar for up to a year.

27

Yearning with a Vengeance

E'VE ALL READ BOOKS ABOUT THAT SEMINAL YEAR ABROAD THAT some see as a rite of passage. An American moves to Paris and spends the year discovering the glories of raw milk cheese, comes to love the gentle snarl of the passersby, and revels in the city's nearly unbearable beauty. Or maybe the writer goes farther south, to Italy, and chronicles the first time she sits down to a meal of homemade tagliatelle at a little no-name *osteria* in the Roman ghetto, strolls the streets of a tiny hilltop town that time forgot, or falls prey to the devastatingly handsome carptener-cum-ladykiller who teaches her Italian and how to love.

Germany, with its overcast skies and its inescapable history, often gets the short end of the stick when it comes to capturing the imagination of food lovers and romantics. There's not much use in competing with sleepy Provençal towns and picturesque Italian villages. But Germany is still the place where seasonal eating is so much a part of the daily social fabric of people's lives that plum cakes are for sale in bakeries only during the months when local plums, known as *Zwetschgen*, are actually in season. Fresh chanterelle mushrooms, golden brown and smelling delicately of apricots, reach markets and restaurant tables only when people can forage for them in their own backyards. And for six weeks a year, the country's dinner tables groan with white asparagus only as long as it's being harvested in German fields.

There is little more heartening than being in Berlin when the first bundles of local white asparagus show up in the city's greenmarkets just as the days begin to warm up. It feels, in those moments, as though the entire city has given a great sigh of relief. Hand-lettered signs proclaim the arrival of the white asparagus at the city's outdoor markets: *"Spargelzeit ist da!"* The sound of sellers calling out their wares echoes across the market squares, and small vans from Beelitz, just a few hours away from Berlin, selling white asparagus and bundles of flowers, park along some of Berlin's big streets. There are the premium white asparagus, with stalks nearly an inch in diameter, clustered in fat bundles of ten apiece, the midsized asparagus that costs a little less, and as the white stalks shrink in size they grow cheaper and cheaper, all the way down to *Bruchspargel*, which are thin, broken pieces of white asparagus for soup, sold for a pittance.

Blinking in the spring sunlight like a pair of moles, Max and I walked to our favorite greenmarket at Karl-August-Platz on a Saturday morning in April. Set on a square around a red brick church, the market had fishmongers and butchers, local farmers and florists, cheese makers and whole grain bakers. The vendors called out their bargains as we made our way through the aisles, filling our bag with all the harbingers of spring: a small bunch of daffodils, great speckled goose eggs, and an enormous bundle of white asparagus, tinged violet at the tips. People lined up in neat rows, waiting their turn politely. The Turkish vendors smiled and waved, the friendly butcher with enormous hands passed surreptitious slices of ham to little children as their parents ordered pork chops and liverwurst and smoked ham for Sunday brunch.

I loved our Saturday market strolls together. It was such a gentle way to welcome the weekend and plan for a week of meals together. Max carried the shopping bags while I poked and prodded the produce until I found what I wanted. There were small artichokes from Italy bundled into bouquets and tiny new potatoes still wet from the ground. And everywhere we looked there were white asparagus, stacked like fat pencils, glowing with life. Before heading home, we stopped at the southeast corner of the market to share a plastic glass of freshly squeezed orange juice, pulp sticking in our teeth.

White asparagus are, botanically speaking, the same thing as green asparagus. They're simply grown underground, the earth preventing their cell layers from developing green chlorophyll, which is produced in conjunction with the sun. In the United States, thin asparagus are the norm. But in Germany, the fatter the asparagus gets, the better. Although thin green asparagus only need their woody ends snapped off, white asparagus must be peeled before they're cooked. And although we Americans like to roast our asparagus quickly in a high-heat oven or grill them over hot coals, leaving them crispy and blistered, the Germans boil their asparagus with a pinch of sugar to keep them sweet, their cellulose breaking down in the boiling water until the stalks are silky-soft and succulent.

For my first white asparagus foray, I followed suit and boiled our asparagus in salted and sugared water, which felt slightly transgressive after all those years of flash-cooking green ones in nothing but a thin film of olive oil and a sprinkle of salt. Max and I ate the plump, juicy white stalks with thin slices of cold cooked ham and boiled potatoes for lunch. They were surprisingly sweet and almost creamy. It was a relief to be eating something that was such a potent symbol of spring, new life pushing through the earth, incontrovertible proof that the grip winter had on us was finally falling away. But the white asparagus, if I may say so, since we're among friends, was also a little flaccid, a little limp. I missed the strong grassy flavor and snappy texture of the green asparagus that I used to eat by the pound in New York. This white asparagus, well, I wondered if I was somehow missing the point.

At an Easter lunch at my mother's a few days later, I decided to try a different approach. Planning the menu, I spent hours with my nose in an old German cookbook that a friend gave to me and I came away inspired to make a classic *Spargelsuppe*—a delicate, porcelain-colored cream of asparagus soup. Perfect for spring, I thought, for an Easter luncheon on a warm Sunday. What could be better than an easy, elegant soup? Here I must admit that I didn't really bother to look at the instructions. After all, how hard could soup be?

And thus began the most complicated soup cooking I'd ever

attempted: First I peeled a mountain of *Bruchspargel*. Then I made a watery broth with the entire pile of trimmings I had reserved from the peeling. After that, I boiled the peeled asparagus in the watery broth. Then I puréed the contents of the pot into a thin, smooth liquid, pausing only to contemplate the fact that this might have been the most work I'd ever put into a soup. But I still wasn't done. After the soup had been puréed to within an inch of its life, I had to pass it through a fine-mesh sieve. When it was finally fully smooth and white as bone china, I brightened it with lemon juice and topped it with a shower of minced chives. One could have run a marathon in the time it took me to cook the soup, or write a novel, or grow an entire thatch of gray hair.

And then I watched, only slightly horrified, as our guests ate up several hours worth of work in a matter of seconds.

Instead of feeling pride in my work, this maddening, vanishing asparagus soup stuck in my craw. *All that work*, I thought, *for something as insipid as that soup?* It's not that it was a kitchen disaster, it was that all the work just didn't feel like it was worth it. And for once in my life, I understood why so many people were discouraged by the act of cooking or felt intimidated by something that had always come so naturally to me. I'd always enjoyed the whole process of cooking, even more so than the final results. Cooking was, for me, a comfort and a practice to be honed every day, like yoga or meditation. The result was the icing on the cake.

The soup made me never want to buy another white asparagus again. *I'm done!* I thought petulantly. If someone wants to make white asparagus for me, fine, I'll eat it. But I'd rather be eating green asparagus, roasted to a crisp. And that's exactly what I did.

At the end of Spargelzeit, though, Max and I were invited to a Sunday lunch at my friends Muck and Jürgen's house, on a leafy street in the south of Berlin. There were soft-boiled eggs that we ate with mother-of-pearl spoons, tiny thin-skinned new potatoes dripping with melted butter, great flaky pieces of pink poached salmon, and an earthenware crock filled with chunks of white asparagus and masses of chopped parsley, chives, and softer herbs, all floating in a vinegar dressing that was nose clearing and wonderful. The asparagus had almost pickled in the dressing, drawing in the invigoratingly sharp flavor until their soft, juicy fibers were practically spilling over with the vinaigrette. The salad was cooling and refreshing, and after three helpings I found myself reevaluating white asparagus altogether. I looked over at Max midmeal, our eyes meeting as we forked the pickly white asparagus into our mouths. We nodded at each other. I knew what he was thinking: *Now this is good stuff.*

At that point, though, the asparagus season was almost over. We were on the very tail end of those magical six weeks. I spent the final days of *Spargelzeit* going to the market every day, spending a king's ransom on big bundles of white asparagus, and making *Spargelsalat* for dinner each night. We slurped it up lustily—it's almost impossible not to slurp when eating white asparagus—and chased the last dregs of herby vinaigrette around on our plates with bread. And wouldn't you know, when one day the *Spargel* vendor at the market looked at me with a kind smile and shrugged because he had none left for me, not even the sad-looking *Bruchspargel*, I found myself almost panicked with disappointment.

And in the weeks to come, I realized that I was yearning for next spring's *Spargelzeit* with a vengeance.

Spargelsalat (White Asparagus Salad)

SERVES 4 AS PART OF A SPREAD OF APPETIZERS

This salad is best when made with very fresh white asparagus. (White asparagus that isn't that fresh anymore sports a disagreeably bitter undertone.) You can, however, make a pretty good salad with jarred white asparagus, which can sometimes be found in Spanish specialty shops. Do not buy canned asparagus, as you will regret wasting your money and your time. While the salad tastes delicious right away, I suggest waiting a few hours before serving it: this gives the plump asparagus time to soak up the herby vinaigrette, rendering it even more succulent and juicy.

10 fat stalks white asparagus (about 1⅓ pounds)

¼ cup finely minced flat-leaf parsley

¼ cup finely minced chives

2 stalks tarragon, finely minced

3 tablespoons best-quality olive oil

2 tablespoons white wine vinegar or Champagne vinegar

¼ teaspoon salt

1. Break off the woody ends of the asparagus and peel the entire length of the stalks.

2. Bring a pot of salted water to a boil. Lower the asparagus into the water and turn down the heat so that the asparagus cook at a slow boil for 13 to 15 minutes.

3. While the asparagus are cooking, put the herbs, olive oil, vinegar, and salt in a serving bowl. Mix well and set aside.

4. When the asparagus are tender, drain them carefully, and as soon as they are cool enough to handle, cut them into 1-inch pieces. Add the still-warm asparagus to the herb vinaigrette and stir gently to coat the asparagus. Let sit for at least 2 hours before serving.

28

I'll Get It Right Next Time

I T WAS A WARM SUNDAY MORNING AND I WAS STANDING IN THE KITCHEN, one foot on top of the other, looking at the bowl on the counter in front of me. In the bowl was batter for a cake for Joanie and Dietrich's fiftieth wedding anniversary party that afternoon, but something wasn't quite right. Instead of looking thick and creamy the way cake batters usually do, the stuff in my bowl was stiff and grainy. And there was so *little* of it. The recipe I was following told me to divide the batter between two springform pans, but the cake batter I made would barely spread to the edges of one.

Now, I've made a hundred cakes in my life, for birthdays and office parties and for endless Sunday afternoon snacks. I can make cake batter in my sleep: cream butter, add eggs one at a time, a splash of vanilla, the flour and milk in alternating pours. But this bowl of batter was making the hair on my neck stand up. And to make matters worse, I didn't have much time to correct it. In a few hours, there would be an anniversary party in Joanie's son Kim's garden with family and old friends and rented benches and tables and a groaning board of food, not to mention an array of celebration cakes, of which mine was supposed to be one: two layers of yellow cake filled with gooseberry cream and topped with a crunchy meringue.

A month earlier, I first encountered the cake, enigmatically named Hannchen Jansen, at a children's birthday party out in Brandenburg.

Our friends' two little boys were turning two and four, and to celebrate, their grandparents had set up an inflatable bouncing castle for the children in their garden, along with a tent and long tables filled with cakes. While every weekend afternoon in Germany presents the opportunity to drink coffee and eat a slice of cake, birthdays are especially important cake-eating occasions. At this garden party, there were no fewer than seven cakes, all homemade that morning: a Quark cheesecake, a strawberry-chocolate torte, a rustic apple cake, a pineapple upside-down cake, a confection of butter cookies sandwiched together with melted chocolate into a loaflike thing (mystifyingly named *Kalter Hund*, or "cold dog"), a platter of violet cakelets, and finally the towering glory known as *Hannchen Jansen*: a gooseberry-cream-filled masterpiece that was creamy and crunchy and sour and sweet and that bewitched me straightaway.

As the children bounced away on their castle for hours on end, Max and I squeezed in between our friends and their guests, eating wedge after wedge of cake and drinking endless cups of coffee and tea. After the cakes were gone, we took a long walk around the property to digest, stumbling onto impressive red currant bushes and gooseberry thickets. When the party stretched out into the evening hours, chafing dishes filled with slices of roast pork and tangles of sauerkraut, meatballs, and mashed potatoes were set out. Everyone got a clean plate to fill before settling back down to the long tables and benches under the tent. The younger children crawled into their parents' laps for dinner and we all grew full and sleepy. Then just when we thought we couldn't possibly eat another bite, we gathered around an open fire pit in the garden and roasted small sausages on sticks as the last glow of light left the sky and the children fell asleep in their parents' arms.

When we got into the car that night to drive back to Berlin, I was given the recipe for the gooseberry-meringue cake I'd fallen in love with. It was all so promising, the idyllic afternoon in the country, the happy children, the good food, the warm breeze of spring. *It's all coming together*, I thought. *This is my new life and it is starting to feel good.*

But here I was now in my kitchen with a cake batter that portended disaster, I just knew it, and I was starting to feel very hot around the collar. The idyllic Sunday afternoon birthday party felt far away, as did the memory of the slice of *Hannchen Jansen* I ate there. I had blindly followed the recipe my friend gave me, not thinking that I should perhaps have tested it once before such an important occasion. This felt especially foolish since my kitchen mojo was still going through a bad case of hiccups while I adjusted to my new life in Berlin.

Things had gotten better, for sure. I could make a pan of dark and fudgy brownies again without a second thought, and a batch of chocolate chip cookies turned out pretty well too (I made friends who came to visit from the United States tote over bags of moist brown sugar, difficult to find in Germany). But I hadn't yet managed to whip up a proper cake like I used to. It was sort of like my writing lately: I could get a chapter here and there down on paper, but most days I still sat in front of a blank screen for hours and then, late at night in our dark bedroom, I secretly convinced myself that I couldn't possibly write a whole book. The euphoria of signing the book deal felt like a lifetime ago too, even though less than a year had passed.

Staring at the misbegotten cake batter wouldn't, I decided, make things better. And the clock was ticking. I had to get creative. So I pulled out all the ingredients I'd already put away and made a second batch of the cake batter so that I could fill the two prepared cake pans and have the requisite layers for the cake. Then I made a small bowl of meringue, the egg whites quickly going from a mess of translucent bubbles to thick, shiny crests, and gently spooned the meringue, all pointy and tipped, over the batter in one of the pans.

This looks promising, I thought to myself. *This is going to be fine.* I slid the pans into the oven and turned to the gooseberries, which I topped, tailed, and sugared before mixing them with whipped cream. The meringue puffed up in the oven and started to brown nicely. The almonds toasting in the oven filled the air with a delicious smell. Why was I such a worrywart? I could feel the knot in my back relax.

When it was time, I pulled the cake pans out of the oven and let them cool for a little while before pulling open the springform. Everything seemed to be falling into place. The morning drawing to a close, I started to feel rather accomplished. The whipped cream was billowy and beautiful; the sugared gooseberries tasted tart and delicious. And a cap of almond-studded meringue was a pretty good look for any cake. I layered all the elements together. Everything was going to be all right.

Except. The recipe commanded me to cut the almond meringue while it was still warm, so that the whole cake didn't fall apart later in shards of crackling meringue when it was sliced and served. Using my viciously sharp bread knife, I started to cut through it. It was at this point that I realized that the cake I ate at the garden party in Brandenburg didn't really look like the one towering in my kitchen. *At all.* This was very odd. Max walked into the kitchen, saw me cursing under my breath and perspiring, and made a swift turn back out of the kitchen again.

This is the worst recipe in the history of cake recipes, I thought. *I hate that I have to precut the meringue. I loathe this stupid cake and its stupid name.* I started to become aware of just how tense I was. The good mood of before was gone. I was in combat mode in my kitchen now, with less than an hour to spare before we had to leave.

I decided to stop cutting the cake. My sanity was more important than what the recipe said to do. *The cake will be just fine as it is*, I thought. The party would be relatively casual and no one would even notice that the cake has a cut through the top, I told myself. I decided I should perhaps take a shower and get ready.

But when I returned, washed and dressed and ready to leave, I peered down into the crevice that I had cut and saw something rather alarming. Instead of delicately quivering meringue, I saw a strange yellow substance oozing into the crack. I stared at it for a few moments, feeling a prickling sweat break out on my back again, then decided to dip my pinky into the yellow ooze. It felt cool to the touch and a little grainy. I couldn't figure out what it was. Could it be gooseberry juice, released by the sugar? Could it be egg-related moisture seeping out of the meringue? Nobody knew, least of all me.

It wasn't until several hours later, after the cake had been transported precariously to the garden party at Kim's house and we'd eaten our delicious lunch of cold yogurt soup flecked with cucumber and fresh herbs and roasted pork and green bean salad, that I realized what the yellow ooze was. At the moment of clarity, I was standing in Kim's kitchen, knife in hand, cutting the cake into segments. As I cut, the knife growing stickier with each slice, it dawned on me: the yellow ooze was nothing less than raw cake batter. Raw, as in *raw*. As in completely uncooked cake batter. Raw because the meringue that I had layered on top of the thin layer of batter insulated the batter so completely that it simply did not bake at all.

Hot sweat broke out on my neck. My hand trembled. I could feel tears pricking in my eyes.

Really? Was this really happening? I was mortified, angry, and utterly discouraged. If I couldn't even make a simple yellow cake, how on earth was I supposed to write a *book*? Where did all my skills go? Did I leave them behind in New York? Was this the universe's way of evening out the playing field? *You got your dream love story and you got to go home again. In return, I'd like to take everything you're good at, thank you very much.*

I decided I had to make the cake disappear. Never mind that one of the guests at the party was a woman who regularly won baking awards in her home state of Hessen and that this woman had already spotted my cake and declared it to be her very favorite kind of cake. Never mind that my *Hannchen Jansen* was meant to be my gift of sorts to Joanie and Dietrich. My mind churned desperately. Maybe I could blame its disappearance on one of the overexcited children in the garden.

I slipped out of the kitchen and carried the cake down to the basement, hoping that no one would notice me walking down the stairs. I stood there for a while feeling lost, when I heard Joanie's footsteps in the stairwell. She came upon me staring at the cake in the dark laundry room. Kim's wife, Susanne, was right behind her. "What are you doing down here, monkey?" Joanie asked. I pointed mutely at the towering cake and then managed to choke out, "It's raw." I was so embarrassed by my tears.

Joanie and Susanne poked and prodded the cake, pulling off a flake of meringue here and a crumb of cake there, chewing thoughtfully while avoiding all eye contact with me. "It tastes good!" Susanne said brightly. "Let's just take out the raw bits." I managed only to shake my head weakly in defeat. *I'll never bake again,* I thought. *My career as a food*

writer was short but enjoyable. Tomorrow I'll call my editor to cancel the book con-
tract and give back the advance.

"Come on, this isn't so bad," Joanie soothed. "We can fix it. But we have to go upstairs." She grabbed the cake platter and headed back to the kitchen with Susanne while I followed mutely. We prepared for surgery.

First we gently sliced the almond meringue off the top layer of the cake and set it aside. Next we scooped out the layer of raw cake batter in the middle, exposing the gooseberry–cream filling. And then we placed the meringue back on top of the filling. The cake looked slightly demented, a blowsy tarted–up thing next to the more austere, elegant cheesecakes and nut tortes on the buffet table. But at least the offending raw batter was gone. I slunk back to my seat in the garden next to Max, who looked at me quizzically, wondering where I'd been. I told him about the cake surgery that had just been performed and then I sort of slumped into myself and he put his arm around me.

But wouldn't you know, the guests at the party, young and old, threw themselves at my *Hannchen Jansen*. It was, improbably, the first cake on the groaning board to disappear and all afternoon people came up to me to tell me how much they loved it. I smiled at them weakly, convinced that Joanie had told everyone to eat the cake and put me out of my misery. Ischen, the award–winning Hessian cake baker, even asked me for the recipe. "You know, I'm still working on it," I told her evasively, searching her eyes for pity but finding none. "I'll send it to you when it's ready."

At the end of the day, we all gathered in the front yard for a group photo, Joanie and Dietrich, all their children and grandchildren, their siblings, and the people who were at their wedding fifty years earlier. Dietrich still fit into the dark gray suit he wore on his wedding day. My camera captured all of us and later, at home, I looked at the photo on the computer and saw one big happy family, with me and Max included.

The strangest thing was, the next morning, when I sat down to write about the cake disaster, the words fairly flew onto the page. And after that, it was like a dam breaking. All the words that had been so hard to summon before started to come to me, and slowly, page by page, I started to get things right again. For the first time in my life, it was writing that was making me feel strong enough to cook, instead of the other way around.

Hannchen Jansen (Gooseberry Cream Cake)

MAKES ONE 8-INCH ROUND LAYER CAKE

Hannchen Jansen is a blowsy-looking, maximalist thing, with its meringue topping and cream filling, but it is delicious. You may have a hard time finding gooseberries where you live, but this cake is equally good when filled with fresh red currants, blackberries, or raspberries. I'd avoid anything sweeter—you want the tart fruit to balance out all the sugar and cream.

Butter and flour for the cake pans
1 ¼ cups all-purpose flour
½ teaspoon baking soda
½ teaspoon baking powder
½ teaspoon plus a pinch of salt
8 tablespoons (4 ounces) slightly softened unsalted butter
1 cup plus 5 tablespoons sugar
2 large eggs
½ cup buttermilk
1 teaspoon vanilla extract
Grated peel of ½ organic lemon
3 egg whites
¼ cup sliced almonds
2 cups heavy cream
12 ounces fresh gooseberries, topped, tailed, and halved

1. Heat the oven to 350 degrees. Butter two 8-inch round cake pans, line the bottoms with parchment paper, and butter the parchment paper. Dust with a thin sprinkling of flour.

2. In a medium bowl, sift together the flour, baking soda, baking powder, and ½ teaspoon of salt. Set aside.

3. In a large bowl, cream together the butter and 1 cup sugar until light and fluffy. Beat in the eggs, one at a time, scraping down the sides of the bowl.

4. Mix the buttermilk, vanilla, and lemon peel together. Pour half the buttermilk mixture into the beaten butter, and beat until just combined. Add half the flour mixture to the butter mixture and beat until just combined. Pour the remaining buttermilk mixture into the batter and beat until just combined. Add the remaining flour mixture to the batter and mix until just combined. Scrape down the sides of the bowl.

5. Divide the batter evenly between the two cake pans. Bake for 25 minutes, rotating halfway through, until golden brown and starting to pull away from the sides of the pan. Remove the pans from the oven and let them cool on a rack for a few minutes before inverting the pans, removing the cakes, and letting the layers cool upside down. Turn the oven down to 325 degrees.

6. Put the egg whites in a spotlessly clean bowl and add the pinch of salt. Beat until frothy. Then, while beating, slowly add 3 tablespoons of the remaining sugar. Continue to beat until the egg whites are stiff and glossy.

7. Using one of the cake pans, draw an 8-inch circle on a clean piece of parchment and put the parchment on a baking sheet. Pile the beaten egg whites evenly into the circle and sprinkle with the sliced almonds. Put the sheet in the oven and bake the meringue round for 30 to 40 minutes, rotating it halfway through.

8. When the almonds are fragrant and the meringue is a toasty brown, turn off the oven and let the meringue cool completely in the oven.

9. When all the elements of the cake have completely cooled, whip the heavy cream. Mix the gooseberries with the remaining 2 tablespoons sugar or to taste. Set aside a few spoonfuls of whipped cream, and then fold the sugared gooseberries into the remaining whipped cream.

10. Put the first layer of cake upside down on a cake platter. Cover with the gooseberry whipped cream, leaving just a small border at the edge. Top with the second layer of cake right side up. Spread the top layer with

the reserved whipped cream. Gently peel the parchment paper off the meringue round and cut the meringue into 8 or 10 wedges (depending on how many people you plan to serve) with a serrated knife. Don't worry if it makes a bit of a mess—all the shards can be piled on top of the cake. Arrange the meringue wedges on top of the cake, cut the cake into slices with a very sharp knife, and serve.

29

I Decide to Be Brave

I'VE ALWAYS THOUGHT OF MYSELF AS A BIT OF A SCAREDY-CAT. WHEN I WAS a little girl, I hated the dark, imagined monsters under my bed, and was deathly afraid of shots. At the doctor's office, my whole body would seize up and I'd be gripped with terror as the needle approached. My mother would hold me and whisper into my ear, "Be brave," until I stuck out my arm. On the first day of first grade, I developed a full-blown panic attack. I clutched desperately at my father's suited legs, certain that I wouldn't survive being left behind, as he tried to move toward the doorway. He bent down and hugged me. "Be brave, Lui. You can do this, but you have to be brave." As I grew older, I learned to say it to myself. Just before an interview, before walking into a huge anonymous work party, on the first airplane ride I took after September 11. I'm not one for tattoos, but if I were, that'd be my ink: *Be brave.*

I had been brave to move back to Berlin, leaving my settled, established life in New York for a love story back home. And I'd been rewarded for my bravery, it's true, with happiness and contentment. That grand love story was thrilling and the transcontinental move was all well and good, but now the dust was settling and my daily life was taking on the easy, pleasing rhythm of a routine. The only thing I was really missing was some girlfriends.

In Berlin I worked from home, where the only other women sat sedately on my bookshelves. They were good company, it has to be said, but a little quiet. My mother and her friends were always around for museum trips, city walks, and fruit-picking adventures, but as a woman just barely into her thirties, I could tell as much as the next person that it might be good, important even, to have a few friends my own age. Max couldn't be my whole social life and I didn't want him to be.

I talked to my faraway friends on the phone and over Skype, a shaky computer picture filling me with joy. Teri and Jenny and I met up at Betsy's house in London for a long weekend of gossip and shopping and made hopeful plans to meet again a few months later. But I was kind of scared of making new friends in Berlin. I didn't even know where to begin. So I didn't. I kept telling myself I would and then I didn't. One day, Teri gave me a stern talking-to over the phone. "You have to make an effort. It's hard! I know. But you have to," she said, not unkindly. "We'll always be here for you. We love you, Lu. But you need people around you there. You have to be brave." I nodded. I *knew*.

With Teri's words echoing in my head, I went to a meetup of young American women freshly arrived in Berlin. It turned out to be very strange. The girls were nice, but none of them spoke German and Berlin was like Fiji to them. I felt so out of place and foreign that all of a sudden I was in fifth grade again, tongue-tied. I walked all the way home from Kreuzberg after that dinner in the dark, along the elevated subway tracks, past neon-lighted snack bars and Internet cafés. *If this is where I belong,* I thought, *and it is, my people must be out there somewhere. But how do I find them?*

The next day, on a solitary walk through Berlin, I snapped photos of an elderly couple holding hands as they took a stroll. I photographed a crumbling building that looked like it had just survived World War II and the clean, expensively restored buildings next to it. I shot walls of graffiti and, from afar, a group of tables on a sidewalk in front of a café. At home later that day, I uploaded the photos to my computer and clicked through each one. When I got to the photograph of the graffitied wall, I stopped cold. There, standing out at me so clearly I could hardly believe my eyes, were two words scribbled in red. I hadn't seen them when I shot the photo, but they were hard to miss now: "*Sei mutig.*" Be brave.

After that, I said yes to everything, every invitation and every extended hand. I met a nice young woman at tea at an acquaintance's house and I asked her if she wanted to go out sometime. She did! A blog reader e-mailed me about where to buy whole wheat tortillas in Berlin and I asked her if she wanted to make them together sometime. She did! I developed a whole new respect and appreciation for the hard work that men did when courting women. We were intimidating creatures, I saw that now. But I also saw that, especially in an expat community, no one can have too many friends. And with each brave thing I did (bear with me—this shy person's bravery is another person's everyday routine, I know), I felt bolder and less intimidated. And before I knew it, I had friends. Real-life, honest-to-goodness friends.

And one of them, in particular, was even more of a mongrel than I was. Suzy was half Jordanian, half Romanian, but she grew up in Greece, went to university in France, and had the lilt of a woman who had spent her adult years in London. She moved to Berlin with her family a few months after I did. Her husband worked just outside of Berlin and his weekly commutes from their home in London to Berlin resulted in their baby daughter not recognizing him when he walked through the front door on Friday nights. For the good of the family, Suzy told me, she had decided to leave London and move the family to Berlin, not knowing a word of German. Talk about being brave.

Best of all, Suzy was a *cook*.

Now I don't mean a cook in a restaurant. And I don't even mean a home cook like you or me. Suzy was a Cook with a capital C, the kind of person who thought nothing of whipping up a batch of finger-sized coffee éclairs on a Tuesday afternoon or sourcing veal bones, veal meat, and veal liver for a Michelin star–worthy dish of homemade tortelloni in broth. She read complicated restaurant cookbooks like novels. She went to three-star restaurants as if it were a sport. She had a degree from an English cooking school where she had learned every classic French sauce, every pastry preparation, every little kitchen trick that would have taken me years to figure out on my own. And she was willing to share.

Suzy taught me to sprinkle sliced avocados with lime juice, salt, and *nanami togarashi*, a Japanese spice mixture. She taught me to make fennel-spiced crisp quinoa flatbread that was so good I would willingly give up salt-and-vinegar potato chips if I could be guaranteed a lifetime supply. For a dinner party, she puréed boiled artichokes into a pale green, silky-smooth cloud and plopped juicy seared scallops on top.

The first time Suzy cooked for me and a group of other friends, she made a deconstructed salade Niçoise—blanching tiny green beans, boiling finger-sized waxy potatoes, making boiled eggs with lush orange yolks, roasting tiny tomatoes still on the vine, plucking meaty olives out of their brine, and plating everything separately so that each one of us could assemble our own salad. It was, I could tell right away, the best salade Niçoise of my life. I couldn't stop eating it. I couldn't stop talking about how good it was. I wept on the inside, thinking: *I will never eat a salad as good as this one again.* Until the next time I went over for lunch at Suzy's and she made it for me again. She's good like that.

But Suzy also met me for last-minute lunches, went on little walks through the city with me, made me laugh when I need to be cheered up, and brought me magazines and a single velvety brownie when I was in the hospital with appendicitis. Soon enough, I could barely remember a time when I didn't know her. And I couldn't imagine Berlin without her.

That's the funny thing about good friends. You can never remember what life was like before they came along.

The Best Niçoise Salad

SERVES 4

The key to this salad, besides using top-quality ingredients, is to cook all the separate elements in advance and then layer the salad together just before serving it. This requires a few good storage containers and some time, but the payoff is worth it. This truly is the best Niçoise salad I've ever eaten.

1 large fennel bulb

Good-quality olive oil

Flakey salt, such as Maldon, and freshly ground black pepper

1 pound cherry tomatoes, on the vine

¾ pound green beans

4 large eggs, room temperature

1 pound fingerling potatoes

1 tablespoon plus 1 teaspoon Dijon mustard

2 tablespoons white wine vinegar

1 9-ounce can or jar of qood-quality preserved tuna in olive oil (I like Ortiz brand)

Fresh lemon juice to taste

½ cup Niçoise or Kalamata olives

1. Heat the oven to 250 degrees and line a baking sheet with aluminum foil. Slice the fennel thinly through the core and toss with a bit of of olive oil and salt and pepper. Put the sliced, dressed fennel on the baking sheet and bake in the oven for 40 minutes. Then scrape the fennel onto a plate and set aside. It can be stored in a turned-off oven for a day.

2. Drizzle the cherry tomatoes with olive oil, sprinkle with salt and pepper, and put them on the baking sheet. Bake them in the oven for 1½ hours. Then turn off the oven and let it cool down with the baking sheet inside. The tomatoes can be stored in the turned-off oven for up to a day before serving.

3. Top and tail the green beans and cut them in half. Bring a pot of salted water to a boil. Add the beans to the boiling water and cover. Cook the beans until they are crisp-tender, about 5 minutes. Drain the beans in a colander and run cold water over them to stop the cooking process. Dry the beans and put them in a storage container lined with a piece of paper towel; then store them in the fridge for up to a day before serving.

4. Bring a small pot of water to a simmer, and then lower the eggs gently into the water. Cook for exactly 6 minutes; then drain the eggs and set them aside to cool. When they've cooled, peel the eggs and put them in a storage container in the fridge for up to a day before serving.

5. Scrub the potatoes. Put them in a pot and cover them with cold salted water. Bring to a boil and cook for 20 minutes, or until a fork pierces a potato easily. Drain the potatoes and peel them while they are still warm. Keep them in a storage container in the fridge for up to a day before serving.

6. About 30 minutes before you're ready to serve the salad, make the dressing: Put the Dijon mustard, salt, and pepper in a bowl. Add the vinegar and whisk to combine. Then add ¼ cup olive oil in a thin stream, whisking continuously until you have a smooth, creamy vinaigrette.

7. Take all the prepped ingredients from the fridge and let them come to room temperature for 30 minutes. Slice the potatoes and dress them with half of the vinaigrette. Season with additional salt and pepper, if needed. Arrange the slices on the serving plates.

8. In the same bowl that you used to dress the potatoes, put the green beans and dress them with the remaining vinaigrette. Arrange the beans on top of and around the potato slices on each serving plate.

9. Open the can or jar of tuna and drain off the oil. Then flake the tuna in good-sized chunks into a bowl and sprinkle with lemon juice, olive oil, and a pinch of salt. Divide the dressed tuna among the serving plates.

10. Quarter the eggs and arrange the wedges (1 whole egg per person) on the serving plates.

11. Drape some fennel and a vine of roasted cherry tomatoes on top of each serving plate. Arrange a few olives on each plate. Drizzle each plate with olive oil, and serve.

30

Friends and Neighbors

I N NEW YORK, THE RULES FOR DAILY SURVIVAL THAT GOVERNED THE sidewalks and the subways (head down, poker face on) also seemed to hold true for relations with your neighbors. You spent the bulk of your adult life interacting with them as if they had the potential to become the kind of person who would, under the guise of borrowing a cup of flour or the morning paper, break into your home to dismember you and steal your identity. The logic went: there were crazy people all over the city, so who's to say there weren't some in the apartment right next door?

In Germany, good relations with your neighbors are de rigueur. Germans may snap at a stranger for crossing the street at a red light, but they treat their neighbors with such tenderness. One girlfriend of mine lives in an apartment building where her neighbors spend hours on the landings chatting with one another, making love matches, becoming clients, and also throw big parties together in the courtyard every year. Another friend tells me her neighbors across the landing are part of the reason she will never move out of her apartment. She leaves her front door open on the weekends so that her toddler can run back and forth among the apartments for snacks and games.

I met our neighbor, Herr Schulze, the first day I saw our apartment. I accidentally rang his doorbell when I came to meet the broker and the door swung open almost immediately. A genial older man with white hair stood smiling in the doorway. I apologized for bothering him, though he didn't seem bothered in the least. He gave me a wink and told me not to worry, the apartment for rent was across the hall. *Huh*, I thought. Berliners have a reputation for not being, let's say, the easiest people in the world to bother unannounced, and here was someone winking and smiling at me despite the fact that I'd done so on a Sunday morning, of all times. I decided it must be a good sign.

When we moved in, Herr and Frau Schulze welcomed us with a potted sunflower plant and an invitation to come over for coffee and cake. We sat in their kitchen drinking coffee and eating big slices of raisin-studded panettone and eventually, when the coffee dried up, we moved on to room-temperature Asti spumante and talked about their childhoods. Herr Schulze had grown up just a few blocks away and had never left the neighborhood. He could still remember playing with his friends in the bombed-out remains of the buildings that littered the streets just after the war. Frau Schulze had grown up in East Prussia and had made the dangerous journey from Königsberg to Berlin after the war with her mother and sisters. Her face pulled together when she started to speak of it, though, and she soon fell quiet. Many Germans died during that period, of starvation or in reprisal killings, while Soviet soldiers were raping and pillaging their way through the German territories. I wondered what she had seen.

After that, the Schulzes stopped us almost daily to chat and check in, asking us to join them for handball games to which they had season tickets or inviting us over for a drink before dinner. At first it was sweet and I felt welcomed in the building. But I soon started to feel ambushed each time Max and I had to stop for a twenty-minute conversation with the Schulzes in the hallway. *Why is it so bad that New Yorkers ignore their neighbors*, I would think as we made polite small talk, heavy bags full of groceries digging into our shoulders, a phone ringing distantly in the background. I wondered if the Schulzes' interest in our lives wasn't starting to feel a little predatory. I decided to politely keep our conversations to a minimum and declined any advances to spend time together. We were busy with work, we would say, begging off, or just on our way out the door to meet friends. Eventually, they got the hint and sometimes a whole week would go by in which we wouldn't see them, though Max, whose next-door neighbors growing up were like substitute grandparents (his own were inconveniently stuck behind the Wall), was always unfailingly kind to them, helping them to order a new dishwasher online or fixing their computer.

The rest of the people in our apartment building seemed to keep to themselves. We'd say *"Guten Tag"* brightly in the hallways when we passed one another, as is the custom in Germany, but I didn't really know any of their names, and although I nursed a sneaking suspicion that I should have been the one to introduce myself when we moved in, the remains of my New York attitude kept me away. I soon identified an American woman on the second floor, a male couple on the third who looked so alike that I could never tell them apart, a Turkish family with three children on the ground floor, and a hatchet-faced Bolivian-German couple on the third who were the superintendents of the building. They were the only ones who complained about the loud music the night we had had friends over for a party, far more in line with the grumpy Berlin style I'd expected from our neighbors.

Then one day Herr and Frau Schulze, or Hans and Brigitte, as they insisted we call them, told us about the barbecue party the tenants held in the courtyard every June. "It's a very nice occasion," Brigitte explained. "We all get together and grill and chat, you know, have a good time." She smiled at me shyly. "We want you to be there." "What weekend in June would be good for you?" Hans asked, pen poised to write down the date. My heart sank. I glanced at Max, who had an impenetrably polite look on his face.

A whole evening in the company of people I didn't really want to get to know? I felt cornered but as far as I could tell there was no way of getting out of it. "June tenth", I said. "We can definitely make it then. Right, Max?" He shrugged and smiled. I told myself to look on the bright side: I liked cooking for parties. "What can we bring?" Hans and Brigitte told us to buy whatever kind of meat we wanted to grill for the two of us and said that if I wanted to bring a salad or something else to share I was welcome to.

The evening of the party rolled around and up in my little office at the top of the house I could hear my neighbors in the courtyard, setting up the party and lighting the two charcoal grills (one for the Turkish family and one for everyone else's pork chops and sausages). I had baked a batch of cookies, and Max washed and filled a big bowl with strawberries I'd picked that morning at a U-pick field in Potsdam with Joanie and her grandsons. But I was still dreading the party. I wondered what Joanie was doing that evening and wished I were in her kitchen instead.

I dragged my feet, checking my e-mail one, two, three last times, wiping down the kitchen counters, and straightening up our bedroom, while Max waited for me patiently in the living room. Finally, half an hour after the official start of the party, we headed downstairs, cookies and strawberries in hand. "Let's just stay an hour, okay?" I whispered to Max in the stairway.

In the courtyard, all of our neighbors were gathered around. The Turkish family manned their grill, turning out spicy homemade lamb burgers and tender chicken breasts. The Germans took their turn at the other grill, where sausages of different lengths and sizes slowly sputtered and crisped. The family who lived below us, a German-Iranian couple and their three handsome sons, brought pots of rice pilaf, a spicy zucchini sauce, and shredded chicken. Our American neighbor had brought a plastic bowl filled with pasta salad. There was homemade garlic butter to spread on Turkish pide bread made crusty over the coals. Max and I slid our offerings onto the table and took a seat, feeling slightly awkward, like the new kids at school.

My neighbors, it turned out, had held this party every year for the past twenty years. They considered themselves good friends, even if many of them still referred to one another by their last names and used the formal "*Sie*." (Germans are a formal folk.) There was Herr Reichenberger, a tall man with a craggy, weathered face, who lived in the back garden building and asked Ms. Moore, the American, a law professor whose apartment abutted his, if his late-night rock 'n' roll sessions ever bothered her. There was the kindly Herr Kruse, who liked to keep watch over our street from the driver's seat of his red Volkswagen sedan, which he always parked near the front door, proudly cleaning it every day, waving cheerfully to all who passed him on the sidewalk. There were the Ergüns, whose dark-eyed children were all born in Berlin but who spoke only Turkish among themselves as they sat shyly at a separate table.

And there was Herr Schiller, who had moved into the building in 1945, when he was four, and never left. After the Allied bombing of Berlin, our building, built in the early nineteenth century, was the only one left standing on the block. But the cast-iron staircase from the grand building next door remained, reaching five stories high, and he and his friends would clamber up to the top and keep watch over the neighborhood from their perch. It took ten years for that staircase to be torn down and a squat postwar apartment building to go up in its place. I tried to imagine our neat, clean street as it must once have looked like under a pile of rubble and came up short.

"Your apartment is where the laundry room used to be!" he said with a laugh, explaining how, until the early 1990s, people would trek up to the top floor to do their laundry in the attic and then hang their wet laundry up to dry under the eaves of the house. He could also remember how, when he was still a child, his father and the other men in the building would set off for the other side of Charlottenburg on the first day of every month to pay the month's rent. But their landlady, Frau Schwarzer, was no ordinary landlady. She was a madam with a nose for real estate, owning several apartment buildings and requiring payment in person on the first of every month at her office, a brothel near Savignyplatz. Every man who paid the rent on time would get a glass of Schnaps as a courtesy. Another round would follow the first and inevitably the crowd would end up at a local bar, accompanied by Frau Schwarzer's ladies for the rest of the evening. What Herr Schiller could remember specifically was all the women in the house waiting angrily for their drunken husbands to come home from their night out and the arguments that would ensue, echoing from each floor's open windows down into the courtyard below.

Back in the late summer of 1988, the year I moved to Berlin to live with my mother again, I was restless and uneasy before the first day of school. I had desperately wanted to come back to Berlin, but alone with my thoughts in my dark bedroom, I worried about what lay in store the next day, the faceless classmates awaiting me. *Will they be nice to me?* I wondered. *I just want them to be nice.* Suddenly I pictured my father in the sprawling Brookline apartment all alone and I got a roiling stomachache.

My mother was out for dinner with Florian that evening at their friends Muck and Jürgen's. When she came home, she slipped into my bedroom to give me a goodnight kiss. "I brought you something," she whispered and pulled a blue ceramic bowl from her bag. "Muck made *rote Grütze* and gave me a little bowl for you." I peered inside and saw a dark red pudding flecked with seeds and almost-black cherries. "There's even some vanilla sauce to go on top." My mother showed me the little pitcher, lifted off the plastic wrap for me to stick my nose inside the jug. The sauce smelled milky and sweet. She pulled a spoon from behind her back and gave it to me and I spooned up some of the *rote Grütze*, which turned out to be cool and sweet-sour. The seeds crunched in my teeth. It tasted like nothing less than all of summer concentrated in that one bowl.

"You can have the rest for breakfast in the morning. But now go to sleep. And stop worrying about tomorrow. It's going to be fine. *Sogni d'oro*," she said as she stood up and smoothed my hair. And then she was gone and the bedroom door was closed again. I could hear her soft voice, mingling with Florian's, on the other side of the wall, the floorboards creaking with each step they took in the hallway.

With those few spoonfuls of *rote Grütze* in my belly, a calm stole over me and warmth spread through my body. I fell asleep thinking I was in the right place.

After dinner in our courtyard, when the sky grew dark, Brigitte brought out two big bowls of thick, dark, quivering *rote Grütze*, studded with fat cherries, sweet raspberries, and tart currants. We each helped ourselves and even the Turkish children were drawn out of their seats to spoon up bowls of it topped with cold vanilla cream.

As we ate, Brigitte shyly confided that it was actually Frau Romero, the woman who had lived in the apartment Max and I now rented, who always brought *rote Grütze* to the courtyard party. It was the staple dessert without which the party wouldn't be the same. So ever since her death a few years earlier, Brigitte had taken over the *rote Grütze* duties. Suddenly I was ashamed that I hadn't known about this small detail. "I would have loved to have been assigned the *rote Grütze*! I have a pretty great recipe for it." I said. "There's always next year," Brigitte said, smiling, and then she whispered in my ear, "Frau Romero always bought hers from the store. Mine is homemade."

When the last light drained from the sky just after 11:00 P.M., Max and I said goodnight and walked the four flights back up to our apartment. Lying side by side in our bedroom before falling asleep, we could hear the last neighbors in the courtyard below, talking softly and laughing, the notes rising high up past our bedroom windows. I had that same warm feeling from all those years ago after eating Muck's *rote Grütze*, listening to Florian and my mother murmuring in the room next door. "That wasn't half as awful as I thought it would be," I whispered to Max. "They were all so nice." I could see his profile as he turned toward me. "I can't believe I'm saying this, but I'm looking forward to next year."

Rote Grütze with Vanilla Sauce

SERVES 6

Rote Grütze is a summery pudding made by only very briefly cooking raspberries, sour cherries, and red currants together with juice, a bit of sugar, and cornstarch for thickening. My friend Muck makes her *rote Grütze*, which I consider the gold standard, with a base of puréed wild plums called *Spillinge* in German. Since the rest of us don't have access to that sour, crimson stuff, I've adapted the recipe to use prune juice or sour cherry juice (as long as there's no additional sugar in the juice) instead. Slippery-smooth, sweet-sour, and refreshing, *rote Grütze's* berry bite is tamed with a creamy pool of vanilla sauce (recipe below) on top. Don't skip it.

¼ cup cornstarch
2 cups prune or cherry juice, no sugar added
¼ cup sugar (I like my *Grütze* on the sour side, but you can add more
    sugar if you like)
Optional flavorings: grated lemon peel, vanilla bean, cinnamon stick
2 cups raspberries
2 cups red currants, destemmed
2 cups sour cherries, pitted

1. Put the cornstarch in a small bowl, and whisk in ¼ cup of water to make a lump-free slurry. Set aside.

2. Pour the juice into a heavy 4-quart pot and add the sugar (if using one of the flavorings, add it now). Set over medium heat and stir until the sugar has dissolved. Add the fruit to the pot and bring just to a boil.

3. Give the slurry another whisk and pour it into the pot just as the fruit mixture starts to bubble. The *Grütze* will start to thicken almost immediately. Bring it back to a boil and then remove the pot from the heat. If using the vanilla bean or cinnamon stick, remove it from the pot.

4. Pour the hot pudding into a large serving bowl or into individual dishes, and let it cool completely before refrigerating it overnight. Serve cold, with a jug of vanilla sauce for pouring over it (see below).

Vanilla Sauce

SERVES 6

2 tablespoons cornstarch
2 cups plus 2 tablespoons whole milk

¼ cup sugar

½ vanilla bean, split and scraped, seeds reserved

Up to ¼ cup heavy cream (optional)

1. Prepare an ice bath.

2. Put the cornstarch in a small bowl and whisk in the 2 tablespoons milk until no lumps remain. Set aside.

3. Pour the 2 cups of milk into a 2-quart saucepan. Add the sugar, the split vanilla bean, and the scraped seeds. Set over medium heat and, whisking, bring to a boil.

4. As soon as the milk boils, whisk in the cornstarch slurry very slowly. The sauce will start to thicken immediately. (If you like a thinner sauce, use a little less of the slurry; if you like a thicker sauce, use all of it.) Whisk for a few more seconds, until the sauce is completely smooth, and then remove it from the heat.

5. Put the pot in the ice bath (taking care not to let the cold water get into the sauce) and continue to whisk the sauce until it has cooled considerably. If you'd like to thin the sauce a little, whisk in heavy cream until you get the consistency you'd like.

6. Serve the vanilla sauce at room temperature with the *rote Grütze*, or refrigerate until ready to serve (if you find the sauce has thickened in the fridge, simply whisk in a little more milk or cream until you get the pouring consistency you'd like).

31

We've Come a Long Way

MY FIRST SUMMER BACK IN BERLIN WAS A HOT ONE, AS IF THE GODS wanted to make up for the long, hard winter that so tested my resolve. The sun shone for weeks on end and it was utterly glorious, even when our attic apartment filled with what felt like a hot desert wind that blew around our ankles as we walked down the hallway to the living room. The heat was unusual for northern Germany. At night, in lieu of air-conditioning, I took to soaking bath towels in cold water and draping myself with them as I nodded off to sleep. When Max and I bought ice cream cones in the leafy warren of streets near our apartment, we had to eat quickly before the melting cream started dripping down our wrists. We watered the tomato plants and flowerpots on the balcony morning and night, since they tended to start drooping rather alarmingly in the midafternoon sun.

But the tomatoes that I promised myself I would plant were flourishing in the warmth, nestled against a wall that was bathed in sunlight every afternoon. Little green tomatoes had recently burst into color and neither Max nor I could resist grabbing a handful of them to pop in our mouths each time we passed them by. Sometimes they were all we could bear to eat, besides pickles straight from the fridge, cold soups, and cheese sandwiches cobbled together in the strange half-light that fell over the city sometime around 10:00 P.M.

Berlin's turn-of-the-century apartments with their ten-foot ceilings were perfectly suited to withstand a heat wave; they remained cool and dark. But our apartment, constructed so recently, was miserably insulated and the air inside soon became oppressive. One day, we found we could barely breathe. By the next morning, I was feeling a little panicked.

"I don't know if I can handle another weekend of this," I said to Max, who was lying on the cool tiled kitchen floor for temporary relief. My mother was in Italy at the time and her apartment, one of the old ones that stayed mercifully fresh, was empty. "Should we go stay at my mother's place for the weekend?" Max lay there silently in contemplation, then sat up with a start. "No. I have a better idea. Let's go to the beach. You've never been to the Baltic Sea before and it's not that far away. This is the perfect time to do it. The weather here can be so iffy that driving that far north usually doesn't make sense. But it's supposed to stay beautiful for weeks. And if we leave in the next hour we'll be there by lunchtime." His eyes were shining. "Now? As in right now?" I asked incredulously. We didn't usually make plans for a weekend trip on a Friday morning. "Yes, now," Max said. "We don't need much beyond the car and our bathing suits." He added, "Also, it'll be a celebration of sorts. Think about it: A year ago this weekend you flew to Berlin to see me for the weekend for the first time. And now you're here, you live here. With me!" I joined him on the floor and we sat there grinning at one another. It was hard to argue with that. We needed to celebrate.

While Max packed our things, I called a few hotels to see about rooms. Every hotel I called was booked, except for a Pension in a town called Ahlbeck, which had one room left. "But it has two single beds and the bathroom's down the hall," the receptionist said apologetically. Then she added, "We're forty yards from the boardwalk." That was all I wanted to know. "We'll take it!" We threw a few sandwiches and a handful of tomatoes in a plastic bag and ran downstairs to the car, giddy with anticipation.

For someone partially raised in Germany, I had seen remarkably little of the country beyond Berlin. There had been a few school trips down to Bavaria in high school, and I regularly flew to Frankfurt and Munich in my old publishing life. But the huge region around and north of Berlin, all the way to the sea that abuts Denmark, was terra incognita. As we drove north to the sea, we passed fields filled with waving poppies, electric windmills, and cows. There was no air-conditioning in our car, but the roads were so empty that we soon rolled down the windows and breathed in the fresh, clean air as we munched on our sandwiches.

As Max predicted, we arrived in Ahlbeck by lunchtime. Ahlbeck was a resort town at the turn of the century, filled with old pastel-colored villas that had all been carefully restored in the years since German reunification. Our pensione was in one of those villas and our room, with its two single beds, was clean and spare. We dropped our things and went straight to the beach. When we plunged into the cold water, relief rose off our bodies like steam. We stayed at the beach, swimming and reading, until long past sunset, listening to the soft crash of the waves and watching the seagulls circling over a distant pier. For dinner, we picked out a homey-looking restaurant nestled in the dune grasses and ate fried pickled herring and potato salad, along with tall, frosty glasses of beer. That night, we left the windows open to hear the sea and let in the cool air.

At the beach the next day, we lay next to one another in the sand remembering the previous summer, when I was still in New York and Max was in Berlin and we were tentatively, carefully, trying to figure out our next steps. On one of Max's trips to New York in late summer, we had spent a day on Fire Island. He had marveled at the little houses, quiet paths, and the deep blue color of the Atlantic Ocean, and at lunchtime we sat side by side at the bar of a local restaurant eating hamburgers while we looked out at the waves lapping at the edges of the pier. We were just getting to know each other again. Things had felt so thrilling and new, yet familiar at the same time. At the end of the day, when the beach had emptied and just before we packed our things to head back to the city, a doe stole carefully onto the beach to root through an overflowing garbage bin as we watched her from a safe distance.

Here we were a year later in Ahlbeck, and although the view was relatively similar—a quiet beach, crashing waves, the hoarse cries of seagulls—our life looked so different now. We'd both risked a lot to make a life together, but it was working. Our big gamble was paying off. I lay back and closed my eyes, feeling the hot sand press into the back of my neck. That afternoon we bought fish sandwiches from a hole-in-the-wall shop in a nearby mall. Big flakes of freshly smoked mackerel and haddock were piled into crisp white buns along with snappy leaves of lettuce. The sandwiches were so good and we were so hungry that as soon as we finished them we bought two more. Later on the beach for a midnight stroll, we gazed out at the thin strip of red sunlight at the very edge of the horizon, delineating the border between water and sky.

By the time we drove home on Sunday night, it felt like we'd been gone for a week. And even though the heat wave wouldn't break for another two weeks, somehow it wasn't so hard to bear anymore. After all, although we didn't have the cool night air or the dark Baltic Sea twenty yards from our front door back in Berlin, we did have a reliable source of pickled herring and smoked fish just ten minutes from our apartment. Rogacki was a legendary Berlin delicatessen that still smoked all its own fish, from tiny golden sprats to slabs of pink salmon, tuna, halibut, and more. They also sold every kind of preserved herring under the sun, from pickled to rollmops to *matjes*. I figured that a steady supply of Rogacki's fish specialties could help prolong our mini-vacation just a bit.

I had always had a soft spot for pickled herring, which at Rogacki was sold as whole skin-on fillets floating in a sharp vinegar brine. It was called *Bismarckhering*, the name never failing to conjure in my mind a solemn-looking fish with whiskers and a long face, maybe even a helmet. Germans tucked these fillets inside crisp white rolls with sliced pickles for lunch, and they cut them up into small pieces and mixed them into potato salads. They even suspended pieces of *Bismarckhering* in white wine aspic, though I'm going to go out on a limb and hazard a guess that wobbly aspic plus pickled herring probably appeals to only about seven people on this entire planet.

When I was a little kid, I thought pickled herring was about as appetizing as a wet rag. On our trips to Philadelphia to visit my grandparents, the fridge was always stuffed to bursting in anticipation. Holding her place with the best of Jewish grandmothers, my Grandma Ann asked us at breakfast what we wanted for lunch and started lunch with a query about dinner. She made noodle casserole with canned tomato soup, stewed pears, and pot roast. There was coleslaw and prune juice, Jell-O cubes and sliced beefsteak tomatoes. And for my father there was always pickled herring and onions in cream sauce. He and my Grandpa Dave would drape the fish over their toasted bagel halves and slurp them up with a grin. I had had good table manners hammered into me night after night by both my parents, but it took an otherworldly amount of restraint not to fall out of my chair in revulsion.

But all little girls eventually grow up and along the way some might even realize that their fathers may have been onto something. I learned to love pickled herring one adventurous year in college when I saw my father eating it on squares of matzo, the crisp bland cracker a perfect foil for the small chunks of velvety, vinegary fish. For many years thereafter, that's the only way I'd eat it. I'd buy a jar of herring and a box of matzos and I'd make the two last for weeks, plucking out a piece or two of fish from the jar and a half-square of matzo from the box each night before dinner until I had my fill.

Now, my hair still coarse and salty from the beach, the two of us hungry for more than just a predinner snack, I decided to make the pickled herring the focus of our meal. I found two potatoes in the stoneware jug under the counter, found a few beets knocking around in the fridge, and pulled out a jar of sour pickles. I boiled the potatoes and beets, and when they had cooled I cut them into large dice along with the herring and pickles, layering everything into a large white bowl and staring at it until I figured out what might still be missing. I minced a large pile of parsley and added it to the bowl before dressing the salad, at which point the diced beets bled into the salad, quickly staining the potatoes and fish pink. I took a taste, trying to get a little cube of every element onto my fork. The strong-tasting fish needed the earthy, sweet beets and potatoes for balance, and the pickles added much-needed crunch to an otherwise soft salad. The dressing was sharp enough to pull all the disparate elements in line, while the parsley added freshness.

I was a little nervous about what Max would think of the salad; pickled herring isn't exactly an easy thing to love. But when he came into the kitchen to take our dinner out to the balcony, his eyes widened. "Is that *Bismarckhering?*" I nodded. "And potatoes and pickles and beets too," I said hopefully, pointing out the different things in the bowl. "It looks good," Max said, and went on to have three helpings for dinner, chasing the hot pink sweet–sour dregs of the salad around the bottom of the bowl with a piece of bread. It wasn't long after that that we decided to drive back to Ahlbeck the next summer and the one after that too: our very first tradition in what we both hoped would be a long life of anniversaries.

Pickled Herring Salad with Potatoes and Beets

SERVES 2 AS A LIGHT MEAL

If you have a source for freshly pickled herring, then by all means buy your fish from them. If not, a jar of pickled herring from the grocery store will do just fine. Mix the salad only just before serving, so that the beets don't bleed too much. Serve with some crusty bread for sopping.

¾ cup drained pickled herring pieces; or if you have a source for
    freshly pickled herring, 2 fillets, cut into bite-sized pieces
1 large dill pickle, diced
2 medium boiled Yukon Gold potatoes, room temperature, peeled
    and diced
½ cup loosely packed flat-leaf parsley, minced
1 teaspoon Dijon mustard
Salt and freshly ground black pepper
1 tablespoon white wine vinegar
3 tablespoons extra-virgin olive oil
3 small boiled or roasted beets, room temperature

1. Place the herring, the diced pickle and potatoes, and the parsley into a serving bowl.

2. Put the mustard in a small bowl and add salt and pepper to taste. Stirring with a fork or a small whisk, add the vinegar and then drizzle in the olive oil until the vinaigrette is emulsified. Drizzle the vinaigrette over the salad and mix well.

3. Just before serving, peel and cut the beets into medium dice. Add to the bowl and toss once or twice. Waiting until the last minute to add the beets means you get to see the salad's colors bleed like a watercolor.

32

Turning Up the Heat

IT HAD BEEN A LONG TIME SINCE I GOT OVER MY GREEN LEAFY VEGETABLE resentment. It was hard to feel resentful of anything lately. It was full summer and Berlin's markets, with their striped canvas awnings, were bursting with glowing heads of lettuce, piles of bright tomatoes, phalanxes of cucumbers, fresh mushrooms, and a seemingly endless array of berries picked from local fields. Max and I ate salads every day and we went for bike rides through Berlin's sprawling Grunewald Forest whenever we could steal away, the warm air brushing our bare legs as we cycled. The days blended into one another and I felt like I was living in a haze of happiness most of the time.

But the one thing I hadn't yet adjusted to was how bland everything was. The Germans, it seemed, were allergic to spice. And when I say spice, I mean heat. Chile heat. Eye-stinging, bum-tingling, tongue-cramping heat.

I went to a Mexican *taqueria* and begged them to make my order of shredded pork tacos spicy. The waiter nodded politely, but when the tacos arrived, well salted at least, there was nary a sliver of chile in sight. I went to two Vietnamese sandwich shops, figuring there would be no way around the chile there—what was a *banh mi* without jalapeños and Sriracha sauce other than just a ham sandwich? Unfortunately, in both places my *banh mi* was nothing more than a ham sandwich.

Even the hot sauce that got slathered on Turkish kebab sandwiches barely put a bead of sweat on my brow.

So I decided to turn up the heat at home. Max and I stocked our fridge with Indonesian *sambal* and Korean *gojuchang* and Vietnamese Sriracha sauce that we bought at the Asian grocery stores that had cropped up all over Berlin in the past ten years. We dabbed the pastes and sauces on our baked beans, stirred them into fried cabbage, and basted them on eggs. I figured that if the city wouldn't give me the spice I craved, I'd just have to make it myself. We stockpiled dried Mexican chiles that friends sent us from the United States, I asked my mother to tote back envelopes from Italy filled with tiny dried Calabrian chiles, and we dared each other to lace our plates with more and more lashings of hot sauce.

When Max's birthday rolled around in July in the middle of the heat wave, I convinced him to have a party at home. Our living room was the perfect size for a party, with plenty of room for late-night dancing. "You won't have to do a thing," I said, "besides buy the beer. I'll take care of the food and everyone will have a great time. Come on! You only turn thirty-four once." I wanted to celebrate his birthday with all our friends and a big spread of food. I had a winter birthday, when the days were short and cold, so I firmly believed that summer birthdays needed to be celebrated in a big way, taking advantage of the long days and warm nights. And in Germany, birthdays, even for adults, were a really big deal. I couldn't wait to get down to business and plan the menu.

Cooking for a crowd requires some thought, as I'm sure you'll agree. I wanted to serve bright, attractive-looking food, with lots of colors and textures, like a cooling salad to balance the heat outside, and something that people could eat with their fingers, but nothing that required too many napkins, especially if they were walking around the apartment, out to the balcony for a smoke, and back again. And because Max would lie down in traffic for a good meatball, I knew those had to go on the menu too.

I picked an Asian-style cold peanut noodle dish spiked with plenty of chile-garlic paste. I planned a huge pan of chewy cocoa brownies, slightly underbaked for irresistibly gooey middles. And, as the pièce de résistance for my meatball–loving, spice–mad German sweetheart, a huge pot of Mexican meatballs stuffed with fine bits of onions and zucchini, swimming in a delectable sauce of chipotle chiles and ground tomatoes. Max approved the menu with two thumbs up. We were good to go.

But the day before the party, at the very last minute in cooking terms, I came down with a bad case of qualms about serving such spicy food to our German friends. What if they balked at the taste of the first chipotle meatball and the first forkful of spicy noodles on their plates? *I can't do this to them*, I thought. I wanted our party food to be the kind of stuff that made people clean their plates and beg for more, not run for the water faucet, eyes watering. So I headed to the butcher at my local greenmarket and I grudgingly bought a big slab of pork shoulder than I turned into goulash, shot through with paprika, onions, and a big healthy tangle of sauerkraut. It turned out rib–sticking and reddish, more winter food than anything else, but it was pretty tasty too. "We should be safe," I muttered to myself as I cleaned up the kitchen late that night.

The next day, Max showed an admirable amount of restraint by keeping his fingers out of the pot of Mexican meatballs as he set up the buffet and got the living room ready, moving the coffee table out of the way and putting out plenty of extra chairs for our friends. When they arrived, it didn't take long for them to crowd around the buffet table, filling paper plates and grabbing forks. And after an hour, when I took a closer look, I couldn't believe my eyes. The bowl of spicy peanut noodles (I'd tripled the original recipe) was almost empty. The pot of Mexican meatballs had one lone meatball in it (and Max was eyeing it ferociously from across the room). But the mild pork goulash was entirely untouched.

During the rest of the party, which lasted until 4:00 A.M., friends came up to me, fanning their mouths. "What was in those noodles? Those meatballs were insane! I need the recipe. And another beer." The only thing still left on the table the next morning when it was time to clean up was the goulash. And as we lugged the heavy cast–iron pot of goulash back to the kitchen to divvy up and freeze, Max turned to me and said, "Next year, will you please make a triple portion of the meat–balls? They ate every last one before I even got to the table."

Meatballs in Tomato-Chipotle Sauce

MAKES APPROXIMATELY THIRTY-FOUR 1½-INCH MEATBALLS

This recipe is adapted from one in Diana Kennedy's *The Cuisines of Mexico*. I love that each meatball is studded with finely diced zucchini and onions. But even better, there's no messy step of browning the meatballs in this recipe. You simply make a flavorful tomato-chipotle sauce and then plop the raw meatballs in the sauce to cook, resulting in tender, delicious meat–balls and a clean stovetop. The recipe makes an enormous amount of sauce, but it's so good I doubt you'll find yourself complaining about it. Put these out on a buffet table for a crowd (the recipe is easily doubled or tri–pled, as Max would like me to tell you) or serve them for dinner with steamed white rice.

Meatballs

12 ounces ground pork
12 ounces ground beef
1 medium zucchini
8 black peppercorns
¼ teaspoon cumin seeds
¼ teaspoon dried Mexican oregano
2 eggs, lightly beaten
⅓ cup finely chopped onion
1½ teaspoons salt

1. Place the ground pork and beef in a large bowl. Trim the ends of the zucchini and chop it finely. Add to the bowl.

2. Finely grind the peppercorns and cumin seeds in a spice grinder or mortar and pestle, and add to the meat. Add the oregano, eggs, onion, and

salt, and gently use your hands or a spatula to thoroughly combine all the ingredients.

3. Gently form the mixture into 1½-inch meatballs. Place on a baking sheet, loosely cover with plastic wrap, and refrigerate, while making the sauce.

Sauce and finish

2 pounds tomatoes
2 to 4 chipotle chiles in adobo, to taste
3 tablespoons vegetable oil
¾ cup chicken broth
Salt

1. Bring a large pot of water to a boil. Core the tomatoes and place them in the boiling water. Reduce the heat and simmer for 5 minutes. Drain the tomatoes and let them cool for a few minutes.

2. Process the tomatoes and chipotle chiles in a blender or food processor until smooth.

3. Heat the oil in a large skillet and add the tomato sauce. When it comes to a boil, reduce the heat and simmer for 5 minutes. Add the chicken broth. When the sauce comes back to a simmer, add the meatballs.

4. Cover the pan and simmer the meatballs over low heat until they are cooked through, about 50 minutes. Adjust the seasoning by tasting and adding salt just before the end of the cooking time. This dish can be prepared a day ahead or can be frozen and reheated.

33

Such Abundance

I N LATE SUMMER, THE FLOWERS THAT TRANSFORMED BERLIN INTO A PER-
fumed paradise in spring were long gone. Lilac bushes once heavy
with blossoms sprang back to their regular upright posture; linden
trees no longer dropped sticky, sweet-smelling leaves and blossoms
onto the cars below. In their place, now, was fruit, as far as the eye
could see.

There were sour cherry trees studded with bright red cherries on
gritty streets in Friedrichshain and fat black sweet cherries in the front
yard of quiet blocks of houses in Marienfelde. Elderberry bushes sprout-
ing blue-black sprays of berries stood in every park. The fields around
Berlin were crammed to bursting with berries. My friend Jürgen took
me to his friend's backyard, where two wild plum trees stood, their
branches spangled with marble-sized bright purple orbs. We picked
pounds and pounds of the plums, filling both our cars with crates of
fruit, and spent the rest of the day in Jürgen's kitchen boiling the plums,
straining out the pits, and filling glasses and jars and bottles with the
magenta pulp, to be used later in the year for jam and *rote Grütze*.

Every weekend it seemed I was out in another field picking some
kind of fruit. One hot afternoon, my mother and I filled huge straw
baskets with blueberries growing in the midst of a Brandenburgian
pine forest and ate handfuls of them at a nearby picnic table, staining
our gums purple. Joanie and Dietrich and I went to Potsdam's strawberry

fields to get the sweet second crop, and came across long rows of raspberry bushes studded with velvety berries while we were there. The trunk of their car groaned with fruit on our way back home.

Picking the fruit was the languid part of summer. Out in the fields, there was never anything more pressing than the fruit trees to empty and the sun beating down on your back. Preserving the bounty was when things got busy. Back home, I had only a day or two to process all that was picked before it started to go soft and moldy. I made jars of puckery sour cherry jam and my kitchen looked like a butcher shop, every surface covered with dots of blood-red cherry juice. I cooked strawberries with thin slices of lemon until the berries and the lemons were suspended in ruby-red jam. I broke down fresh raspberries to put them in vinegar or mixed them with mint into a fragrant preserve.

One weekend in August, Max and I got in the car with his parents and drove to the very northernmost tip of Berlin, to a huge abandoned orchard just past where the Wall had once stood. Berlin is an enormous city, geographically speaking, and although we had driven nearly an hour away from our apartment, we were still within the city limits, though just barely. We parked the car along a tree-lined country road, grabbed our baskets, and waded through knee-high grass to get to the orchard, passing a small sign marking where the Wall had been. I cast a sideways glance at Sepp, Max's father, who had been imprisoned in the GDR for almost two years before he, his wife, Kerstin, and Max and his brother were allowed to leave East Germany in the late 1970s.

The orchard had long gone wild and was slightly overgrown. I wouldn't even have known in which direction to head if Sepp and Kerstin hadn't led the way. There were gnarled pear and apple trees, though the fruit on them were still small and hard, and as we progressed through the orchard, getting deeper and deeper into the silent copses, we found trees full of marble-sized yellow and red mirabelle plums and oblong dark purple plums covered in a silvery dust. We were almost entirely alone, save for a few Russians who tramped past us occasionally, holding long wooden ladders. This was apparently their unofficial foraging ground. We were careful to keep an eye out for the wild boars that had proliferated in recent years in and around Berlin.

Kerstin explained that the orchard had probably once been someone's personal property, but that the original owner must have been forced to relinquish it to the state during the Cold War and then, after the Wall fell, there was no one left to claim the land. It was similar to what happened to her family's plot of land in Meissen. In the GDR, her grandparents were forced to give the land on which their house was built over to the state. After they died, the state built public apartments on the land. When the Wall fell and Germany reunited, the property rights should have reverted back to Kerstin and her mother, but because there were apartment buildings on the land, that didn't happen. Kerstin and Sepp pooled their life savings to buy back the house she'd grown up in. A few weeks earlier, Max and I had visited Meissen and Kerstin showed me how far her grandparents' land had once stretched. But none of it was theirs anymore.

We started picking plums and worked for what seemed like hours, a faint wind cooling our necks as we filled our bags and baskets and bellies with the sweet-sour fruit. As we worked quietly, each of us at a different tree, doing our best to avoid the moldy or worm-bitten ones, I thought about how marvelous it was that in Berlin you could still find such natural abundance all around. The city still had a special, wild feel to it. There was something so innocent and untouched about an abandoned fruit orchard, open for the picking, just a few miles from the city center, making jelly from berries found on bushes in the park across the street, and finding wild plum trees in people's backyards.

At home later, I tried to pit the mirabelle plums before cooking them, but their bright yellow flesh clung stubbornly to the tiny, stonelike pits. So I cooked the fruit whole, in the hopes of straining the pulp later. But I didn't fare much better with my hand-cranked food mill and I was forced to leave the pits in the jam. I marked the jar labels with warnings and exclamation points and then I spread the remaining dregs of jam that didn't fit into the many jars I'd filled on a heel of bread and ate it standing up. It was agreeably tart, with a lovely sticky texture, and the color had mellowed to a warm amber. The tender skins almost dissolved under the pressure of my knife.

The prune plums were easier to deal with. I quartered them quickly, slipping out the pointy pits, and sugared them, leaving them to macerate overnight in a heavy pot. The next morning, the plums were swimming in their own juice. I pushed a cinnamon stick and a few cloves down into the fruit and put the pot in the oven to cook for hours, where the fruit bubbled and reduced into a thick, pastelike jam, fragrant with spice and a rich, almondy scent. *Pflaumenmus* filled sweet yeasted dumplings and jelly doughnuts across the country and I loved it too, for pouring into jam tarts or spreading on butter-spackled bread for breakfast. It had a surprisingly deep, earthy flavor.

Preserving is more than just putting up fruit before it spoils. It also preserves a moment in time. And when you've foraged the fruit yourself, I swear the jam tastes even sweeter. In the winter, months after our foray into the wild orchard, each jar of *Pflaumenmus* I opened reminded me of that hot, quiet day when Max and his family and I picked fruit together companionably. And each jar contained everything that I loved about this city in its rich, dark depths.

Pflaumenmus (Spiced Plum Butter)

MAKES 4 TO 5 JARS

If you've been scared of making your own jam, this is a great recipe to start with: you simply mix the pitted plums, sugar, and a few spices in a heavy pot and put it in the oven to cook for hours, stirring it only occasionally. Spread *Pflaumenmus* on your morning toast (it's especially delicious over a layer of cottage cheese) or fill doughnuts (page 166) with it.

4 pounds Italian prune plums
2 cups sugar
1 cinnamon stick
2 whole cloves

1. Pit and quarter the plums and put them in a heavy 4-quart pot. Add the sugar, the cinnamon stick, and the cloves. Stir well and let sit overnight or for 8 hours.

2. The next day, heat the oven to 350 degrees. Put the pot, unlidded, into the oven and cook for 2 hours, stirring the mixture occasionally.

3. Sterilize glass jars and lids in boiling water.

4. When the plums have broken down and the liquid has reduced to a thick jam, remove the pot from the oven and fish out the cinnamon stick (if you can find the cloves, fish them out too). Purée the jam with an immersion blender until it resembles a fruit butter, and then fill the sterilized jars with the hot purée, screw on the tops, and immediately turn the jars upside down. If you prefer a jam with discernible chunks of fruit, however, don't purée the jam; simply ladle the hot jam into the sterilized jars. (Technically, this is *Pflaumenmarmelade*; *Pflaumenmus* means the fruit has been puréed.)

5. Let the jars cool completely before turning them right side up again and labeling them. The jam will keep for at least a year.

34

Stunningly Complete

AUGUST IS A FUNNY MONTH IN BERLIN. IT'S NOT RELIABLY WARM; IN fact, it can often feel downright autumnal. But it's the last chance for people to take a little time off before school starts up again. The city empties as people head north to Scandinavia for camping trips or down to the mountains of southern Germany to hike among wildflowers and waving grasses. Some even go to the beaches of the Baltic and hope for warm weather to temper the steel-gray skies.

After the turbulence of the winter, when we were adjusting to life together, Max and I had settled into an easy rhythm. Our apartment smelled reliably of his detergent and my cooking. My *New Yorker* magazines shared space with his German newspapers on the coffee table I found on eBay. While the weather was still good, we went for morning runs together in the manicured park of the Schloss Charlottenburg across the street, our feet hitting the gravel in time as we passed flowerbeds and fountains and small clusters of tourists. I usually had to be coaxed to exercise, but our routine had me looking forward to our runs together.

For a little while that summer, Max was working from home, ensconced in his small office at the back of the apartment while I worked in the front. We took breaks at midday together, meeting in the kitchen for lunch. Then in the afternoon, when we'd had enough of work, we headed to the Lietzensee, a small lake near our apartment. We walked around the lake and stopped for a beer or an apple soda in the Biergarten next to the lake, the setting sun always soft and languid. Our neighborhood, with its mix of Turkish clans, older German ladies with tiny dogs, and families with small children, was feeling more and more like home. We had a favorite vegetable vendor at the farmers' market and the three Turkish men who ran a small snack bar around the corner from us, turning out delicious lamb-stuffed peppers and brick oven—fired spinach-and-feta *börek*, smiled with recognition each time we walked in the door for lunch.

Our days were, in a sense, unremarkable. But they felt special too. I loved how they stretched into one another, ordinary and lovely at the same time. The days of having Max home all the time were numbered—he would soon be starting a new job in another city and would have to commute home on weekends, which is perhaps partly why this time felt so luxurious even in its ordinariness.

August started off wet and rainy. But the day Muck and Jürgen invited us to dinner was a beautiful one, sunny and just barely humid. Max and I met friends in the afternoon in an outdoor café and shared a glass of buttermilk, a soft breeze in the air. After hours of strolling in the heat, the cold glass of sour buttermilk was just the thing we both craved to quench our thirst. The clean, pure flavor of the buttermilk and its thickness cooling my throat lingered with me long after we pushed back from the table, said goodbye, and walked home, sandals slapping gently against the sidewalk.

Muck had told us to bring dessert, so I sifted through my recipes and cookbooks in search of something to make, both relishing the task and feeling indecisive, as I always did, about which direction to go in. I could bake a cake, something rustic and simple, topped with fruit. But in Germany, cake was eaten mostly in the afternoon with a cup of coffee or tea. And although I used to bake cakes for dinner parties in New York, the idea of a slice of cake after dinner no longer appealed to me. A grainy crumb and a thin cap of frosting made more sense in the afternoon now—that was when a substantial snack was needed to bolster blood sugar and creativity. After dinner, especially on a warm summer's day, I wanted something lighter and more refreshing.

I thought about slicing peaches and slipping the wedges into wine, but the truth is that good peaches were not so easy to come by in Berlin. The softball-sized peaches we liked to buy at roadside stands in Italy when we visited my mother, who spent each summer there, were so good, bursting with juice under their velvety skin, that I rarely bothered to buy them anywhere else. I let them remain a seasonal treat at my mother's house, to be eaten over the sink or in the garden, neck stuck out at an angle so that the golden juice dripped down into the grass while the cats watched quizzically from a safe distance.

A pavlova sounded pretty good too: marshmallowy meringue topped with whipped cream and berries, of which there were plenty in the Berlin markets. In fact, I had jewel-like red currants and a basket of fragrant little strawberries in my kitchen already—every time I passed the currants, I couldn't help but pluck off a red berry here and there to pop into my mouth, its thin skin bursting and its sour juice flooding my mouth like candy.

But pavlova felt too fussy for this languid afternoon. I leaned back on the couch and closed my eyes, hearing the faint hum of traffic from the outdoors and thinking about our day. I remembered the buttermilk we'd shared, creamy and sour. It occurred to me that buttermilk and berries would make a perfect summer dessert. In my collection of clipped recipes from so long ago, I found the recipe I was looking for almost straightaway: buttermilk panna cotta.

The dessert consisted of not much more than buttermilk, heavy cream, and sugar, with a little gelatin for suspension and wiggle. To serve with the panna cotta, I decided to sugar the red berries, letting a syrupy, ruby-red juice form. Their sweet-sour pop would be a good contrast to the nursery-dessert quality of the panna cotta.

The panna cotta was simple to make, but when the time came to unmold the set cream from its ceramic mold, I struggled to loosen it from the sides. Max walked into the kitchen just as I was starting to lose my cool and ended up helping me, the two of us giggling at the panna cotta's luxuriant wobble as it settled onto its serving plate. Then I spooned the juicy berries and their syrup all around the panna cotta, almost obscuring the creamy mound. As Max drove us to Muck and

Jürgen's house on a leafy street in Zehlendorf, I held the serving plate gingerly in my lap as the fruit syrup slid back and forth precariously.

Out on their deck at dusk, we ate pink–fleshed lake trout poached gently in fennel broth, small boiled potatoes, waxy and sunflower-yellow and dusted with chopped parsley, and a little salad of soft greens studded with toasted sunflower seeds. There was a cold bottle of Riesling and a sharp and creamy horseradish sauce mixed with grated apple for a bit of sweetness to dollop on the fish, its flesh tender and barely warm. Later, when the sky had grown dark and we sat outside in candlelight, full of fish and potatoes and wine, everybody oohed and aahed as I spooned out trembling portions of panna cotta and sweet-sour berries into little dishes that Muck had brought out.

As we ate, the buttermilk cutting the richness of the cream and the sugared berries a sharp contrast to the soothing blandness of the panna cotta, we listened to the neighbor's children play in the garden next door. The table soon fell quiet and as our spoons scraped against the china and I saw the light draining from the sky, my world suddenly felt so stunningly complete, so full and rich and just as it should be, that I almost lost my breath.

Buttermilk Panna Cotta

SERVES 6

This panna cotta recipe is adapted from one in Claudia Fleming's landmark cookbook, *The Last Course*. It lightens a traditional panna cotta by using a mixture of buttermilk and heavy cream. I serve panna cotta with a mixture of sugared red berries, because I like the tart bite they add to the smooth, vanilla-speckled cream. But you could serve this with any fruit or, of course, plain.

2 teaspoons powdered gelatin
1¼ cups heavy cream
9 to 10 tablespoons sugar

½ vanilla bean, split and scraped, seeds reserved

1¾ cups buttermilk

1 pint strawberries, hulled and quartered

1 pint red currants, destemmed

Juice of ¼ lemon, or a few drops of balsamic vinegar

1. Put 1 tablespoon of cold water in a small bowl and sprinkle the gelatin evenly over the water. Set aside to dissolve for 5 minutes.

2. Put the cream, 7 tablespoons sugar, and the split and scraped vanilla bean (seeds included) in a heavy 2-quart pot and place over medium heat. Warm the cream until the sugar dissolves, whisking constantly.

3. Whisk in the buttermilk. Then add the gelatin, stirring for just a few moments to dissolve it. Pour the buttermilk mixture through a fine-mesh sieve into a measuring cup or jug with a spout.

4. Divide the buttermilk mixture among six ramekins or dessert dishes and refrigerate overnight.

5. An hour before serving, put the strawberries and red currants in a bowl and sprinkle with the remaining 2 to 3 tablespoons sugar. Add the lemon juice or balsamic vinegar and mix well to combine.

6. If you would like to unmold the panna cotta before serving them, dip the bottom of each ramekin in warm water for a minute or two, then turn them over and gently and carefully loosen the delicate cream onto serving plates. Serve the berries with the panna cotta.

Part 5

35

The Happiest Man in the World

I T HAD BEEN ALMOST A YEAR SINCE I LEFT NEW YORK, AND BERLIN FELT like it belonged to me again. Eleven months had passed since I arrived in that snowstorm, but when I thought back to January and February, they felt like a lifetime ago. It took me a lot longer than I expected to find my footing, but now that I had my little circle of friends and a routine, I woke up most mornings feeling that I was right where I should be. Sometimes I still had to check to make sure: I'd poke myself and think of New York to see what would happen. But nothing ever happened. There was no sickening twinge or tug at my heart. All I felt was calm. I was home.

The days grew shorter and the streets filled, once again, with children toting their huge square backpacks on their way to school. Dead leaves from the trees that line the majestic road leading to the palace clustered in the gutters and on the windshields of cars. We had to pull out the heavy comforter again. The salads and simple sandwiches of late summer gave way to long–cooked beans and beef stew. I spent hours in the kitchen roasting apples for applesauce or caramelizing onions for soup.

A week before I was scheduled to fly to Boston and New York to see my father, my friends, and my editor, Max left a little note on my desk asking me out to dinner the night before my flight. I figured it was just to squeeze in a romantic evening before we didn't see each other for two weeks. He wanted to take me to a restaurant called Renger–Patzsch, on one of my favorite streets in Berlin. Renger–Patzsch had big black–and–white photographs of quiet landscapes hanging on the wall, a long, gleaming wooden bar, and simple wood tables laid with cloth napkins. It had a little bit of old West Berlin glamour, which was so easily drowned out by the louder, brighter, shinier Mitte these days. "Yes, yes!" I shouted with glee when Max came home later, waving his note at him. I'd always wanted to go in to drink a glass of wine there and eat squares of *Flammkuchen*, their specialty, a thin crispy Alsatian flatbread topped with onion slivers, bits of smoked bacon, and crème fraîche.

But the evening of our dinner reservation was a busy one. Teri was visiting us from New York for business and wanted to meet for a drink after dinner, I had to pick up a cell phone from a friend before I left to use in New York, and Joanie had a few things she needed me to deliver to her sister in Boston. There were a dozen other small errands to run, as there always were the day before a transcontinental flight, and I was a ball of tense nerves, as I so often was when I traveled. We rushed from appointment to appointment and even had Joanie meet us with her packages at the restaurant, where we talked for a little while until our table was ready. Then, just as we were seated, Max realized that our waiter, Victor, was an old acquaintance from high school. They spent ten minutes catching up before Victor excused himself to get back to work.

We ordered glasses of sparkling wine, and when our *Flammkuchen* was ready it came to the table on great wooden boards, cut into squares. The *Flammkuchen* was singed delicately in spots and was crisp and savory, the perfect thing to eat with the flinty Alsatian wine. As we ate and talked, I realized that Max was dressed very nicely, in black slacks and a black cashmere sweater. It was a sharp contrast to the jeans and sweatshirts he usually wore. *Huh,* I thought. I could barely remember if I had even brushed my hair before leaving the house that morning. The wine was just starting to help me relax.

Victor stopped by every so often to check in during our meal, and then a loud, happy family collapsed at the table next to ours and Max and I ended up spending the rest of the meal eavesdropping happily on the people around us. Sometimes I caught him smiling at me. *I'll never tire of that*, I thought.

When we got home, Teri was waiting for us with a drink and the three of us talked in the living room while I packed my things. Teri and I were flying back to the United States together in the morning. After midnight, our eyelids heavy, we said goodnight and headed to bed, alarm clocks set. It wasn't until we were under the covers, teeth brushed, face washed, and reading, that Max turned to me and cleared his throat, once, twice, before I finally realized he was trying to catch my attention. Then it slowly dawned on me that he might have been trying to get my attention all night.

"Yes?" I put down my book and smiled at him. "Well, um . . . ," He smiled apologetically. "It was kind of a busy evening . . ." "I know! Can you believe that Victor was our waiter? We have to go back there soon. I loved it. Thank you again for dinner." I leaned over to kiss him. He obliged, then drew his head back and looked at me. "Do you know what date it was today?" I thought for a moment and then said, "October twelfth?" "Yeah. October twelfth. Well, I don't know if you remember, but October twelfth was when we first met in Paris, that night at Le Breguet. Remember?" Of course I remembered; in fact, *he* had asked *me* what day we'd first met just a few weeks earlier. "That was eleven years ago." He smiled at me again, then turned on his back. "So much has happened since then." He dug in the covers and pulled out a tiny envelope, handing it to me. "I wanted to ask you earlier at dinner, but it was so busy . . ." His voice trailed off.

I opened the envelope and pulled out two small pieces of paper that he had filled with a love letter. When I got to to the end, I flipped over the second piece of paper and saw that on the back he had written this one sentence: "Will you make me the happiest man in the world?" I looked up at him and he was beaming at me expectantly, so happy and gleeful that I couldn't help but beam back. Then I started to laugh and he started to laugh and between our laughter and the little pieces of paper in the deep bedcovers, I realized that he was asking me to marry him and so I said yes.

Of course I said yes.

Flammkuchen (Alsatian Flatbread with Bacon and Crème Fraîche)

SERVES 2

The key to delicious *Flammkuchen* (also known *as tarte flambée*) is getting the dough as thin as possible—you want the finished *Flammkuchen* to fairly crackle when you cut it into pieces. When you're rolling out the dough, make it as thin as you possibly can without breaking it, and then work quickly when transferring it to the baking sheet. If you can find lean Speck (German smoked bacon), then by all means use it. Otherwise, relatively lean slab bacon works fine too. Serve the *Flammkuchen* with a cold Riesling.

> 3 cups all-purpose flour, plus more for kneading
> 1 teaspoon instant yeast
> 2 tablespoons olive oil, plus more for the bowl
> 2 teaspoons salt
> 1 scant cup lukewarm water
> 14 tablespoons crème fraîche
> 2 medium red or yellow onions, very thinly sliced
> 7 ounces Speck or lean bacon, cut into ¼-inch batons
> Freshly ground black pepper

1. Put the flour, yeast, olive oil, and salt in a food processor and pulse a few times. Then, with the motor running, add the water. The dough should come together in a matter of seconds.

2. Lightly flour your work surface, and then dump the dough out onto it. Knead the dough a few times until it's smooth and supple. Form it into a ball and place it in a bowl that you've oiled with a drop or two of olive oil. Cover with a dishtowel and set aside for 1 hour.

3. Heat the oven as high as it goes. Divide the dough in half and set aside one piece. Roll the other piece out on the floured counter until it's very, very thin, resting every so often to give the dough a chance to relax. Line a baking sheet with parchment paper.

4. Transfer the nearly translucent rolled-out dough carefully to the baking sheet, pulling the edges of the dough all the way to the sides of the sheet so that the dough is even. Spread the dough thinly with half the crème fraîche, leaving a ¼-inch border. Then distribute half the onion slices and half the Speck or bacon batons evenly over the *Flammkuchen*.

5. Slide the baking sheet into the oven and bake the *Flammkuchen* for 10 minutes, until it's crisp and browned. Remove the sheet from the oven, sprinkle liberally with freshly ground black pepper, cut into squares, and serve immediately. Repeat with the remaining dough and toppings.

36

Thanksgiving in Berlin

NEITHER OF MY PARENTS HAS EVER BEEN BIG ON TRADITION. THEY think traditions are a little stuffy, weirdly repetitive, and too much work. It's something they'd far prefer to leave to other people. Which means, of course, that I have spent most of my life craving traditions of my own. My parents think it's totally bourgeois, but I like doing the same thing over and over again, year after year. It fills me with a deep-seated sense of safety and coziness, for lack of a better word, to have Thanksgiving on the horizon like an anchor, knowing that the stuffing will always taste of sage and leeks, that the tines of the forks will always gleam just so in the candlelight, that there will always be leftover pie for breakfast the next day. It makes me feel settled and secure, when the reality of my life has often been different.

For a long time, it felt like I was waiting for the right time to start getting serious about traditions. I wasn't settled yet, wasn't in the right place to let down my hair and get comfortable with choosing the things that would make a holiday or a celebration my own. But now that Max and I were going to be a family, it seemed like a good time to apply myself. Especially with Thanksgiving around the corner.

When I lived in New York, most years I'd head up to Boston to celebrate Thanksgiving at my father and Susan's house. Thanksgiving in Boston was as close to a regular tradition in my family as I'd ever gotten. I suspected my stepmother had a lot to do with it. We'd spend two days in the kitchen together: I was in charge of making the pies, my father acted as prep cook and errand boy, peeling onions, whittling mountains of Brussels sprouts, running out to the store just one last time, and Susan presided over the turkey, gravy, and stuffing, her delicate fingers knuckle-deep in some cold crevice, tossing cubes of bread, or fiddling with the turkey neck. Each year, Susan made the same stuffing, with celery and sage and chestnuts, worried about the turkey being ready in time, and was happy to manage the kitchen in such a way that all of us felt like we were integral to the fate of the meal coming together.

One year, a banner year, there were twenty-four of us, including friends, colleagues, and my father's and Susan's international graduate students. Tables snaked through the house to accommodate everyone, small children and teenagers and young adults and senior citizens and *really* senior citizens. Someone brought fresh crab claws to gnaw on before the meal. Susan got everyone to say grace. The turkey was enormous. The wine was good. And I made three different pies, apple-quince, pumpkin-gingersnap, and almond-cranberry. It was thrilling.

For our first Thanksgiving together in Berlin, Max and I were invited to celebrate at Kim's house with my mother and other close family friends. My father decided to fly in from Boston for the weekend to join us and celebrate our engagement too, while Susan stayed behind to go to her sister's, whom she hadn't seen in a while, instead.

It became clear rather quickly after my father's arrival that he was not having an easy time of things lately. The summer before my move back to Berlin, my father had gone to a conference in Berlin. "It's so cool here," he said to me over the phone. "I think you're doing the right thing. If I were your age, I would move to Berlin in a heartbeat!" I was so cheered by his good spirits that I didn't say anything about the fact that this was exactly what he had done.

Now that I was here here, though, and the reality that I wasn't going to return to New York was setting in, he wasn't so sure he liked it. He loved Max and he was happy that we were getting married. But he also felt abandoned by me and inexplicably unloved, which made me feel guilty and defensive and a little jumpy. The day before Thanksgiving, we got into a fight on the sidewalk near my apartment. It was awful.

I could see my father's pain lurking right behind his eyes, but I didn't know how to help him. And I wasn't sure I was supposed to.

The next morning my father sat at my kitchen table peeling apples while I made pie dough. I wanted to make a rustic apple tart with a sugar-spangled crust to bring to Kim's that afternoon, and my favorite pumpkin pie, faintly peppery and smooth. My father and I worked on the pie in an uneasy, unspoken truce. The kitchen felt so small and too quiet. Susan was missing, as was the general spirit of Thanksgiving.

As I processed chunks of cold butter and flour together into a waxy lump of pie dough, I realized how angry I was. I was angry at my father for his jumble of emotions and I was angry at both of my parents for having created this situation in the first place—the two of them so far apart that I'd always be forced to leave one behind. How could we still be some kind of a family when we were separated by an ocean? I was tired of doing all the hard work. I wanted to be grateful for everything good in my life—for Max, our love, and our new life together—but right now I just couldn't. So much for new traditions.

That evening at Kim's house, my father sat two seats down from me in miserable silence, resentful of the fact that my mother took the seat next to me. Max's steadying hand was on my knee, but I felt very small and very sad and very young all the same. I hoped the happy chatter from the rest of the table hid at least some of our unhappiness.

In lieu of turkey, Kim roasted wild boar and there were big rosy slices of it alongside sweet braised Jerusalem artichokes doused in gravy so good I would have liked to tip it directly into my mouth. There were delicious Brussels sprouts and a little dish of cranberry sauce that got passed around the table. But the cord of tension running beneath the table like an electrical current between my father and me distracted me from any real enjoyment of the feast. When Kim's sons jumped around us with glee—they adored Max—it was all I could do to keep myself from going upstairs and hiding in their bedroom until the evening was over.

After dinner, Joanie and I put my pies on the table while Kim made coffee and his wife, Susanne, brewed herbal tea with lemon verbena from my mother's garden in Italy. I liked eating the pumpkin pie, its silky texture and sweet autumnal flavor a little zipline back to Boston and happier times. But the apple tart was the real crowd-pleaser. The pastry was flaky as can be—it practically crackled under the knife—and the apples that my father had cut into perfectly even slices earlier that day were tender, their flavor concentrated from the hot oven. The tart vanished in a few minutes as talk turned to our engagement and the wedding we needed to plan.

Later that evening, when Max and I were home again, he told me to give my father some time. "Don't rush him," he said. "He feels like he's lost you again and it must be bringing back some painful memories. Are you where you want to be?" I nodded. "There's nowhere else I can be, really," I said. And I meant it, from the bottom of my heart. "Well, then, just focus on that and give him time to adjust. You're his baby and you always will be. I mean, if I had a daughter and she lived so far away . . ." Max shook his head.

I lay in our dark bedroom thinking of my father in the guest room and the apple tart we made together that was gobbled up so quickly. At next year's Thanksgiving, I thought, Max and I would be married. I curled up on my side, warming my feet on Max's thigh as he breathed evenly, and I started to think about what our Thanksgiving next year would look like.

I saw my mother's dining table pulled out to its full length, laid with our white china and my great-grandmother's silver. I saw shredded Brussels sprouts studded with mustard seeds, jewel-like cranberry chutney, Joanie's chestnut-prune stew, boiled green beans, velvety gravy, and, of course, Susan's stuffing. I saw our living room filled with Max and his family, my parents, our Berlin friends, all the people I call family. Somehow, the table fit everyone. It just kept stretching and stretching. Everyone was happy, crackers spread with fish pâté in one hand and something dry and sparkling in the other. My father was laughing, the little wrinkles around his eyes crinkling up, and Susan was next to him, and none of the murky sadness that so plagued us this evening was anywhere to be found. There were children underfoot. There were pies cooling on the windowsill and my mother couldn't believe I'd made all of them. There was, of course, a turkey at the center of the table, a big, glowing, burnished turkey. And when I looked up to survey all the people crammed into our home, I saw Max across the room, his eyes twinkling and his crooked smile buoying me.

Apple Tart

MAKES ONE 10- TO 12-INCH FREE-FORM TART

This tart is about the pure, clear taste of apples, sugar, and a little bit of butter. There are no spices to muddle the flavors; here, the apples truly shine. I owe this recipe to four different people: To Jacques Pépin for coming up with it in the first place. To Alice Waters for keeping it on the menu at Chez Panisse for twenty years. To Deb Perelman for writing about it on her blog, Smitten Kitchen. And to Melissa Clark, whose tips in a *New York Times* pie crust video about leaving the butter chunks lima bean–sized instead of pea-sized helped me make the flakiest handmade tart pastry of all time.

Dough

1 cup all-purpose flour, plus more for dusting
½ teaspoon sugar
⅛ teaspoon salt
6 tablespoons (3 ounces) unsalted butter, cold, cut into 1-inch pieces

Filling

2 pounds Golden Delicious apples, peeled, cored, and sliced (do not discard the peels and cores)
2 tablespoons unsalted butter, melted
3 to 5 tablespoons sugar, depending on your sweet tooth

Glaze

½ cup sugar

1. Put the flour, sugar, and salt in the bowl of a food processor. Add the butter. Pulse the food processor a few times, only until the butter is broken

down into lima bean–sized pieces, no smaller. (If you don't have a food processor, use two butter knives to cut the butter into the flour mixture in a large bowl.)

2. Drizzle in up to 3½ tablespoons of cold water, 1 tablespoon at a time, processing or stirring after each addition, until the dough just holds together. You might need a little more or less water depending on the weather where you are.

3. Dump the dough out onto a lightly floured work surface, and working quickly, gather it together and flatten it into a 4-inch-wide disk. Wrap the disk in plastic wrap and refrigerate it for at least 30 minutes and up to 3 days.

4. When you're ready to bake, heat the oven to 400 degrees and prepare a lightly floured work surface. Then remove the dough from the fridge. Unwrap the dough and begin to roll it out with a pin, turning it over and over repeatedly so that it doesn't stick to the counter as it gets thinner. Flour as needed. When the dough is a 14-inch round and about ⅛-inch thick, dust the excess flour from the dough with a brush.

5. Place the dough on a parchment-lined baking sheet. Place the apple slices in overlapping circles on the dough, leaving a 2-inch border. Crowd as many apple slices as you possibly can onto the dough; they will cook down in the oven. Fold the edges of the dough over the apples to create a rustic crust, leaving the center of the tart uncovered.

6. Brush the melted butter over the apples and onto the crust of the tart. Sprinkle the sugar over the crust and the apples.

7. Slide the baking sheet onto the center rack of the oven and bake for about 45 minutes, rotating halfway through, until the apples are soft, with browned edges, and the crust has turned a dark golden brown.

8. In the meantime, for the glaze, put the reserved peels and cores in a saucepan along with the sugar. Pour in just enough water to cover, and bring to a boil; then cook for 30 minutes. Strain the liquid, discard the apple trimmings, and return the liquid to the pan and bring it to a low boil. Reduce it until thickened and syrupy, another 10 to 15 minutes.

9. When the tart is finished, pull the parchment paper and the tart from the sheet onto a cooling rack. Let cool for about 15 minutes, and then brush the apple glaze over the apples. Serve warm or at room temperature.

37

Something of an Epiphany

M Y FATHER'S IDEA OF CELEBRATING CHRISTMAS IS LETTING SUSAN string lights on the big rubber plant in their kitchen for a few days. I guess you can't really blame him: he's Jewish, after all. But my mother isn't much better. Oh, she'll gladly celebrate Christmas, but to buy, let alone decorate, a tree or roast a bird or deal with any of the organizational hoopla is definitely beyond her ken. So I grew up celebrating Christmas at other people's houses. To be specific, I grew up celebrating Christmas at Christa's.

Christa and her husband, Rainer, lived across the landing from my mother's apartment on Bamberger Strasse with their daughter, Julia, who was exactly one year and five days younger than me. I can still remember the first time I saw Julia, peering out at me from behind Christa's legs as our mothers stood in the doorways of their apartments chatting. We soon became fast friends, two only children with similar sensibilities, and we would try to convince strangers at the playground that we were sisters, despite the fact that no two children ever looked more dissimilar. While I was a swarthy, dark-haired little girl, Julia was a pale sprite of a child with translucent skin and white-blond hair.

There were sleepovers and dinner swaps (liverwurst on dark bread at their place; spaghetti with tomato sauce at ours) and a general open-door policy. One year, Christa even put a little settee out on the landing because we liked to stand in our doorways and chat so much that she thought we needed a place to sit down.

In those early years, when Rainer and Christa were still married, we didn't yet celebrate Christmas together. But later, when Christa and Julia lived alone in the apartment and I had moved back from Boston to live with my mother again, it just made sense. Christa would buy a big pine tree and her twin brother, who lived two floors below us, helped her schlep it home. They would decorate it secretly on December 23 and then keep the door to the living room firmly closed against our prying little eyes, desperate for a glimpse of the glittering tree and the mountain of presents beneath it.

The next day, at 6:00 P.M. on Christmas Eve, my mother and I would present ourselves at the front door, dressed in our very finest, and wait in the foyer with Julia, squirming impatiently, for Christa to ring the little brass bell that signaled permission to open and enter the land of *Weihnachten*, all spangled and candlelit and warm and smelling of pine needles, with the clear-as-glass voices of the Vienna Boys Choir piercing through the night.

There is no better place in the world to celebrate Christmas than in Germany. No country I know takes it more seriously. And no other place on Earth is still able to infuse the holiday with such a sense of solemn tradition and beauty. *Weihnachten* in Deutschland still retains a sense of the sacred and the divine.

Maybe it starts with the run-up to Christmas, the four Advent Sundays beforehand filled with endless afternoon teas with friends, crunching through all manner of homemade Christmas cookies or moist Stollen or dense fruit bread. Perhaps it's because tradition here dictates that the Christmas tree not be decorated until the day before Christmas Eve, drawing out the thrill until the very last moment. Maybe it's the brass bands at Christmas markets or the Christmas markets themselves, all lit up and smelling of warm *Glühwein* and sausages. Or perhaps it's the candlelight. In Germany, people still put candles, *lit* candles, with actual flames, on their trees instead of electric lights. (A bucket of water for emergency dousing lurks behind every tree.)

But my bet is that it's actually because of the holiday food: crisp roast goose, rich and tasty, a pile of sweet-and-sour braised red cabbage spiked with tender pieces of apples or a bright spoonful of red currant jam, and boiled potatoes bathed in a glorious ladleful of gravy so good you could eat it with a spoon from the pot.

Most Berliners eat something simple on Christmas Eve, like potato salad with steamed hot dogs, saving the big roast for the midday meal on Christmas Day. That's sensible and ascetic and so perfectly in character, really. But we weren't like other Berliners, as you've gathered by now, and because Christa, who comes from Hamburg, grew up eating roast goose on Christmas Eve, that's what we did too.

The first thing to do is to find a goose. In Berlin, it's not too hard. If I'm feeling flush, I like to order one at Bachhuber, an old-time, white-tiled butcher shop in Wilmersdorf hung with hams and salamis. The butcher gets his geese from a farm in Brandenburg that slaughters the birds all the way up to the day before Christmas, emptying the field entirely. The geese are free range and well fed and plump, roasting up into crisp-skinned and golden-brown specimens you would feel proud to display on your Christmas table.

Now, they are not cheap, these birds. They run about sixteen euros a kilo, which means that an average bird that will feed six people (goose meat is far richer than turkey; a slice or two goes a long way) can cost you around eighty euros. That is close to one hundred and five dollars by today's exchange rate. One hundred and five U.S. dollars for a goose! I had to sit down and fan myself the first time I heard this piece of information from the very kind butcher's assistant on the phone. I could hear the bustling Wilmersdorf clientele clamoring in the background as I gathered my wits about me. And then I set about ordering one. After all, it was Christmas. When else would you buy an eighty-euro bird? By the way, that intrepid, can-do spirit is integral to achieving a merry German Christmas.

The second thing to do is to find a roasting pan big enough for your goose. A five-kilo (that's eleven pounds) goose is not a small animal. Luckily for me, I'd come into the possession of a very large roasting pan complete with a rack courtesy of my generous aunt Laura several years earlier. I'd had the good sense (debatable, some would say) to include the roasting pan in the forty boxes of prized possessions I had shipped across the Atlantic. Now it was gathering dust in the basement because it barely fit in our narrow European oven. In fact, I'd almost forgotten about the roasting pan. Almost, until I found my-self perplexedly staring at the massive plucked bird lying defenseless and naked on my stovetop.

Eight and a half flights of stairs later and only slightly out of breath, I was back in the kitchen with the roasting pan. By some stroke of luck, the goose not only fit in the pan (well, the wing knuckles didn't quite, but I figured my Drusilla of a bird could handle it), but the goose-filled pan actually fit into the oven, even if the fit was so tight that the heart-warming sound of metal scraping against metal filled the air. I was triumphant. We were in business. Christmas in Germany was within reach.

I'll be straight with you about this endeavor. Roasting a goose is not for the weak or for the faint of heart. It requires a cool head and well-developed biceps. If you know these things going into it, I think you'll have yourself a pretty good time. And in any case, armed with these tips, you'll know more than I did the first time. So consider yourselves lucky.

Geese are generally well-fed birds. They sport a generous—even enormous, some would say—amount of fat in comparison to their other feathered friends. So if you tried to roast a goose the way you might roast a turkey or a chicken, say, you'd end up with a grease-logged *thing*, for lack of a better word, that wouldn't make for very good eating or celebrating at all.

To get around this situation, you have to start by first cooking your goose in broth, letting most of the bird's fat leach right out of it. You can do this in the selfsame pan you will roast the bird in, just for conve-nience's sake (unless you're the kind of person who has a pot, or a caul-dron, large enough to accommodate a goose covered in broth). The broth you cook the goose in is flavored with beer and onions and bay leaves and a mysterious-sounding German herb called *Beifuss*, which is known in English as mugwort, conjuring up all sorts of Harry Potterian fantasies, and is, in Germany, grown with the sole purpose of being eaten with goose (I suppose you could use thyme instead). The seasoned beer broth not only flavors the goose but later produces a thick layer of pure white fat at the top, tasting wondrously of savory meat and onions and herbs. This stuff is almost worth the price of the bird (almost) and should be saved by you (packed into glass jars and refrigerated) for roasting potatoes throughout the year.

Once you've cooked your goose and most of that fat has leached out, you have to let the goose rest overnight. I covered my pan with aluminum foil and set it out on the balcony, seeing as my adorable European fridge was just big enough for a pot of yogurt and some jam, but certainly not a five-kilo bird and its hulking metal pan. If you happen to live in warmer climes like, say, southern California or the entire continental United States, I'm going to go out on a limb and assume you also have a fridge large enough to accommodate a goose.

The next day, Christmas Eve or Christmas Day, as the case may be, your goose will be ready for the roasting. These are not leisurely times. There are children to lock out of the living room; there are the final presents to be wrapped, not to mention the preparation of the braised red cabbage and boiled potatoes that are tantamount to the meal. (Here's a tip: Make the braised cabbage a day or two before the meal— no one will know the difference. Some people even say it tastes better with age.)

Do not think for a moment that you can attempt to do things on your own. You must have an assistant, a loving fiancé or someone similar, to help you. Otherwise, you might find yourself swearing that Christmas comes but once in a lifetime by the end of it all. Have that someone else set the table. Corral the kids. Warm up the cabbage. Peel and boil the potatoes. Light the candles. And if you still find yourself, in a fit of desperation, downing a glass or two of wine in the middle of the afternoon just to steady your frayed nerves, know that you are not alone.

Besides, at this point, the rest of the process of roasting the goose is relatively easy. You put the cooked bird, drained of most of its fat and stuffed with a few peeled onions, an apple, and more mugwort, on its rack in the roasting pan. You put the pan in the oven and baste the bird regularly with a bit of wine. You reserve the liver to fry up for yourself as afternoon snack, because you are the cook and you deserve the treat. You drink another glass or three of wine. You continue to baste. And then, before you know it, you will find a burnished goose in your very oven, fragrant and tender beneath a crackling layer of skin.

While all of this was happening, by some minor miracle you will also have managed to wash yourself and change out of your oily kitchen clothes into your slinky Christmas attire. (Yes, slinky! You don't want to be eating this meal in cords and a fleece jacket, trust me.) Your trusty assistant will have set the dinner table with your best china and the good linen napkins. He will have opened the door for all the guests, hung up their coats in the foyer, and ushered them to their seats, wine in hand. Your house will smell like it can smell only at Christmastime: of candle wax and fragrant pine, of roasting goose meat and the sweet, earthy fug of potatoes.

You will have a few minutes in the kitchen to contemplate the fact that you pulled it all together. Your gravy is smooth and pourable, your goose is toothsome and perfectly cooked, and the brittle skin is a guilty pleasure for all. The cabbage offers just the amount of acidity to cut the richness of the meal and the boiled potatoes provide a much-needed sponge for soaking up all the creamy gravy and sweet-sour cabbage juices from your dinner plate.

And then you will sit at the table with your family, or your tribe, either way your beloveds, and within minutes you will see the meal that took you two days to make disappear, just as you had hoped. It's quite something. And instead of feeling peeved or resentful, you will feel nothing but the deep-seated pleasure that comes from continuing a tradition cobbled together by two friends and their daughters over the years in Berlin.

German food takes a beating in the world these days. It's easy to make fun of Wurst-eating Krauts and to think that Germany's great contribution to the culinary world stops at the lowly sausage. But I would wager that even the most determined naysayers have never tucked into quite so grand and delicious a Christmas meal as this. For it, all by itself, is something of an epiphany.

Roast Goose

SERVES 6

> 1 10-pound goose
> 1 large onion, halved
> 2 stalks celery
> 2 large carrots
> 2 large sprigs flat-leaf parsley
> 1 leek, halved and well rinsed
> 2 big cloves garlic
> ½ organic lemon
> 1 bay leaf
> 10 black peppercorns
> 1 large bunch mugwort (or thyme)
> 2 bottles dark beer
> Salt and freshly ground black pepper
> 1 apple, quartered (your favorite!)
> 2 small yellow onions, quartered
> 1 cup good-quality red wine
> 3 tablespoons (1½ ounces) unsalted butter
> 3 tablespoons all-purpose flour
> ¼ to ½ cup heavy cream (optional)

1. Remove the giblets and the neck from the cavity of the goose, and wash and dry the bird. Place it, breast side up, in a roasting pan that is large enough to hold the bird and the vegetables. Add the onion halves, celery, carrots, parsley, leek, garlic, lemon, bay leaf, peppercorns, and half the mugwort to the pan. Then pour in the beer and enough water to fill the pan halfway. Tightly cover the pan with aluminum foil and set it on the

stove over high heat. When the broth has come to a boil, lower the heat and let it simmer for 1½ hours.

2. Remove the bird from the roasting pan and put it on a large platter to cool overnight in the fridge. Remove all the solids from the broth and let the broth cool overnight in the fridge.

3. The next day, a thick layer of white fat will have formed on the surface of the broth. This can and should be removed and saved for the red cabbage (recipe below) and for roasting potatoes. (Packed in a glass jar and refrigerated, the fat will keep for at least a few months.) Pour the jellied broth into a pot and reserve it for the gravy.

4. Remove the bird from the fridge a few hours before roasting.

5. Wash and dry the roasting pan. Heat the oven to 390 degrees. Cut off the wing tips of the goose, and salt and pepper the bird on both sides and in the cavity. Stuff the cavity of the goose with the remaining mugwort and the quartered apple and onions. Place the stuffed, salted goose, breast side down, in the roasting pan and put it in the oven.

6. After 20 minutes, pour a little of the red wine over the bird. After another 20 minutes, turn the goose breast side up and pour more wine over it. Continue basting with the red wine every 20 minutes until the goose is crisp-skinned and a rich brown, roasting it for a total of 1½ to 2 hours. If the bird seems to be getting too dark before it's done cooking, tent some aluminum foil over it.

7. While the bird roasts, make the gravy: Heat the jellied goose broth. Melt the butter in a saucepan, and add the flour and a pinch of salt, stirring for a few minutes to let the flour cook. Then add small ladlefuls of the hot goose broth to the pan, whisking constantly, until you have a smooth, silky gravy. Keep warm until serving time. To enrich the gravy further, just before serving you can add heavy cream to taste, whisking carefully to incorporate.

8. When the goose has finished roasting, remove it from the oven and carefully transfer the bird to a cutting board. Let it rest for 10 minutes before carving and plating on a serving dish. Pass the gravy with the roasted goose, and serve with braised red cabbage (recipe below) and boiled peeled potatoes.

Braised Red Cabbage

SERVES 6 AS A SIDE DISH

> 1 medium head red cabbage (about 2½ pounds)
> 3 tablespoons reserved goose fat (see recipe above)
> 1 large yellow onion, diced
> 1 apple, peeled and cored and chopped
> ½ cup dry red wine
> ¼ cup apple cider vinegar
> 3 tablespoons brown sugar
> 1 bay leaf
> 3 whole cloves
> Salt and freshly ground black pepper
> 1 tablespoon red currant preserves

1. Cut the cabbage in half and cut out the inner core. Cut the halves into quarters and slice thinly. Set aside.

2. Put the goose fat in a large heavy pot and set it over medium heat. Add the diced onion and cook until translucent but not browned, about 8 minutes. Add the cabbage in two batches, stirring each time so that the cabbage wilts a bit.

3. Add the apple, wine, cider vinegar, brown sugar, bay leaf, cloves, 1 teaspoon salt, and black pepper to taste, and mix well. Reduce the heat to low, cover, and braise for 1 hour, stirring occasionally, until the cabbage is fork-tender. Stir in the preserves.

4. Remove the bay leaf and cloves (if you can find them) before serving. Taste for salt. The cabbage can be served right away or cooled and refrigerated for up to 2 days (it improves with age). Reheat before serving.

38

Full of Rewards

J UST AFTER NEW YEAR'S, MAX AND I THREW A DINNER PARTY IN WHICH everything felt wrong. Not in the way you'd think: our guests ate everything I cooked (two chickens, made using a complicated Palestinian recipe from a trendy cookbook, several pounds of Brussels sprouts, an entire chestnut-flour cake, a whole liter of whipped cream, and six poached quince), and there were no leftovers. But—has this ever happened to you?—when I sat down to eat dinner with our guests I looked down at my plate and thought, "I don't want to eat any of this." (Well, except the quince. Those were pretty great.)

It wasn't that the food didn't *taste* good. It's just that it all felt so strained, my relationship with what I'd cooked, I mean. I'd expended a lot of time and energy on figuring out the menu, planning the dinner, sourcing the ingredients, and cooking the food, and then, once my plate was in front of me, it all just felt so foreign, so far away from what I actually wanted to eat. My throat closed right up. It was an unexpectedly upsetting moment—to be surrounded by nine people kindly devouring all that was laid before them and to feel so estranged from their experience.

As I thought about the dinner the next day, I couldn't help but draw parallels from that dinner party to my life. I'd spent a lot of time and energy in New York putting together a life that, from the outside,

267

looked lovely. Many people would have liked that life and would have been happy to gobble it up. In fact, a few of my friends never understood just how wrong things felt in the end, just how out of place and strange and mistaken it was for me to be there in the long run. They couldn't understand why I would give all that up to chase something intangible and, yes, more than a little risky.

Now, I love dinner parties. I love planning for them, getting the apartment ready, choosing a menu, and watching people settle down at the dining table, unfurling the linen napkins my mother gave me on their laps. I spend days poring over cookbooks and magazines and recipe clippings, putting together a menu that makes sense, finding something special, maybe even a little unusual, to cook. I love feeding people; I love the easy conversations that ensue in the comfort of someone's home, away from the bustle and formality of a restaurant. If I could, I'd throw a dinner party every weekend. (All I'm missing is a cleaning staff.)

After that fateful meal, however, I decided that I needed to approach my dinner parties differently. Clearly the old model was broken. I had to turn away the complicated cookbooks and highfalutin ambitions and just think about the core of the matter. I needed to think about what *I* wanted to eat, first and foremost, when I had guests over. That's really all it was about. It was as simple and as complicated as that.

What do I want to eat? That question reminded me of the more complicated ones I used to think about when I lay awake sleepless in New York. And after the dinner party that made me lose my appetite, I decided that, actually, Max and I ate pretty darn well when we were home alone. Why did I have to change that winning formula just because we had people coming over? In fact, wouldn't that be just the moment to stick with the greatest hits that made us happy, dinner guests or no dinner guests? I already knew that Max trusted my taste; he was always happy with what I cooked. And as the cook, you are entitled to be selfish. It's part of the reward for all the hard work you do before a dinner party and afterward too. You are allowed to do what you want, to do what makes you happy. The challenge is learning to believe that in other aspects of your life too.

I wanted tried-and-true dishes that I could make without breaking a sweat, things that would satisfy and feed our guests but that would still make me feel true to myself. That was the crux of it all, really. To find a menu, to find a life, that would be *mine*. That would feel genuine and true. Rather simple, really. But it took me over thirty years to figure it out.

To test out this new method of dinner party cooking, I threw my mother a dinner party for her birthday. We invited several of her closest friends and I put together a menu of things I'd woken up craving just that morning: panade, salad, and those fantastic poached quince. That was it.

I'd discovered *panade* a few years earlier, a sort of savory baked casserole from the southwest region of France, made by layering pieces of really good and chewy peasant bread with sautéed greens, long-cooked onions, Gruyère cheese, and chicken stock. I'd made *panade* many times before just for Max and me, relishing the preparatory shopping trips to gather peasant bread and nutty Gruyère, dark bunches of Swiss chard, and papery-skinned yellow onions, and I fell in love with it a bit more each time I made it. It was the perfect winter meal—meatless yet still full of richness and flavor, shot through with dark greens to shape the mind and a little cheese to comfort the soul. Simple yet celebratory.

The salad was made up of soft butter lettuce and mâche with cubed avocados and slices of juicy oranges, bound together with a shallot vinaigrette. We had a few good bottles of red wine to pass around and then, for dessert, those same poached quince from the dinner party disaster, topped with a spoonful of thick Greek yogurt and a shower of toasted chopped hazelnuts.

The dinner was a huge success. People took seconds, thirds, licked their plates, and—thrillingly—I joined in. My mother, a tough critic, was still raving about the meal days later. It was just the thing to make this hostess who, in truth, really does love throwing dinner parties, feel like a million dollars again.

It was all so *easy*, if you know what I mean. Like I was cooking for just the two of us, safe and secure in the knowledge that I could be trusted to make the right decisions for me and Max, picking the right meal, and the right life. And while it's true that everything tasted good, that part was almost incidental. What really had me glowing was the fact that I'd listened to my instincts and that that had been enough. It turns out that following your heart in the kitchen is the same as in real life: full of rewards.

Swiss Chard and Gruyère *Panade*

SERVES 6

Panade is sort of a cross between a gratin and a bread pudding, but only sort of. Chewy cubes of bread, sautéed chard, long-cooked onions, and savory shreds of Gruyère cheese are layered carefully and then baked very slowly in the oven until the *panade* is plush and satiny, almost wobbling, the top crusted perfectly. It's peasant food for the gods. The recipe takes some time, but I promise it's all worth it. This recipe comes from Judy Rodgers's *Zuni Cafe Cookbook* and is absolutely perfect as is, though I keep meaning to slip a few thin slices of butternut squash into the baking dish to see what happens. One request: Please take the time to make your own chicken stock for this dish. Canned broth simply will not give you the same sublime result.

½ cup olive oil
1½ pounds yellow onions, thinly sliced
6 sprigs thyme, stripped
6 cloves garlic, thinly sliced
Salt
1 pound Swiss chard, leaves sliced 1-inch wide
10 ounces day-old chewy peasant-style bread, cut into 1-inch cubes
4 cups chicken stock
6 ounces Gruyère cheese, coarsely grated

1. Put half the oil in a heavy 4-quart pot, add the onions, and mix. Over medium-high heat, cook for about 3 minutes, until the bottom slices are starting to turn color; then add the thyme leaves and mix again. Cook for another 3 minutes, and then add the garlic and ¼ teaspoon salt. Mix well and cook, stirring occasionally, for another 20 minutes. The onions should be a pale golden brown and tender, but not mushy. If, during the cooking, the onions look as if they are drying out, lower the heat a bit and cover the pot to trap some of the moisture. Taste for seasoning and add more salt if needed.

2. Heat the oven to 325 degrees.

3. Derib the chard; wash the leaves and cut into 1-inch-thick slices. Place the still-wet chard in a large skillet with a drizzle of olive oil and a large pinch of salt. Set the pan over medium heat and cook until the water begins to steam. Then reduce the heat and stir the chard until it has just wilted, 3 to 4 minutes. You may have to do this in batches. Taste for salt and set aside.

4. Toss the cubed bread with a few tablespoons of olive oil, a generous ¼ cup of the stock, and a few pinches of salt, or to taste.

5. Set out an ovenproof baking dish or enameled cast-iron Dutch oven. Assemble the *panade* in layers, starting with a layer of onions, followed by a handful of bread cubes, a second layer of onions, a layer of chard, and a handful of cheese. Repeat until the dish is brimming. Aim for two to three layers of each component, and then make sure the top layer displays a little of everything. Drizzle with any remaining olive oil.

6. Bring the remaining stock to a simmer and taste for salt. Pour the hot stock slowly around the edge of the dish until it's about ½ inch below the top layer of ingredients. Wait a minute for the stock to be absorbed, then add more if needed to get to the desired depth. The *panade* may rise a little as the bread swells.

7. Cover the baking dish or pot with aluminum foil and put it in the oven. Bake until the *panade* is piping hot and bubbly. The *panade* will rise a little, lifting the foil with it. The top should be pale golden in the center and slightly darker on the edges. This usually takes about 1½ hours, but varies according to the shape and material of the baking dish and oven.

8. At this point, uncover the *panade*, raise the temperature to 375 degrees, and bake until golden brown on top, 10 to 20 minutes. Slide a knife down the side of the dish and check the consistency. Beneath the crust, it should be very satiny and it should ooze liquid as you press against it with the blade of the knife. If it seems dry, add a few tablespoons of hot stock and bake for 10 minutes longer. Serve immediately.

Slow-Baked Quince

SERVES 8

This recipe is adapted from one in Paula Wolfert's brilliant cookbook *The Slow Mediterranean Kitchen*. After 5 hours in the oven, the slow-baked quince have the consistency of sliceable fudge and a magically fragrant taste (they also do a wonderful job of perfuming your house). Be careful when peeling, halving, and coring the quince—they are very hard and sometimes a knife can slip and nick you. Serve the quince, warm or chilled, with yogurt for breakfast or, paired with whipped cream, alongside a rustic autumnal cake.

6 small quince
¾ cup sugar
2 whole cloves, or ½ cinnamon stick
Juice of 1 lemon

1. Preheat the oven to 250 degrees.
2. Peel, halve, and core the quince. Reserve all the peel and trimmings. Combine the sugar, cloves or chinnamon, and lemon juice, with ⅔ cup of water in a shallow flameproof baking dish set over low heat. Stir to dissolve the sugar. Put the quince halves in the syrup in one layer and cover with the reserved trimmings (this will keep the quince from drying out).
3. Cover with aluminum foil and bake in the oven for 5 hours. The quince will be soft and will have changed color—either a deep rusty red or

a pale pink, depending on the provenance of your quince. Discard the trimmings and transfer the quince to a container with a lid.

4. Pour the cooking liquid through a fine-mesh sieve over the quince (there won't be much liquid, but if it seems too much, reduce it before pouring it over the fruit). Serve right away or store in the fridge for up to a week (let the quince cool completely before refrigerating).

39

The Perfect Place

M Y MOTHER TAUGHT ME TO LOVE FIGS FOURTEEN YEARS AGO. SHE was living in Rome at the time, after her boyfriend, Florian, broke her heart and she'd had to move for Italy for work. I'd flown to visit her during my first summer break from college. She was staying at her cousin Paolo's apartment until she could find her own place. There was a narrow balcony that stretched along the length of the entire apartment, which had cool marble floors and a tiny kitchen. A jeroboam of Veuve Clicquot Champagne stood in the living room. I wondered what Paolo was saving it for.

After dinner one evening, my mother and I sat in the kitchen at the small table built for two—it was dark outside—and slowly ate our way through a big plate of peeled green figs that she'd bought at the market earlier that day. It was very hot out and my mother's heart was raw and I was terribly confused, because I loved Florian too. I'll never forget how the cool flesh felt in my mouth, the surprise of those hundreds of crisp little seeds, the impossible depth of each fig's sweetness. My mother was back in her hometown and I was far away from mine and we were both sad, for the same and such different reasons.

I didn't eat figs again for a long time after that. The figs for sale in grocery stores in Boston and New York never tasted as good as they did in Italy anyway. But one summer, the last one that he was alive, I decided to visit my grandfather in Italy just around Labor Day, much later

274

in the summer than I'd ever been to see him, and I found ripe purple figs hanging heavily on the two sprawling trees in front of his house. My mother and I stood under the trees, picking and eating the sweet, swollen fruit for hours, my grandfather watching us from the shade of the house. Whatever we didn't eat, peeled and speared after dinner, we turned into jam studded with lemon peel or bits of ginger.

Five months later, he was gone, three days before his ninety-ninth birthday. After his death, when I returned to Italy to visit my mother, now the main caretaker of his house, I missed seeing my grandfather and his gnarled knuckles, his dirty T-shirts, and his toothy smile as he sat on his bench in the shade. My grandparents had bought the house when it was not much more than a ruin and my grandfather had spent years of his retirement fixing it up, putting it back together again. But my grandmother died only a year after they moved to the village of Torre from Rome. My grandfather had had to live out the rest of his life, nearly another quarter of a century, alone in Torre, save for our annual visits.

As the years passed since his death, the house became wholly my mother's. She planted a sour cherry tree in the garden, along with raspberry bushes and a lettuce patch. Each November she harvested the olives from the gnarled trees my grandfather planted so long ago, hauling them to the local mill to be pressed and storing her olive oil in a large metal canister in the basement. And whenever I visited the house at the right time in late summer, I could stand below the two fig trees that stretched over the lawn and the cliff on the other side and eat fig after fig while looking out into the valley below, a drop of milky sap on my wrist.

I never wanted to have a big white wedding. My girlhood fantasies mostly revolved around pinafores and bonnets and the fervent wish to time travel back to the pioneering times of Laura Ingalls Wilder, so that I could learn how to make green tomato pie by Ma Ingalls's side. I had never liked being the center of any room's attention and I was a little embarrassed at the prospect of saying our very private vows in front of so many people. The thought of all those *faces* watching me as I walked down the aisle scared me. As much as I'd enjoyed going to other people's weddings over the years, they mostly seemed like an awful lot of work and not the kind of work I'd enjoy, either. But mostly I was just shy.

"Shouldn't we just go to Vegas?" I asked Max every so often after we got engaged. "Just the two of us? We'll rent a motorcycle! And drive to Los Angeles afterward for our honeymoon!" I loved Los Angeles—its piercing bright sun, its masses of pink flowers, its gritty corners and Chinese palaces. I wanted to take Max there, walk down the huge Santa Monica beach with him, and watch him fall in love too, so that we could both dream of living there one day. Even Max's father, who at nearly sixty still regularly rode his Ducati on the autobahn, thought Vegas and a honeymoon by motorcycle was a great idea.

"We can do that if you really want," Max would say. "But think about it. This is our one chance in life to gather everyone we love in one place. Your girls from New York. Our families. My friends. Joanie and Dietrich. Everyone. I don't think we'll regret it. And there's nothing to be afraid of—I'll be there, right by your side, the whole time."

He had a point. Maybe, I thought, if we could figure out a way to have a wedding on our terms, it wouldn't be the exhausting, nerve-wracking experience I always figured it would be. Maybe it could even be fun. And when we thought about it, there really was no better place for a wedding than my mother's house in Italy.

We both loved being there; Max felt just as home there as I did. Torre was in a spectacularly beautiful and relatively unknown part of Italy, nestled amid rolling hills near the Adriatic coast and fully off the beaten path. When I was young, my mother and I would fly to Milan, then board a train for Pesaro, which wobbled through the picturesque countryside for hours. In Pesaro, my grandfather would pick us up in his car and drive back home, along flat beachside roads and then slowly up into the hills beset with wildflowers, white butterflies, and sheep. In Torre, his house was set up away from the road and it was always a surprise, when we made that final turn, to see it above us, framed by a blue sky and fluttering acacia leaves.

That was the only drawback of the place, really: our guests wouldn't have an easy time getting there. But if they could make it, it would be spectacular. There was a flat piece of lawn on one side of the house where we could set up benches for people to sit on while Max and I said our vows in front of the two sprawling fig trees. And behind the house, on a promontory overlooking our neighbors' fields and the surrounding hills, was a clearing just the right size for a tent and a dance floor. The panoramic view of the Montefeltro hills all around the property was stunning.

My mother was ready for the challenge of hosting the wedding in her backyard. "It'll be fun!" she crowed over the phone when Max finally won me over in January. The wedding date was set for the end of June, five months away. "Antonio and I will get to work right away." Antonio was her friend and neighbor, who helped her out regularly in the garden, cutting trees and building fences to keep the deer away from her painstakingly tended garden. The clearing where we fantasized about putting a tent and dance floor had been a fire pit for the past twenty years. They would need to fill the gaping hole with sod, plant grass, and then hope for an even result. And while the house my grandfather had built up from ruins and the property my mother so carefully tended to were beautiful, they were not ready for a hundred guests coming in from all corners of the globe. My mother and Antonio would have their hands full.

While my mother and Antonio dug and planted and watered and waited, Max and I put together our idea of an ideal, relaxed wedding— a garden party, really—back in Berlin. We decided to borrow picnic benches from the local men's club to set up near the fig trees. Instead of a priest or minister, we'd ask our two close friends, Dave and Tilman, dressed in black suits for the occasion, to speak from the heart and marry us. We planned for a cocktail hour by the front door with Champagne that my uncle Pietro said he could buy wholesale from his friends in France and little paper cones filled with fritto misto and prosciutto–stuffed rounds of flaky savory pastry. And after the cocktail hour, we would get everyone to walk past the little wooden tool-shed that my grandfather built when he was a relatively spry eighty-year-old, through a small copse of pine trees, down to the rented clear plastic tent that looked like a greenhouse set on the edge of the property, looking over the valley and the surrounding hills. If the weather cooperated, we might even catch a glimpse of the sea on the horizon. We'd have dinner and we'd dance and that would be that. We'd be married.

When it came to wedding dress shopping, I realized quickly that a long white wedding gown wasn't going to be quite right for me. I tried on a few, but felt intensely awkward in the fitting rooms when I gazed at myself in the mirror. It was like I was playing dress-up with someone else's clothes. I couldn't wait to tear the dresses off again. Then on a stroll on the KuDamm one day, I saw a shiny mannequin in the Yves Saint Laurent storefront across the street wearing a pretty white frock. I stood for a while outside in the cold looking at the dress—strapless, knee-length, with a full skirt—before getting up the nerve to go inside.

When I slipped on the dress, made of thick, stiff linen, and did up the back zipper, I felt instantly at ease. The dress, hardly a wedding gown, was completely unadorned save for two little ruffles placed at pocket height, and it was exactly what I felt like wearing. It took me a while to buy it; after all, I'd never so much as looked at an Yves Saint Laurent store before that day. But nothing else came close to that dress. And when you know, you know.

Next, Max and I had to figure out our menu. Fourteen years earlier, my cousin Valeria was also married in Torre, at the house my aunt and uncle owned on the other side of the hill. Valeria and Jack's wedding had been fantastic, with dancing late into the night and lots of laughter and happiness. But the thing I remembered best from that night was the risotto with big pink shrimp that we were served for dinner, spooned out family style by kindly waiters. *Wouldn't it be so easy if that caterer was still in business?* I thought one day. I soon found out that he was. Before long, Signor Perugini and I were exchanging daily e-mails.

Max and I wanted to serve a rustic Italian meal, with local dishes like tagliatelle sauced with *ragù* and simple grilled fish and long-cooked vegetables. Food in the Marche was uncomplicated and delicious and I thought that serving the simple meals I'd spent my summers eating would fit the slightly haphazard homemade wedding we were planning.

For Signor Perugini, however, this was tantamount to sacrilege. After all, these were peasant dishes we were talking about—meals that farmers ate on Sunday afternoons and certainly not the kind of thing a lady would serve at her wedding. My mother and I tried to reason with him, promising him that the Italians at the wedding wouldn't be appalled and that the foreigners would be delighted with whatever we put in front of them. But Signor Perugini was to not be budged.

He turned his nose up at our requests for roast rabbit and rosemary potatoes, for tagliatelle and plain green salads. He wanted tiny lamb chops with white frilled collars and whole langoustines, simply grilled. He wanted fish-stuffed *margherite* and beef-cheek-filled *mezzalune*. The e-mails batted politely back and forth for weeks, until Signor Perugini did the unthinkable. He told us we should serve sushi.

After sputtering in outrage at the computer for some time, I sat down to compose one last e-mail to Signor Perugini. I had an idea about what might work. Max, arms crossed, stood behind me. "Most honorable Signor Perugini," I typed. "Thank you for your latest suggestion, which is indeed most elegant and special. However, after much discussion with my fiancé, I must deliver the information that he has had his heart set on rustic Italian food since he first started envisioning this wedding. My mother and I, of course, understand the lengths to which you have gone to conjure up a most spectacular and delicious meal for our joyous occasion. But my future husband's desire is one I cannot bear to deny. I hope you understand my predicament. With my most affectionate greetings, Luisa Weiss." I turned around to Max, who smiled down at me. "Italian men are such machos. Want to bet this does the trick? Let's go have dinner."

The next morning, I had an e-mailed response from Signor Perugini in my inbox, as apologetic as anything. "But of course, Signora. I understand completely," it began. Attached was a revised menu that contained everything we'd been requesting all along. With no sushi in sight.

Fig Jam

MAKES APPROXIMATELY 5 JARS

The truth is that if you are lucky enough to come into a few figs, they are best eaten raw, out of hand, your teeth crunching down on a hundred tiny seeds. Nothing can improve on nature, especially not when we're talking about figs. But if you happen to have a source for an abundance of fresh figs, you'll find that they often ripen so quickly that you simply can't eat fast enough to keep up. That's where preserving comes in. Fig jam can often tend to the too-sweet side of things, which is why the addition of a bit of lemon juice or zest is crucial.

> 1½ pounds fresh purple or green figs
> 2 cups sugar
> Juice of ½ lemon and/or grated peel of ½ lemon
> Pinch of ground cinnamon

1. Clean the figs with a damp cloth, but don't peel them. Cut them into quarters and put them in a heavy 4-quart pot. Add the sugar and the lemon juice or peel (or both) and mix well. Cover and let sit overnight, or for at least 4 hours.

2. Put the pot over very low heat, uncovered, and bring to the gentlest simmer. Cook for 2 hours, swirling the contents of the pot every once in a while (stir only once or twice). By the end, you want the sugar to be almost caramelized.

3. In the meantime, sterilize the jam jars and lids.

4. When the jam has finished cooking, take it off the heat and stir in the ground cinnamon. Then ladle the boiling-hot jam into the jars, screw on the lids, and turn the jars upside down to cool completely.

5. Turn the jars right side up and label them. The jam will keep for a year.

40

All of Me

I FLEW DOWN TO ITALY TWO WEEKS BEFORE OUR WEDDING. THERE WERE last-minute things to figure out, like the flower arrangements for the tables, whether I was going to get my hair done by Milly, the village hairdresser, or whether I'd just do it myself, and exactly which gelato flavors we wanted Claudia, the *gelataia* from the neighboring town, to pack into her little rolling wagon and serve for dessert.

My mother and her friend Antonio had spent months working on her garden and the large expanse of grass where we wanted to set up the tent for the reception. After the last bonfire in the pit, when there was nothing but a big scorched circle of soot and blackened earth left, Antonio came day after day to rake it and shovel fresh earth onto the pile. He sowed grass seed and then watered it daily, coaxing tender green shoots from the ground. By the time June rolled around, the promontory was lush and verdant. It almost seemed a pity to plop the tent on top of all that hard work.

When I arrived in Italy in mid-June, my mother and father were waiting for me. For five days, until Max's family arrived from Berlin and my stepmother flew in from Boston, it would just be my mother, my father, and me. Max wouldn't arrive until two days before the wedding because he had to work. Having both of my parents to myself was a rare treat. We spent a few days running errands together, seeing our old friends in town, getting on each other nerves, and making zucchini flower frittata for lunch.

I was having a little case of dress regret. I'd bought the white Yves Saint Laurent dress six months earlier and then forgotten about it. Now, seeing it hang in my bedroom, I was a little unsure. Should I have bought a long dress? One with sleeves? Or with lots of lace? Should I have, in other words, made a bigger deal about my wedding dress? "You'll look beautiful no matter what," my father said, getting misty-eyed at the lunch table. "Don't be ridiculous! The dress is beautiful," scoffed my mother as she pitted cherries for jam at the worktable, bright red juice spraying everywhere. Luckily, there wasn't much I could do at this point. Torre didn't have much in the way of wedding boutiques. Besides, I had the very distinct impression that this was my equivalent of cold feet. My parents wanted to move on to more important things.

My father: "I still cannot believe you aren't having any music."

Me: ". . ."

My father: "Really? Are you really telling me you're not going to have any music?"

Me: "Nope, no music. None."

My father: "I'm pretty sure that's the worst idea ever. Are you sure you won't change your mind? Can I call Max?"

But I held my ground. Max and I had long ago decided to eschew music for walking down the wedding aisle. Much like we didn't want a first dance or a wedding program or a cake or even a religious officiant. We wanted the wedding to be plain and simple. And I wanted to hear nothing more than the wind in the acacias that towered over the house. While my father was happy to go along with most of our idiosyncrasies, the no-music thing bugged him to no end.

Those were busy days. Each morning started with lists and errands run along the winding country roads that snaked through the country-side like veins. But there were also moments I wanted to hold tight. My father listening to a Beniamino Gigli recording from the 1920s on the tinny little orange radio in the kitchen as I stood at the counter and sliced zucchini for dinner, the setting sun streaming in through the screen door and illuminating the wall behind him. The three of us standing at the counter of the florist's shop that was filled with fake flowers, looking at each other helplessly as the kind florist filled a pot-bellied vase with white rubber pebbles that were meant to resemble stones and then plugged in a handful of acid-yellow chrysanthemums. Huffing and puffing up the steep hill in Urbino to get to the Saturday market in time to buy vegetables for lunch and then heading to the *vinoteca*, where we tasted the local red and white wines we wanted to serve at the wedding that was now just a few days away.

The weeks leading up to the wedding felt like the first three quarters of a relay race, each step solidifying the team, bringing them closer, allowing them to perfect the baton handoff. I relished just being together, the three of us, even if we were such a motley little unit, hearts bared, tempers high, so full of nervous excitement. I cooked simply for my parents in those days: spaghetti, frittata, and salads from the heads of milky lettuce that I picked in the garden. One afternoon, my father and I waded into the raspberry patch and picked berries in silence for an hour, filling the bowl. We ate them for dessert with our fingers. The figs wouldn't be ripe for another few months.

Then, slowly, our table started filling up. First came Susan, who flew in from Boston, radiating calm in the midst of three rather anxious individuals. After we told her about the acid-yellow mums at the florist, Susan told me she'd take care of the flowers for the wedding. There was plenty of material in the fields around the house and along the roads. Wildflowers sounded much better to me than mums, and my mother dug out her great-aunt's crystal glasses for Susan to use as vases. One day at lunch, my mother cooked a simple two-pot stew of dried chickpeas and pasta, shot through with shreds of tomato, spiky rosemary, and chile for the four of us. My mother, unused to cooking for more than just two, miscalculated how much she needed to prepare and we finished lunch still hungry. She beamed as we scraped our plates and told her how delicious it was.

When Max's family arrived from Berlin, we boiled big piles of tagliatelle and heated up trays of lasagne that our neighbors had made for us. Max's mother promised to help me make the place cards and table seating chart, which I'd left to the very last minute, and before long she and Max's grandmother were sewing fresh lavender from the garden to little sachets filled with Jordan almonds, Italian wedding favors that my mother insisted we pass out. When my mother's companion, Maurizio, arrived from Bari, he brought plastic boxes filled with freshly braided mozzarella, cool and milky, for us to eat with potato focaccia and salad. And then I started getting impatient for Max to arrive. All these special little moments were slipping by without him there to see them. I wanted to squeeze his hand when I came across his grandmother resting in the shade after lunch, or when I saw his brother head up to the fruit trees, basket in hand, to pick fruit for dessert.

After Laura and Pietro and their family arrived, they took over the kitchen, and we gladly let them. They bought piles of bitter greens, which they painstakingly trimmed and cleaned before boiling them or sautéeing them in garlic and olive oil, and dressed boiled potatoes with my cousin's boyfriend's artisanal balsamic vinegar, thick as molasses. My father cooked then too, venturing into the kitchen to make a zucchini–potato gratin studded with shredded olives and baked in milk. It didn't look like much, but everyone clamored for seconds and asked him for the recipe. He sheepishly admitted it came from a brochure in the Conad grocery store down the road.

Those busy, crowded dinners we had outside at dusk were some of the loveliest moments of the run–up to the wedding. As more and more people arrived, we kept adding chairs and plates to the long wooden table out on the stone patio behind the house. While my mother and father and I had still been alone, tiny lizards would dart along the stone wall from time to time, before being chased away by one of the cats. But as the table filled up, all the animals kept away and the air filled with a jumble of languages—German, Italian, French, and English. And finally Max was there too. When Betsy and her husband and their baby daughter arrived, they put Isla's Moses basket in the hammock near the dinner table and she slept as we ate and talked.

Night after night, I watched our dinner table swell: Max and my in–laws at one end; my girlfriends from New York, who'd come early to help with the preparation, in the middle; my Italian family at the other end; and all my parents next to each other in the corner. And as I saw all of them eating together, passing big plates of pasta to each other, laughingly trying to make themselves understood in different languages, I thought: This *is everything. This is enough. I don't need a wedding. Just having all these people here together now is enough for me.*

When you have one parent in one country and one in another, when you are the one who travels back and forth, you learn to split your life very carefully. You have your German life and your American life, your Berlin friends and your New York friends. With a few exceptions, there's very little overlap. I was the one who bounced between all these factions the easiest, slipping in and out of languages and their lives. It was a little lonely, to feel that the people dearest and closest to me didn't have a complete picture of me. But I'd learned long ago that this was how it always would be. It was all I'd ever really known. The fact that now everyone from all these different parts of my life was in one place, right in front of my eyes, was almost more than I could handle.

Max had figured out right away, all those years ago in Paris, that there was more to me than what I was showing him. I had been very good at the careful compartmentalizing dance I did to manage my life. It was how I existed, how I made things work. When Max fell in love with me, he understood that unless he pushed for it he would only ever get one part of me. But I wasn't ready to be pushed and so he knocked me clean off my ledge. It took me almost a decade to figure out that he deserved to see every part of me: the Italian, the American, the Berliner with the divided heart, the strong career woman, the writer, and the goofball. Max made me realize that I didn't need to hide any part of myself anymore. Doing so would only be letting him play with half a deck of cards. He wanted all of me. He was ready for it. All I had to do was open up and let him in. The rest would follow. The rest had already followed.

So it was with this sense of total peace that I watched our dinner table fill up, saw all the people who populated all the parts of my life come together, knowing that Max had made it possible by convincing me to have the wedding. He'd motivated me to gamble my life in New

York for a new one in Berlin. He'd showered me with gratitude for taking the huge step and had been patient with me all the way, as I sobbed with loneliness, missed my girlfriends, resented the harshness of the Berlin winter. He had let me fantasize about moving back to the United States when I got homesick for New York, promising we'd always be together, and he hadn't smirked, not even once, when I told him I never wanted to leave Berlin again. Max knew, he understood, that to keep me, he would have to let me feel that I was free to go.

Feeling myself fill up with gratitude and happiness and a sense of completeness, I thought that that would be the best thing about the wedding. Until, of course, the wedding itself.

Pasta e Ceci with Rosemary and Chile

SERVES 4

This is a spicier, sunnier take on the classic Italian *pasta e fagioli*. Don't be tempted to substitute canned chickpeas in this recipe—dried ones have a slightly more delicate texture and flavor that comes across beautifully here. As for the hit of spicy heat, I like to use tiny dried Italian *peperoncini* (Calabrian are best), but you could use crumbled *chiles de arbòl* too.

    1½ cups dried chickpeas
    1 bushy sprig fresh rosemary, stripped
    1¼ teaspoons salt, plus more to taste
    3 plum tomatoes
    2 tablespoons olive oil, plus more for drizzling
    1 plump clove garlic
    2 small dried Italian chiles
    4¼ ounces dried *pennette* or *maccheroncini*

1. Soak the chickpeas in cold water to cover for a minimum of 8 hours or overnight.

2. Drain the chickpeas and place them in a 3- or 4-quart pot with the stripped rosemary leaves and fresh water to cover by 1 inch. Bring to a boil, then reduce to a simmer. Cook the chickpeas, covered, for 1½ hours or until they are tender. During the last 10 minutes of cooking, season the chickpeas with 1 teaspoon of the salt.

3. When the chickpeas are tender, move the pot off the heat. Using a slotted spoon, take out 1 cup of chickpeas and set aside. Then, using an immersion blender, purée the remaining chickpeas in their broth until smooth. Set aside.

4. Core the tomatoes and sliver them lengthwise. (You may, if you like, peel the tomatoes before coring and slicing them, but I never do.)

5. Pour the olive oil into a small pan over medium heat and add the garlic. Cook for a few minutes, letting the garlic color only slightly. Add the chiles, the slivered plum tomatoes, and ¼ teaspoon salt, and cook for 10 minutes, stirring occasionally, until the tomatoes have broken down. Discard the garlic.

6. Scrape the cooked tomatoes into the pot with the puréed chickpeas. Add the reserved cup of whole cooked chickpeas and mix well.

7. Bring a pot of salted water to a boil and cook the pasta until al dente. Drain the pasta and add it to the chickpeas. Stir well to combine. Taste for salt and adjust the seasoning. Serve immediately, drizzled with a little additional olive oil if you like.

41

The Luckiest Girl

T HE NIGHT BEFORE THE WEDDING, IT RAINED, AN HONEST-TO-GOODNESS thunderstorm. Max and I had put in earplugs before going to bed because sometimes the wind around the house could be relentless at night and we wanted to be well rested on the day of the wedding. So we didn't hear a thing. But the next morning the sudden rain was all anyone wanted to talk about. "Can you believe it?" my aunt crowed at breakfast. "You're so lucky it's over!" And, in fact, it was a beautiful day, sharp and clear and just warm enough without being hot.

I spent the morning in the basement with Max's mother, making big flowers out of green and pink and white tissue paper to decorate the garden and the gate. She carefully lettered the place cards and seating charts by hand. My stepmother took my girlfriends out to the surrounding fields to gather flowers and then sat out behind the house with great buckets of wildflowers and the cut-crystal water glasses and a pile of pebbles from the driveway, making the table arrangements, her head cocked carefully to one side as she contemplated her work.

It was hard to stay focused on the morning's many tasks with so many of my dearest friends within spitting distance. At midday, Max went to spend time with his parents while I drove to the pensione where Betsy, Jenny, and Teri were staying and found them setting up lunch with provisions bought that morning in town. It was a fancy little picnic: wedges of melon, silky slices of prosciutto, spicy little olives, fat tomatoes, good olive oil. We ate with our legs in the pensione's pool beside the owner's olive grove as their husbands splashed in the deep end, until I realized with a scream that the wedding was scheduled to start in three hours and I hadn't even showered yet.

Back at the house, I discovered my mother running around frantically and clutching the telephone. There was an unexpected problem with the septic tank. It was backed up and because it was a Saturday afternoon she couldn't find a plumber to come and fix the problem. We couldn't shower or flush the toilet until someone came to figure things out. So I sat out on the front stoop with my cousin Valeria and her kids and waited while my mother called every person she knew who might be able to fix a clogged septic tank. Soon Bruno, our neighbor from down the road, came to the rescue.

When the water was running again, we all took showers, my aunt and her family upstairs, Max and my mother and Maurizio and I downstairs. I loved bustling around in the full house, watching Signor Perugini's team in the distance from our bedroom window, looking down at the benches assembled just so in front of the fig trees. In the distance, we could see our friends, Dave and Tilman, conferring over white pieces of paper. We'd given them a little directive about what kinds of vows we wanted to say, but we'd never rehearsed anything. I was so excited to hear what they'd have us say.

Max and I got ready in our bedroom together, with the photographer peeking in now and then to take a shot of us as we got dressed. I didn't care that Max and I would see each other before the wedding; he was the only one who made me feel calm now. "Are you nervous?" I asked him as he did up his tie. "Because I'm a little nervous." Max smiled. "Nah, not really. We're already married, remember?" We'd had a brief civil ceremony in Berlin a few weeks earlier. "Just think of this as a party."

"Totally. You're so right! It's just a party." But my palms were sweating.

When I was dressed, I tried my best to make a smooth chignon, just as I had in Berlin, practicing in the bathroom mirror until I got it just right. But today I would have no such luck and had to stick my hair in a bun instead. With Valeria's ten-year-old son's careful supervision, I put on my own makeup and my girlfriends pinned chiffon flowers in my hair. Max wore a dark blue suit and Susan made him a little boutonnière out of lavender from the bush by the front door and a white roselike flower plucked from a bouquet the neighbors had sent over earlier that day. We ripped up a bunch of roses from my mother's garden to fill a basket for our flower girl, Emma, who had been training for the past week to walk very slowly as she strewed petals carefully all along the aisle.

Suddenly, it was time. I hadn't even really noticed people arriving, but when we looked out of our window, the benches by the fig trees were filled with our family and friends. Max kissed me goodbye and left to find his spot under the fig trees with Dave and Tilman standing behind him. My father came in to get me and Emma walked out ahead of us, head held high, little hands dropping the flower petals like a princess. *It's just a party, it's just a party*, I said to myself as we walked out the front door, down the steps, and around the corner to where our guests were assembled. *Stay calm, you're already married. Remember?* But I felt like I was trembling inside.

My father had worried so much about the lack of music as we made our way down the aisle that he had tried, once again, to change my mind that morning. But I couldn't get over the feeling that piping classical music through a boom box balanced on the living room windowsill would feel artificial. With all the natural beauty around us, and the sound of the wind in the acacias above us and the rustle of grass as we walked through it, I didn't need any music at all.

But as we approached the makeshift aisle and I could see Max beaming at me, his hands clasped in front of him (he was a little nervous, after all), our guests, *all* of them, starting humming the "Wedding March," getting louder and louder as my father and I passed each row. It was the funniest, most beautiful sound, so strong and pure and perfect that I thought it might reach all the way to where I hoped my grandparents, all of them, were watching. I wanted to laugh and cry and hug everyone around us all at once, but instead I just grabbed onto my father's arm and I squeezed as hard as I could.

A few weeks earlier, after our civil wedding that had been so easy and quick, just six minutes long including the officiant's jokes, the official signatures, and our kiss, there had been no music and no tears. It was as I had hoped: a quick, lovely thing that made Max and me man and wife under the law. After that, we had schnitzel and white asparagus and beer for lunch in a simple Berlin restaurant. And after that, I secretly questioned the wisdom of having a second ceremony.

But now that we were here with everyone around us—all the people who had been with us along the way as we grew into the people we were now—beaming with love and happiness and not a few tears, the crowd standing and cheering and hollering, waving kerchiefs and clapping—I finally understood why people have wedding ceremonies. Why it's so important to mark the occasion with proper vows and with people bearing witness to your innermost love and promises. As Max and I stood up by the fig trees, trying not to cry, and were told by Dave and Tilman to turn around and look at all the people who'd come from so far, from Berlin and New York and Jakarta and Los Angeles and Seattle and San Francisco and Brussels, I realized finally that this was no nameless, faceless mass to be afraid of. These were *our people*, our families, my many mothers, my sisters, my tribe. They had all come here, to this faraway, hard-to-get-to place for us, to bear witness to our love, to cry with us, to sing for us. They were there because they loved us and it was as profound a realization as I've ever had in my life.

Understanding that I was truly loved, not just by Max but by all the people who had raised me and accompanied me along the way, was a watershed moment. That all these people would be there, long after the party ended, caring for us, being a part of our lives, listening to our struggles, rejoicing in our joy, was the most important message of that day, of my life. Not only were Max and I deeply blessed to have found each other a second time, to be given the rare chance to start anew, we had the gift of all those loving people in our lives too.

The one thing we hadn't done at our civil ceremony in Berlin was exchange rings. We had wanted to save them for Italy. Dave and Tilman had the simple gold bands tucked away in their jacket pockets and pulled them out after we turned back to each other to say our vows.

Max's eyes were filled with tears and it was so very hard to keep my chin from wobbling as I listened to him repeat his vows after Dave. Our love story had been so impossible to imagine just a year earlier, and before that, my own happiness had felt so completely out of reach. And now here we were. It was so wonderful, I didn't know what to do. So I simply followed suit, let Dave guide me in my vows, did my very best not to sob, and married the love of my life. When we kissed and hugged after that, our guests stood and cheered. If I could have bottled the sound, I would have done so on the spot.

And then it was time to celebrate with the Champagne that Pietro had driven down from a vineyard in France and little kraft paper cones filled with the crisp seafood that had been fried in a huge kettle of oil set behind the house. The little ones ran around as everyone ate and drank and the garden filled up. Later my father's beautiful, funny speech, timed perfectly to end with the setting sun. The sun was low in the sky and Max's arms were around me when I looked out over the crowd and saw all the people who had helped raise me, who had opened their families to me, along with my friends from New York and Max's family, and sitting at a table together, my mother in her new lavender silk dress, my father in his good blue suit, and my stepmother, Susan, in a gold shift, hugging each other. My family. My families. We danced, music echoing into the valley below, until the sun came up and two local *carabinieri* were summoned because of the noise, but very quickly dispatched once they realized it was just a wedding ("A wedding! We had no idea! *Auguri! Auguri! Scusate!*") and not an illegal outdoor disco. The last stragglers staggered home as the birds awoke.

After it was all over, after everyone stopped by the house to say goodbye the next day—my father and Susan heading to Rome with his brother's family, my friends flying home to New York, my new in-laws driving to Berlin, and even Max leaving to go back to work—the house grew very quiet. It was just my mother and me again. I took a hundred photos of the sun casting its special evening light over everything, the way I did every time I came to Italy. I snapped the cats dozing on the stacked firewood, the lone horse drinking from a creek in the distance, the terra-cotta tiles of our neighbor's house, the shed my grandfather built, the fig trees. Then I walked down to the promontory where the empty tent still stood and looked out over the hills.

It felt a little dreamlike, then, the fact that only two days before people had gathered right there to eat and dance and celebrate with us. I spotted a few blue sequins from a friend's dress in the grass, a couple of squashed cigarette butts, an abandoned fork, a napkin. I walked around picking up these talismans and putting them in my pocket. They felt like precious finds, proof that we'd been there.

I am the luckiest girl alive, I thought as I surveyed the land stretching out in front of me. To have had that day, these days. To love and be loved. I willed myself to remember every moment of the wedding, that one marvelous moment in my life when all my worlds were gathered in one place, when I had everything that mattered in a single gaze in front of me.

And then I too packed my things and headed home. Home to the city I was born in and where my husband awaited me, where I could feel my heart swell every time I arrived in its funny gray streets, where I knew I belonged. I went home again.

Acknowledgments

UNLIKE MANY FIRST-TIME WRITERS, I HAD THE VERY GOOD FORTUNE of having an audience before I ever dreamed of writing this book. So the first thanks go to the readers of my blog, without whom there would never have been a book at all. Thank you for always coming back for more, for your thoughtful comments over the years, for being there with me through lemon chicken and braised zucchini, heartbreak and triumph. You helped me make my dream of becoming a writer come true.

My incomparable agent and friend, Brettne Bloom, extended unwavering support and inspiration throughout the entire process of cooking up *My Berlin Kitchen*. My editor, Joy de Menil, worked tirelessly to make my manuscript the very best it could be. I also owe a debt of gratitude to Molly Stern, Laura Tisdel, Jane Cavolina, Clare Ferraro, Roseanne Serra, Hal Fessenden, Carolyn Coleburn, Lindsay Prevette, Langan Kingsley, Christopher Russell, and Beena Kamlani at Viking.

Thanks too to those cooks whose recipes I have adapted for this book and who have kept me so well fed over the years: Samuel Chamberlain, Melissa Clark, Andrew Feinberg, Claudia Fleming, Suzanne Goin, Diana Kennedy, Jim Lahey, Jamie Oliver, Jacques Pépin, Deb Perelman, Judy Rodgers, Suvir Saran, Bill Telepan, Paula Wolfert, and Alice Waters.

I have been blessed with the joy of having several families. The Klakows were the first ones to teach me that love transcends blood, especially Joanie, my first cooking teacher, my second mother, and my tireless champion. My aunt Laura Gangemi helped me peek at what lay below while her husband, Pietro, inspired me in the kitchen, as did the the Carlonis, Maurizio Catalano, the Crone von Gosslers, the Klakow-Kaufholds, the Marsch–Zieglers, the Müller–Stühlers, the Wertheimer-Schönings, and Sepp, Robert, and especially Kerstin Beuchel.

And no mention of family could be complete without Susan Ernst, my favorite person to cook with and the best stepmother a girl could ask for.

My friends on both continents who cheered me on in countless ways as I worked on this book include Jördis Anderson; Stephen Bitterolf; Serena Carloni; Traci Ergün; Cynthia Barcomi Friedman; Becca Gordon; Sylee Gore; Joanna Gröning; Marguerite Joly; Kim Klakow; Liana Krissoff; David Lebovitz; Sharmaine Lovegrove; Sonia Kassel Mandelbaum; Mathias Meyer; Ian Mutch; Ulrike Nicolaus; Julie Rath; Ellen, Steve, and Leah Rosenblum; Karen Roth; Gemma Saylor; Bettina Schrewe; Suzan Taher; Yvonne and Philippe Vom Bauer; Gisela Williams; Anna Winger; Molly Wizenberg; and Andrea and Scott Zieher.

I would especially like to thank my soul sisters Jenny Bailly, Betsy Robbins, and Teri Tobias for their love and friendship. I am unspeakably lucky to have them in my corner. As well as David Bressler, a prince among men. Dervla Kelly and Kate Norment kept me afloat with laughter in the dark days. And Tara Austen Weaver, who was so generous with her wise editorial eye.

Thanks to the Holstein family, for embracing me with such love.

Paula Glickman, in the understatement of the century, helped me find my voice. She has my everlasting gratitude.

I once read that writers should never include dead people in their acknowledgments, but *my* dead people kept me going in so many ways as I wrote that I simply must: Ninì Cosentino, who always wished to have written a book herself; Ann Weiss, for long ago instilling in me that cooking is love; and Florian von Buttlar, who ate everything to come out of the Bamberger Strasse kitchen when I was learning how to bake and whom I miss every day.

It is most difficult, it seems, to find the words to thank those closest to us. I tried to fill a whole book and I still came up short. So I'll just put it simply: my mother and father, Letizia Cosentino Weiss and Richard Weiss, are the sun and moon in my sky. Thank you both, for everything.

And finally, this book is dedicated to my husband, Max, for his love, his constancy, and for helping me to be brave, every step of the way. He is the pearl in my oyster, the love of my life.

Index